Tending Fire

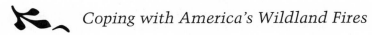 *Coping with America's Wildland Fires*

STEPHEN J. PYNE

Island Press / *Shearwater Books*

WASHINGTON . COVELO . LONDON

A Shearwater Book
Published by Island Press

Copyright © 2004 Stephen J. Pyne

All rights reserved under International and Pan-American Copyright Conventions. No part of this book may be reproduced in any form or by any means without permission in writing from the publisher: Island Press, 1718 Connecticut Ave., Suite 300, NW, Washington, DC 20009.

SHEARWATER BOOKS is a trademark of The Center for Resource Economics.

Some passages from the prologue have been published in *Conservation Biology* (2004).

Some passages from "Fire's Narrative" have appeared in "Fire Creature, Fire Planet," published by *History Compass* (2004).

Library of Congress Cataloging-in-Publication Data.

Pyne, Stephen J., 1949–
   Tending fire : coping with America's wildland fires / Stephen J. Pyne.
      p. cm.
   Includes bibliographical references and index.
   ISBN 1-55963-565-7 (cloth : alk. paper)
   1. Wildfires—United States—History. 2. Fire management—United States—History. 3. Wildfires—United States. 4. Fire management—United States. I. Title.

   SD421.3.P96 2004
   363.37'9—dc22

                              2004008094

British Cataloguing-in-Publication data available.

Printed on recycled, acid-free paper

Design by Teresa Bonner

Manufactured in the United States if America
10 9 8 7 6 5 4 3 2 1

To W. G. WYMAN

"PACKER BILL"

WHO TAUGHT ME THE KNOTS AND

SHOWED ME WHAT THEY WERE GOOD FOR

AND SONJA

ENDURING TO THE END

Out of heaven he made thee to hear his voice, that he might instruct thee: and upon earth he shewed thee his great fire; and thou heardest his words out of the midst of the fire.

—DEUTERONOMY 4:36

From this standpoint, the history of environmental protection is as discouraging as the history of environmental pollution. Anyone who is willing to argue, for example, that the industrial policy of clear-cutting forests is more damaging than the ecological policy of fire suppression ignores the fact that both policies have been carried out with utter conviction, and both have altered the virgin forest irrevocably.

—MICHAEL CRICHTON, *Prey* (2002)

We're not putting them out. We're putting them off.

—COMMON SAYING AMONG AMERICAN FIRE CREWS

CONTENTS

Preface

THE FIRES RETURN, year after year, like some biblical plague. On TV screens the sights and sounds mimic a war zone: helicopters circle overhead, lumbering bombers dump their pay-loads, convoys of fatigued fighters and mechanized armor rumble over remote roads, villages evacuate, angry thunderheads of smoke boil upward like exploding munitions, and ugly palls darken whole regions. The American West eerily echoes the West Bank, or the too-familiar images of many war-torn places. Worse, the land itself has become a shambles, a fire-bulimic biota, suffering fire binges and fire purges. There is too little of the right fire and too much of the wrong. The land bounces from fire drought to fire deluge and back again.

Fire has suddenly become visible. For decades it had steadily receded from everyday life. It left America's homes, its lawns, its fields, its woods. Now it has—apparently—returned. For those with longish memories, it may seem that the fires have suddenly over-spread the country, like an ecological infection, a flaming Ebola or SARS, bubbling out of some long-suppressed hellhole. There are more fires and they are more virulent. For most casual observers, the fires have simply inscribed themselves into a media liturgy. Not so long ago big fires might break occasionally into national attention, but they seemed a curiosity of western violence, like a grizzly bear attack. Now fire season has joined tornadoes, hurricanes, and spring floods as part of a cycle of annual disasters. Each year the nation spends more to fight them, each year the fires rip indifferently through the public wildlands and gnaw into towns, each year critics hurl slogans about who to blame, caught in an ancient blood feud in which each side apparently believes that the only way to save the forest is to destroy it. One group would stand aside and let the fires roar, a "natural" cleansing of abused lands. The other would haul off the woods or convert it to buildings to spare it from the flames. One polarity would have us try to abolish fire; the other, to remove ourselves from its ecological presence. A people that take pride in being a nation of pragmatists are behaving as though we were debating the finer points of canon law rather than what to do in the nation's backcountry. The whole sorry, extravagant, savage spectacle could stand as a dictionary definition of a vicious circle. There might seem no basis for humanity and fire to coexist.

Amid the shouting and roar, a central fact remains. Fire isn't listening. It doesn't feel our pain. It doesn't care—it really, really doesn't care. It understands a language of wind, drought, woods, grass, brush, and terrain, and it will ignore anything stated otherwise. It will burn oblivious to congressional resolutions, presidential initiatives, court injunctions, NGO manifestos, and federal or state agency programs. This is what is missing from most analyses and proposed solutions. They fail to see the world as fire does. They fail to speak in terms that fire understands. Instead, the "fire problem" is hijacked to advance other agendas. It becomes an item in quarrels over clean air or the Kyoto Accord, over an endangered species or the ruination of rain forests. Free-burning flame becomes an argument that management inevitably fails and the land should be wild, or that unmanaged land is inherently dangerous and uncontrolled flame is an ecological terror. It is as though critics stood around a great fire, but with their backs to the flames, addressing their particular audiences, using the fire to animate some other message. The fire isn't listening.

My intention is to examine America's wildland fires from a perspective that is both historical and that more closely tacks to fire's. Why is there fire? Where is there fire, and how has its geography changed? How is America's fire scene like and unlike that of other nations? How have fire policies and institutions evolved? What options exist for relating to fire—not only general principles, but policies and practices that existing agencies can absorb? Is reconciliation possible between humanity and fire? Or is America's current fire crisis a synecdoche for our relationship with nature generally? In brief, how might we cope with fire?

This is a complex task, since fire is a creature of its context; it synthesizes its surroundings. Everything that affects how fire appears—its sources of ignition, the arrangements of its fuels, the structure of the land and the weather that washes over the flames, and all the things people do to shape each—properly belongs in such an analysis. But this comes close to being a history of everything. Instead, I have parsed the saga into three narratives—a fire-history triangle, if you will. Braiding these three strands together can explain much of why the country is burning, or not burning, as it is. Projecting them beyond today's horizon suggests some likelihoods for the future, and why policy alone can neither explain nor cope with the consequences.

There is, first, the general story of Earthly fire. The past 150 years have witnessed a revolution in planetary burning. Industrial combustion—the burning of fossil fuels—has substituted for and suppressed open flame in living biomass. The ecology of this process is poorly understood, but it has fundamentally altered how, through fire, we interact with nature. Industrial combustion explains why, with or without Smokey Bear, fire has withered from the landscapes of developed countries everywhere, not least America. Second, there is the peculiar story of European expansion and its creation, over the past two centuries, of a handful of nations with extensive, fire-prone public lands. These lands remain the prime habitat of free-burning fire, and the nations holding them are the world's natural fire powers and America's fire cognates. The fires roaring across the West are burning on public, not private, lands, and they burn nominally wild, not agricultural lands. The political economy of land use is shaping America's fires as fully as transmigration policies in Indonesia and Brazil have restructured the geography of fire in those nations. Most of the Earth's fires are embedded within agriculture. That is no longer true for America.

Third, there is the evolving story of how Americans have devised fire-related institutions. There are national traditions in fire practices, just as there are in literature, art, politics. One can examine their expressions as one can scrutinize a culture's architecture or its legal system. Europe differs from Africa, America from Europe, Australia from Russia. Europe's ideal nature is a garden, for which fire is a tool, and (in the minds of intellectuals and officials) an unsavory tool for which other implements might better serve. America's ideal nature is a wilderness, for which fire is a natural event, one removed only at peril. American fire institutions evolved out of the political cauldron of the Progressive Era, catalyzed by the Great Fires of 1910. Australia's, by contrast, responded to the Black Friday fires of 1939, building on traditions of volunteer bushfire brigades and rural burning, as the country slid into a world war. Russia's modern era coincided with the Soviet state; a Great Transformation of Nature for which fire control was a paramilitary means to wrest taiga and steppe into forms suitable for rapid economic development. These distinctions reflect not merely environmental circumstances, but choices made by the planet's most powerful fire creature. Those choices are matters of values, knowledge, beliefs, politics. Fire, too, has its clash of civilizations.

A braided history of these three narratives explains why certain options for dealing with fire are available, and not others. America can learn from more places than its public-land West about what options exist for coping with fire. The American West, after all, is only one small cluster of tiles in the planetary mosaic of fire; globally, it accounts for less than 5 percent of open fire on the planet, and often less than 1 percent. Other nations, too, have fire-prone national estates—Australia, Russia, and Canada, most prominently. What can we learn from their collective experiences?

We can learn some common principles—policy options about what to do with fire. These options boil down to four: do nothing, suppress, prescribe burn, or change the combustibility of the land. Each has its particular power, and each suffers the vice of its virtue. Each succeeds or stumbles according to the details of its circumstances. What the lengthening history of American fire history illustrates is that all four need to be in play, with the actual proportions adjusted to the particulars of setting and society. How to decide on a suitable mix has spawned a cottage industry of ideas, to which I will add a smattering.

But as America debates those pyric compounds, we should appreciate that the future of fire involves more than policy within the Washington Beltway. Like the shifting channels of the upper Platte, the flow of fire history is a braided stream. The evolving saga will follow the channels of fire's grand narratives. The American fire scene will adjust to that of other nations. And, too often forgotten, fire will fashion its own synthesis, indifferent to policy altogether.

My interest in these questions dates from June 1967 when I signed on for the first of fifteen seasons on the fire crew at the North Rim of Grand Canyon National Park. The North Rim Longshots had a practical knowledge of fire and a keen, if hapless, concern over what fire policy was appropriate. Ten years later I launched the research that led to *Fire in America*, the first of a dozen books about fire. All included an exegesis on policy, if only implied and refracted through historical scholarship. That focus has endured, but tangentially, with policy only one aspect of fire themes among many, and America but one country amid a combustible world. The politics of fire had to compete with its ecology, its literature, its anthropology, its moral drama. The one exception was a booklet, *America's Fires*, which I wrote for the Forest History Society's "issues" series. That survey climaxed with the 1994 season, although it managed to shoehorn in elements of the 1996 outbreak during its editing.

Much has happened since. Critics have reviewed my recent books in the expectation that they would speak directly to matters of policy; they did not. Friends and colleagues, too, have urged me to lay out my thoughts more explicitly. They have wanted me to unpack my dense historical narratives into a leaner text, to abstract from my world-trekking essays the critical insights, to move my self-described pyromanticism from a playful literary shamanism into a more political pyromancy—to see meaning in the flames and explain that to others. This brief survey is my response.

I thank Bill Wyman for prodding me to do it; my wife, Sonja, for providing a cushion for my wounded self to work on; and Len Dems, Jane Maienschein, and Packer Bill (again) for reviewing the outcome, about which they had many misgivings. Special thanks go to Jonathan Cobb for accepting the manuscript and for forcing me to be emphatic where I had tried evasion and to be clear where I had trusted in ambiguity. Any errors of fact are of course mine, along with misreadings, howlers, ugly malaprops, and ornery interpretations.

More than once, contemplating the American fire scene, I have recalled Dr. Seuss's young Gerald McGrew, who had found the zoo pretty good and the zookeeper proud, but had his own ideas about what such a place might contain. While it has been made economically impossible for me to quote directly from Gerald's fantasy, I can frame my contemplation with his, capturing perhaps a similar touch of whimsy. Yes, in the work that follows here's what I'd do, if I ran the zoo.

Seeing Meaning in the Flames

々

AT LAST IT HAPPENED: California got its Big One in October 2003. But that long-anticipated jolt came not from shaking earth but from flames before a shattering wind. Fire poured across Southern California's mountains like an avalanche. Before fog and drizzle quenched it, the contagion of combustion had swept 740,000 acres, incinerated 3,00 structures, and killed twenty-two persons. The fires formed an arc between the mountains and the sea. One alone, the Cedar fire that burned into San Diego, was the largest in California since the monumental Matilija burn of 1932. The collective destruction of buildings dwarfed even the horrific Oakland fire of 1991. But the California conflagrations were only a coda to a long year of burning, and that year was a relatively mild peroration to an extraordinary cycle of wildfire.

The loss of life shamed a nation newly dedicated, at enormous cost, to homeland security. A near double-decade of drought and fire had torched the American West and turned to ash many presumptions about how we might best oversee uninhabited public domains and increasingly congested private landscapes. With metronomic rigor, the fires had come, and come again, and then come back, gorging on lands blasted with drought, encrusted with beetle-killed pine, starved of nutrients, choking on its own heaped combustibles. An ill-used land had kindled a savage retribution. The cynical and the meditative might ponder if this could be nature's attempt at regime change—shock-and-awe fires intended to blow away an odious landscape.

Out of this long cycle of drought and flame, an intifada of nature, the 2003 California conflagrations were the most stunning. It was one thing if Idaho wilderness or Montana backcountry or a handful of hard-scrabble towns along Arizona's Mogollon Rim burned. It was something else when California—the self-proclaimed future of America, a state with one out of every nine Americans, the world's seventh largest economy—went to its knees. Scoffers might dismiss the eruption as another violent quirk of Southern California, an aftershock of the 1993 outbreak. But the 1996 fires had blasted Northern California, an echo of that region's even more virulent 1987 fire "siege." The fire plague was not confined to one or a small clutch of unorthodox sites. The fires ran everywhere. It was as though something long vanquished, like a medieval pestilence, had suddenly revived. This was after all a region sophisticated in fire suppression, chocked full of fire expertise, overflowing with spin controllers. The fires burned regardless. They were, in Hollywood imagery that California's newly elected governor might understand, a Terminator. They heard only their own programming, supremely indifferent to everything said about them and responsive only to anything done, or more often not done, to stop them.

Surely, critics muttered, this time there would be real reform. The fires had swept up the blather about causes and the rhetoric about philosophies about nature like so much vapor sucked into its collective maelstrom. But then observers had said the same thing after the 1987 fires. And after the 1988 season, and 1994, and after the 1996 conflagrations, after the 1998 fires that forced the evacuation of a 100,000 Floridians, the brutal 1999 California fires, the millennial 2000 season, the 2002 monster fires—the Hayman and Rodeo-Chediski—which were the worst recorded for

Colorado and Arizona, respectively, and the Biscuit fire, the most severe for Oregon since the early nineteenth century. The succession of great fires over a handful of years appeared as a crash in nature's economy as profound as those in the stock market. Surely, however, California would be the tipping point, it was thought. Surely, this time we would invest our cleverness and technologies and political will to grapple with fire and end such catastrophes once and for all. When the flames disappeared from the TV screens, however, they vanished from the news, and outside its wracked landscapes, the fires were replaced in the public mind by celebrity trials, new-release movies, a grinding guerilla war in Iraq, and political ads. The war on fire was likely to resemble the war on cancer. "Surely" was not a betting proposition.

How Had It Come to This?

For most of the twentieth century the issue had seemed simple. One could batten down fire in wildlands as one could in cities, and this would be a good thing. It seemed self-evident to right-thinking elites that fire was unnecessary, dangerous, and destructive. All it took was sufficient ingenuity to devise tools and institutions, enough money to buy and staff them, and adequate social will to apply them. And for decades, the results seemed spectacular. Burned area declined. The greater the effort to abolish free-burning fire the greater the plunge in acres incinerated. Even friendly fire—controlled burns to remove slash or burn up autumn leaves—faded before new technologies that buried combustion within machines or dispensed with it altogether. It seemed that free-burning fire would continue to flourish only in remote places, rather like an endangered woodpecker or the bubonic plague.

The fire community, those who dealt with fire as a career, knew better. It had long had its dissenters, counterexamples, and ironic reversals. From the onset critics of simple suppression had argued for a strategy based not on fire's exclusion but on its calculated use.

In fire-prone landscapes fire's attempted abolition would, they forecast, only stockpile more fuel, corrupt woods into bug-ridden and disease-infested jungles, and ecologically pervert the lands under protection. The critics could draw support from other parts of the world. British India, for example, underwent the same debate as the United States, although thirty years earlier, and came to the same conclusion as America's fire skeptics. Rural Australia, too, fashioned a working compromise between fire control and controlled burning. But in this matter, as in others, American exceptionalism triumphed. Americans found the tools, the money, and the will, and suppressed fire and critics with equal relish.

By the 1960s, however, the conceptual foundations of fire protection shifted and the bureaucratic edifice cracked. The fire community converted to a doctrine of fire by prescription—the belief that fire belonged in wildlands and that controlled burning under suitable guidelines was essential. For economic and ecological reasons both, federal land agencies would have to reverse a half-century policy of attempted fire exclusion. This institutional sea change resulted in new policies and practices for "managing" rather than suppressing fire; for the National Park Service these came in 1968, for the Forest Service in 1978. The argument over a proper strategy toward fire went public a decade later when conflagrations swept Yellowstone National Park.

Over the past twenty years, two long waves of fire have swept over the West. That future was not obvious during the 1982–83 seasons, which set near records for fire's absence. The Great Salt Lake overflowed its levees; a soggy West worried about mudflows rather than firestorms; and climate scientists warned of an impending ice age. If critics fretted over fire, it was the specter of the sooty pall that would conclude a thermonuclear exchange and plunge the planet into a fire-kindled nuclear winter. Then the West began to dry. The 1986 season approached the burned-area norm. The next year sparked the Siege of '87, a prolonged campaign of firefighting centered mostly in Northern California. Then the rising tide of fire deluged Yellowstone in 1988. The question of fire on public lands splashed out of bureaucratic pigeonholes and became an object of national, even international attention. For weeks the national media tracked the drama as fires burned some 45 percent of the park before bolting beyond. A resort community outside the park boundaries, Cooke City, became Cooked City. Throughout, the public received a spectacular tutorial on the natural power of fire in the wild. The deeper issue—not whether fire belonged but how—got sloughed aside as cloud-hugging flames bore down on Old Faithful. The experience announced an era of celebrity fires.

Then, a pause. The drought abated, and western conflagration seemed suitably contained within preserves, like mountain lions and bighorn sheep. When fire returned, it moved from the backcountry to the urban fringe. The 1990 Painted Cave fire blasted into Santa Barbara and sacked 641 structures. The 1991 Oakland fire ravaged exclusive communities across the Berkeley Hills, consuming 2,449 houses and 437 apartment and condominium units. These were not natural fires romping through natural landscapes. They were set, perhaps maliciously; they savaged suburbs; and they would not remain, as the public might imagine, as another freak of California. The planets and stars of the national environment began to align for disaster. The Long Drought set in, worsening year by year throughout the West; urban (or suburban, or exurban) sprawl exploded, a veritable recolonization of rural America, slamming houses against wildlands; land management agencies fumbled through new programs and practices; and the long-deferred fuel bill, a legacy of misguided fire policy over the past century, fell due. The convergence of these events sparked the second great wave of fire. This one would begin in Southern California in 1993 and, after galloping over the West (and elsewhere), return to morph into the Southern California conflagrations of 2003.

A few highlights are worth recalling. One is the impact of the 1994 season, a tipping point that stunned the fire community and, with the full glare of media attention, forced that community's ambitions and doubts upon the nation as a whole. The

5

year's burned area was the largest in decades, fighting those fires rang up the first billion-dollar suppression invoice, and thirty-five firefighters died. The final phase of federal fire reforms, a collective fire policy, followed in December 1995. The 2000 fires proved suitably millennial as they mocked fire fighting and fire lighting equally. Wildfires roared through the Northern Rockies, eerily echoing the formative Great Fires of 1910, while a rogue prescribed fire blasted out of Bandelier National Monument and crackled through Los Alamos. It was as though nature challenged humanity's nuclear pretensions with a reality check in the form of its own lethal fireballs. The 2002 season flushed out small communities throughout the West, most spectacularly the 30,000 residents of Show Low, Arizona. Regions that had traditionally known a lot of small fires now had large ones. Wildfires burned with a biotic savagery that many wildlands could not accommodate. The roster of fallen firefighters swelled. Between 1994 and 2002 alone, some 171 firefighters died, a higher toll than suffered in the conquest of Baghdad.[1]

Meanwhile the long shift in U.S. fire policy quickened. A small service industry pumped out reviews and audits, congressional inquiries, agency mission studies, and consultant reports. From the Forest Service to the GAO to the Sierra Club and the Brookings Institution, analyses have poured forth, while agencies have restated policies, experimented, fretted, and reformulated policies again, and then, when the smoke billowed up, did what they considered necessary and unavoidable: they fought the fires. With preternatural cunning the big fire seasons arrived every two years, syncopated with national elections, forcing fire onto the agenda of national politics (or in California, with gubernatorial recalls). Wildfire, it seems, has become a matter of homeland security. A century of massive federal efforts ended in an uncontrollable contagion of combustion. America's war on fire uncannily resembles its war on drugs. The off-budget costs for fire suppression in 2000 soared to $1.3 billion, almost exactly what the country committed for drug interdiction with Plan Colombia.

Those who could see beyond their shovels or minicams would have observed a larger context. The 2003 fire season, despite the California aftershock, actually fell below norms. Over the course of the Long Drought, the country had averaged 80,000 fires that burned annually 4.3 million acres. The 2003 season—in reality, a quieter season but one given full media glare—experienced 59,000 fires that blackened 3.8 million acres. Increasingly, public attention reflected a manic media that scanned the flames for "stories," simple episodes with clear human-interest drama. Celebrity settings like Yellowstone and Southern California were usable stories; so were cavalcades of fleeing residents, dot-com millionaires scrambling to hose down the roofs of their threatened trophy homes, and Hollywood stars like Zsa Zsa Gabor pleading for shelter for horses dispossessed of burned stables. The world media followed suit, ogling over formulaic fables of American extravagance and violence. But all this was far from full-bodied cultural criticism: one could find commentaries more varied, abundant, and insightful about golf, TV, or yoga.

Americans might be forgiven then if they thought their fires a special curse, another burden of American exceptionalism. Yet they would be wrong.

A quick world tour, following fire's 2003 calendar, will show why. Begin with a supernova of fire in the Australian Alps, where a throng of lightning fires combined with human ignitions to overrun newly ordained nature reserves, burning more than 75 percent of Australia's flagship national park, Mount Kosciusko, before sending venomous streamers of flame northward to lash Canberra, incinerating suburbs and the Mount Stromlo observatory. In the mountains that joined Victoria and New South Wales, more than 6 million hectares burned, as much as the United States suffered during its two nominally millennial seasons, 2000 and 2002, combined. So much of its Outback burned that Australia had to wait upon satellite records to tell it all. Meanwhile, the 2003 springtime in Siberia, dry and windy, erupted into flame.

7

The fires were many, most of them set to clear fields and pastures, before the dreaded *burya* blew them out of control. By the end of May more than 13 million hectares had burned in the Transbaikalia region. Smoke plumes extended to Alaska. By August 4, as old and new fires moved eastward, an estimated 22 million hectares had burned, an area equivalent to fifty fires on the order of the Yellowstone complex. While the American West broke out in fires that summer, like some landscape measles, vast smoldering burns smothered Indonesia and Malaysia with a pall of smoke, the annual fire season in Brazil quickened its tempo, a drought-hardened east Africa began to burn, and with far more media impact, fires crackled through a Europe sweltering under record heat. Major fires blistered Italy, France, Portugal; forests in Scotland burned, while officials banned open fires, including barbecues, on England's moors; Adriatic islands off Croatia caught fire, along with the Canary Isles in the Atlantic. By mid-August, Portugal alone tallied its fires' damages at $1 billion. On August 10 the Pope prayed for rain. Despite evacuations, and occasionally because of them, the fires turned lethal. Portugal saw twenty die, Spain eight, and France five, most of them elderly, many of them tourists. Assisting with the firefighting, the Russians lost a helicopter fire crew of twelve. Then, as large fires mustered in the Northern Rockies, and as officials fretted over the likelihood that a couple might breach the Canadian border, an outbreak of new fires, many kindled by lightning, plastered the interior of British Columbia and the land along the Alberta border. Unchecked flames, evacuated towns, burned homes, a forest weakened by drought and plagued by beetles—it seemed that NAFTA had encouraged a free trade in fire as well as softwood. And the Earth still had a lot of burning yet to do. Amid this outburst, no one reckoned how much fire had not gotten on lands that needed it.[2]

How then to situate the American scene in world context? Consider the 2000 fire season. The United States racked up 3.5 million hectares burned, which seemed astronomical in its magnitude. That same year the global estimate of burned area was

350 million hectares. America's contribution was a paltry 1 percent. Mongolia, India, Indonesia, even Bolivia, all burned on annual average an area that what was double the amount burned in the United States during an extreme year. The American fire scene is real; discouraging, damaging, deadly. But it is easy to exaggerate its size and its exceptionalism. It shares global trends.[3]

Along with the chiaroscuro of flames and a media frenzy—after all, few phenomena are as telegenic as free-burning fire—a narrative has evolved about how the national fire story had all gone wrong. By the 2003 season this explanation had so saturated the popular mind that Michael Crichton could use misplaced fire suppression as an example of ironic environmental protection, as part of his introduction to *Prey*, and expect to be understood by readers of glossy-paper pulp fiction. The received history goes something like this:

Fire had been a natural feature in North America, and in some ways—perhaps minor, maybe massive—pre-Columbian peoples had altered those aboriginal conditions by their own burning practices. Regardless, European settlement upset this putatively prelapsarian world. The creation of public lands attempted to halt the havoc, but early administrators did not understand the true significance of fire and mistakenly sought to exclude it. The 1910 fires catalyzed a national mobilization, led by the Forest Service, a campaign to battle fire to the death. The source of a fire did not matter: its consequences, universally baleful, marked it for suppression. The New Deal granted this agenda enormous resources, particularly the Civilian Conservation Corps. Then a world war and a cold war kneaded national security considerations (and Smokey Bear) into the mix until, by the mid-1960s, protest against this fire-suppression agenda blossomed into a fire counterculture that viewed the war on fire rather like the war in Vietnam.

The full costs of fire suppression, both economic and ecological, had become increasingly apparent and progressively unacceptable. Besides, the Wilderness Act forced the agencies to confront the unblinking absurdity of excluding a natural process from natural areas. Led by the National Park Service, the federal agencies began revising their policies to accommodate fire—lightning fire where possible, controlled burning where a purely natural regime was regrettably denied. The Forest Service followed a decade later.

By 1995 all the federal agencies accepted a common policy of fire pluralism. In brief, the policy was to take "appropriate response" to fires and fire needs—to fight unwanted wildfire, to light needed prescribed burns, to allow fire to ramble in the back-country, whatever. The agencies became deeply committed to fire's management, not its suppression. But distressingly little happened on the ground. The reason, it was argued, was a lack of public understanding, waffling administrators, and a gut-wrenching scarcity of funds. The 2000 fire season provided a climax, a horrible mockery of a century's bold presumptions. Meanwhile, combustibles had stockpiled like a toxic dump, and an exurban sprawl complicated the scene by scrambling homes and wildlands into an ecological omelet. The drama ends in a Wagnerian climax, to which the 2002 season added a staggering coda and on which the 2003 California conflagrations piled an unwanted anticlimax.

This narrative includes an interlinear text that tells the sad saga of fire science. From the onset, real science had been ignored, or compromised by politics. Through the 1920s the Forest Service shamefully suppressed even research from its own field stations that suggested fire served legitimate ecological purposes or that might question the political imperative for fire suppression. Foresters closed ranks—and this mattered enormously because the Forest Service controlled virtually all federal funding for fire research. Still, dissidents arose. Many of the early critics came from wildlife biology or range management; later, forestry found its own voices. Herbert Stoddard, E. V. Komarek, Harold Biswell, Harold Weaver—these have become revered names, brave scientists who dared to challenge the Establishment, voices crying out quite literally in the wilderness, warning that fire suppression was self-defeating and ecologically mad. The Tall Timbers Fire

Ecology Conferences, begun in 1962, became a major forum for an alternative vision of fire, happily coinciding with more sophisticated models of ecology that found value in regular "disturbances," of which fire is an archetype.

Eventually the weight of scientific knowledge forced the political power structure to bend. The process continues, though compromised: too many politicians remain hostile to conservation, too few of the public have heeded the fire prophets, serious science remains starved for funding, politics still refuses to accept a fully science-based solution to wildland fire. Had the federal agencies only listened to its scientific savants a century ago, had it harkened to its fire-ecology Jeremiahs, had it staffed research adequately, had it founded policy on the empirical rock of natural science, we would not have today's crisis. However well-intentioned (by some), the whole suppression project had been a ghastly mistake, propelled by bad ideas, power politics, loose money, institutional inertia, and the occasional truly scary fire.

This story is loosely correct, badly incomplete, and fitfully helpful in suggesting what we should do next. The Received Standard Version seems written to reinforce the consensus that fire is inevitable because it is natural, that fire is necessary because it is useful, that we require more fire (and less logging), and that policy simply, unequivocally must be science based. In brief, it sustains the prevailing beliefs of most of the American fire community.

The difficulty is that it is simplistic in ways that may make reform more difficult and that, having become canonical, it tends to exclude all the other stories. The western fire scene is not the outcome of misapplied science and misguided policy. It is the sum of all we have done and not done over the past century; not only the logging, the grazing, and the road building, but the biosphere reserves, the wilderness areas, the recreational sites; the loss of old species, the invasion of new ones; the fires suppressed, the fires no longer set; the whole rearranged biotas of the public domain. There is a good case to be made that policy, of any sort, however informed, cannot alone undo that legacy. The story identifies protest with a small claque of prophets from fire's Old Testament era; dissent today mostly means recycling those jeremiads. The narrative focuses almost exclusively on public lands, when most fires lay outside them. The Southeast still commands the national statistics on ignitions, area burned, and prescribed fires. The received narrative says little about restoration, which is arguably the most critical task ahead. It ignores the deeper forces of fire's history, notably the prime-mover power of industrial combustion, and the wholesale shifts in land use that determine what is available to burn, itself often a by-product of industrial fire. And its belief that science can and should drive policy goes beyond naïveté into near delusion. The revolution in fire policy did not come from science: it emanated from esthetics, ethics, and economics, from beliefs and values for which its holders sought scientific sanction. Fire science appears as a scaffolding constantly raised, removed, and rebuilt again on the hard pilings of art and philosophy. Science can inform and advise; it won't decide. That synthesis belongs with politics.

The more one peers, the murkier the scene becomes. The complications compound. Prescribed fire, or controlled burning, is no longer a new policy, and in truth, looks a bit shopworn. The Forest Service accepted burning for fuel reduction in the South in 1943. The National Park Service announced the restoration of fire, including prescription burning, in 1968; the Forest Service agreed a decade later; and some federal agencies, like the Fish and Wildlife Service, have always had it on their books. If we date the advent of modern fire policy from 1910, then we have fifty-eight years of fire protection as a goal, followed by thirty-five years of fire by prescription. More than a third of the modern era has had what most observers would consider a suitable policy, one that accepts the ecological value of fire and acknowledges the limits of a suppression-only strategy. The hard-core era for federal fire protection—the epoch of the 10 AM policy, the decree that every fire should be controlled by 10 AM the morning following its report—lasted thirty-three years for the Park Service, and forty-three for the Forest Service. A policy of all-out suppression accounts for less than half of the modern era, a proportion shrinking with each new season. The policy issue is not the alleged dominance of suppression, with its lingering pathologies, but the colossal disappointment of the prescribed reform. In fact, many of the worst (and most expensive) fires of recent years have resulted from prescribed burns gone bad: Gallagher Peak, Lowden Ranch, Cerro Grande, among others, and yes, the 1988 Yellowstone burns.

There is not much natural or moral clarity to this narrative. Of the three monster fires of 2002, lightning kindled one (Biscuit fire in Oregon), while people kindled two (Hayman fire in Colorado, and Rodeo-Chediski fire in Arizona). The latter were the largest of record for their states. New Mexico's conflagration of record occurred in 2000, the Cerro Grande fire. This suite would seem to support the thesis that conditions are indeed worsening, that fuels have metastasized to uncontrollable masses, that fire is inevitable. Yet all three fires were set not merely by people but by people associated with the fire community—Hayman by a fire-prevention technician for reasons that are still obscure, Rodeo-Chediski by a job-hunting Apache hoping to be hired to fight it, and Cerro Grande by a prescribed fire crew. On all these lands, fire was probably inevitable; these particular fires were not.

A year after a dramatic firefight spared Show Low, Arizona, from the Rodeo-Chediski fire, the leader of crews who had held a critical line by burning out along Hop Canyon, an Apache Indian named Rick Lupe, died when a prescribed fire he was attending outside Whiteriver blew up on May 14 and trapped him; he died five weeks later, almost exactly a year after his spirited firefight. The Sawtooth Mountain prescribed burn was part of a larger scheme for reintroducing fire that had been scrapped after the first burn of a series had escaped control in April 2001; officials then rescinded their approval of the rest. Two years later fire crews went ahead, regardless. On the third day Lupe, otherwise uninvolved, showed up at 11 AM, and when a flare-up developed, went to inspect it. The patch blew up, overrunning him and his hastily deployed fireshelter. Within a month, lightning kindled a new start, the Kinishba fire, which forced evacuations of the major Apache communities, including Whiteriver, and then burned over the Sawtooth Mountain region.[4]

Still more irony, in a saga already drenched in it? Delve deeper, however, and the veils of irony draping that tragedy dissolve. Fire's story will not insert itself neatly into narrative templates— of nature vs. people, of suppression versus prescribed burning, of bold firefighters versus. bumbling bureaucrats. Humanity's pact with fire was our first Faustian bargain. Fire's story is not wholly ours to narrate.

That reservation is not restricted to the United States. The same deep drivers of planetary combustion are wrenching landscapes into new patterns everywhere, but they express themselves in various ways.

Consider some examples. Most of the world's burning still comes from traditional sources (the firing of pastures, fallow fields, and slash-and-burn cultivation), and much of that in the developing world. That is, most of the open fires predated industrialization's pyric transition from the burning of living biomass to the combustion of fossil biomass or occur within countries still undergoing that profound transformation. This would include not only Brazil and Kenya, for example, but Portugal and large chunks of Transbaikalia. The most violent outbreaks followed massive changes in land use that liberated landscapes of otherwise inaccessible combustibles. Australia's transfer of land into "natural-regulation" nature reserves, Indonesia's transmigration schemes for encouraging population to move from Java to Borneo, the northern Mediterranean's shift from close-tended cultivation to coarse-cropped forests, scrub, and villas—these made available fuels on a scale not previously known. Where such lands were prone to fire, large fires ripped. Some countries experienced vast conflagrations because their apparatus for social control and fire protection had collapsed, no longer able to discipline careless fire or arson and unable to fight fires, as with Mongolia, or had fallen into institutional disrepair, as with Russia's Avialesookhrana, its fabled aerial firefighting service; here, suppression could no longer keep up with ignition. And Canada—industrialized, efficient, nominally green—seemed destined to confront an environmental nemesis, after a long history of commercial exploitation and attempted fire suppression that left its northern forests in ecological disarray on a scale vaster than America's.

Even the variously labeled fires attacking urban fringes, which American critics treat with special scorn, have afflicted Sydney's suburbs and its Blue Mountain exurbs, and have ravaged France's Departement du Var, otherwise devoted to tourism and holiday homes. The Australian scene mimicked America's in that homes smashed against bush. The French farce resulted from a breakdown in the landscape of traditional agriculture, into which commercial developments and plantation forests thrust themselves in the flume of the mistral. Australia, that is, looked like the American West; Riviera France, like Florida and the American Southeast. The United States is neither as distinctive as it believes itself to be, nor quite so readily absorbed into international conventions as outside observers insist it should be.

All these outbreaks share a similar hierarchy of causes. There is, most proximally, the ideally timed ignition, the extreme weather event, a grinding drought, and a plentitude of combustibles. The deeper drivers are economic and political—cultural in the sense that they shape how people see their relationship to their lands, how people make a living, what institutions people apply to fire. Mostly this relates to where a people stand in the wrenching process of industrializing, how far they have advanced technologically in substituting for open flame, how pervasively they have been in opening new lands or allowing old ones to regrow, how they have imagined fire. Beyond that is the climate, full of newly violent shifts that, among other quirks, expose normally rank forests to drought-sated flame. If the Intergovernmental Panel on Climate Change is correct, then the Earth's climate, under the blows of human-inspired burning, is veering into a new state, one that favors the rapid fluctuations of wetting and drying, and the bouts of aridity, heat, and wind, that sustain fires. If so, the wave of burning is part of a planetary process of reforging fire regimes, again powered by industrial fire and directed by the creature whose hands pull its levers.

America does not, in truth, have *a* fire problem or *a* fire story. It has many fire problems, some of which have technical solutions, others of which have none, but each of which requires different treatments. And it has many fire stories, not easily yoked to a common purpose or even to a common chronicle. There will be no universal prescription, only a universal process. There will not be one narrative, but a swirl. Until society can speak about fire as it does other matters of cultural significance, as something intrinsically woven into the fabric of American life and land-scape, it will continue to interpret fire in terms of technical fixes, and to defer to a simplistic story about good and bad science, right and wrong politics, clever and clumsy policies.

Still, the goals, as defined by fire, seem reasonably clear. We should protect the public lands from those fires we don't want and promote those fires we do. For a group like the fire community that is trained from birth to think of fire as a triangle, we might restate the ambition this way: to remove bad fires, to rein-state good fires, and to otherwise reconcile fire with its natural and social surroundings. But such shared ends say nothing about the means we might use to achieve them or the methods by which we might evaluate those means.

Fire is a cultural matter: it demands a whole culture's judg-ment. A society's fire practices embody choices that reflect val-ues and get encoded into institutions. They align with under-standings about how a people see themselves in nature, for as they think, so they do. Europe, for example, struggles to conceive

of fire as a legitimate ecological agent, insisting that all environmental problems are social problems. Wildfires are an index of
social disorder. Its instinct is to contain fire within its social
model, spinning webs of legal institutions to further regulate
human behavior. By contrast, the United States thrashes about to
find some way to incorporate people into the putatively "natural"
landscape of fire. It is today disposed to promote fire, even at
some human costs.

The fact is, we don't know fire as itself, because it exists only as
a reaction among its sustaining parts. It has no reality apart from
those circumstances. We know it, rather, by its context. The
thicker our description of that context, the richer our historical
understanding of why and how that context has evolved as it has,
the greater our ability to cope with fire in all its protean permuta-
tions and Promethean possibilities. For humanity, there is no evad-
ing that task. We remain a uniquely fire creature on a uniquely fire
planet. For us, fire is less a social problem, a forester's tool, or an
ecological event than it is a relationship. It needs tending. It will
need a lot of tending for a very long time. An explanation why is
the task of this book.

CHAPTER ONE

Why Fire?

THE AMERICAN FIRE community is not, by instinct, historically minded. It obsesses about the coming season, the immi-
nence of blustering winds or dry lightning, about response time.
It reacts, and trains hard to do so. If it contemplates historical
change, its members are most likely to imagine the future, and
run simulations by which to get there. The fire community wants
to *do*.

How much of this indifference to history results from being
steeped in American culture, and how much comes from being in
the fire community, is unclear—and there are bureaucratic ingre-
dients to knead in, as well. When the Brookings Institution can-
vassed high-level fire officers, that group declined to imagine a
past before the 2000 fire season. Before then was prehistory, as
archaic and useless as excavations of Neanderthals. Other
inquiries suggest the same: three years is an average horizon. History's function is archival and bardic—to record and celebrate the
great deeds of the clan.[1]

Certainly, contemporary fire problems can be analyzed as just
that. There is fuel and there is ignition and there are conditions
that cause them to collide. The problem exists now; the solution
is to break that combustion chain now. A leisurely narrative of

how the problem evolved may pique the curiosity but it will not shatter the links that connect spark, oxygen, and fuel. Yet history is a powerful means of explanation, a thickening agent for description, and, while it may not be sufficient by itself, it may be necessary. Even ecologists have come to recognize that, like geology, their discipline is a historical science. The land looks the way it does not simply because it is a physical matrix of parts and processes but because those events and species have occurred in particular sequences. Fire history, broadly conceived, is not an indulgence: no proposed remedy will likely succeed unless it can tease out, analyze, and cope with the historical contingencies that have given the problem its precise shape.

There are many ways to parse American fire history. Perhaps the most punch for the prose comes, as suggested in the prologue, by considering it as the braiding of three narratives. There is the story of fire on Earth: call it fire's narrative. There is a story of public lands and the institutions to administer them: call it an imperial narrative. And there is a story of national particulars: call it America's narrative. In truth, there are thousands of stories; each place will have its own, as in ancient times every landscape had its unique *genius loci*. But the Big Three will block out the critical proportions. Their telling will push our historical horizon well beyond three years.

Fire's Narrative

The oldest story is that of fire itself. This saga comprises the ur-manuscript on which the others, with scribbles and erasures, inscribe a palimpsest. And it *is* a story. Fire has origins; has spread, particularly once allied with human activity; and, while its death is difficult to imagine, has subsided within recent times, a recession that is probably irreversible. Birth, growth, decline— that is the arc of fire's narrative. The story sculpts the boldest contours of combustion's contemporary presence on the planet.

This organic metaphor, moreover, has a firm basis in reality.

What we know as fire is a creation of the biosphere and shares its properties. In simplest terms, fire exists because the Earth holds life. Life pumped the atmosphere with oxygen, life lathered the land with hydrocarbons. The chemistry of combustion is among life's most elemental reactions, for it simply takes apart what photosynthesis puts together. The "slow combustion" within cells we call respiration. The "fast combustion" outside organisms we call fire. From the level of molecules to the planet itself, biological controls shape fire's presence. It makes more sense to imagine fire not so much as a physical phenomenon that acts on a biological world than as a biological phenomenon that expresses itself as a physical process. Earthquakes, floods, windstorms, and other physical "disturbances" can happen without a particle of life present; fire cannot. It propagates through a biotic medium, subject to biological controls. It is a commonly used conceit that such-and-such a disease spread like wildfire. It is equally apt to say that such-and-such a fire spread like a disease. Fire behaves less as a hammer than as an epidemic.

The natural history of natural fire is full of lumpiness. In its basic dynamics, naturally ignited fire occurs in patches and pulses, patterns known as regimes. It is powered by a two-cycle engine of wetting and drying, waiting on lightning's lottery to kindle. A land has to be wet enough to grow combustibles and dry enough to ready them to burn. The possible combinations are legion. There are humid regions that occasionally dry, arid regions that occasionally wet, places that undergo annual rhythms of rain and drought, places that are rich in lightning but only scantily in a state to ignite, and places chronically ready to burn but rarely kindled. While ancient—for more than 425 million years fossil charcoal has littered the sedimentary record—fire is far from universal. Much of the Earth does not naturally burn. It is too wet, too dry, too disconnected from a routine source of ignition. Much of the historical Earth so failed to combust that vast quantities of biomass were simply buried. Nature's economy, in brief, lacked a broker that could match flame with fuel.

This changed with the arrival of the later hominids. It seems that *Homo erectus* could tend fire, could keep it alive in caves, or could hold it in torches or slow matches. Probably not until *Homo sapiens*, however, could humans start fire more or less at will. Still, it was easier to keep fire alight than to continually rekindle it. So it became with nature, also. The sputtering flame became constant, something that accompanied people wherever they went; and they went everywhere. One species acquired a monopoly over fire that it will never willingly surrender.

People exploited fire wherever they could to make their surroundings more habitable. Since the first tread of *Homo sapiens*, fire ecology has thus entailed human ecology. People sought out particularly those landscapes where flame could take most readily, and shunned those places where they could not amplify their firepower. Where fire was possible, they burned for their own ends. They inscribed lines of fire along routes of travel and fields of fire where they paused to hunt, forage, or cook; together these practices, deliberate and accidental, laid down a new mosaic. People preemptively burned, wresting fire away from purely natural forces, much as their myths spoke of stealing fire from selfish potentates. They littered landscapes with flame. They used fire as a force multiplier in foraging and hunting, promoting those plants and animals they most desired, shaping habitats favorable to themselves. Their firepower increased with the extinction of megafauna in fire-prone landscapes, an event that liberated more fuels for anthropogenic flame. People remade fire regimes, imposing new rhythms and inscribing new geography. Under the right conditions, their flame-mediated manipulation could resemble an intensive cultivation, famously characterized by Rhys Jones as "fire-stick farming."[2]

Yet that power had limits. Not every spark took, not every fire could propagate. The fact is, tough limits remained on anthropogenic fire. Mostly, people could only work with what nature presented to them by way of weather and fuels. They could not often bring fire where nature would not allow it. They seized fire-rich sites and regions that lacked only ignition to burst into flame. They sought out places with vigorous wet-dry cycles that could crack open a biota the way a frost-thaw cycle could stone. But they could not break into shade-laden woods empty of dry tinder or hold the frontier against blurred seasons and chronic wetness. The fire stick could nudge vast ecosystems, as it did much of Africa, or even move whole continents, as it apparently did Australia, but only if it had a suitable fulcrum. Fire became more frequent, more pervasive, and, to human sensibilities, less damaging. By whatever reckoning, however, fire regimes were different and it was to these regimes that flora and fauna would have to adapt.

The early keepers of the flame knew full well both their power and its limits. The possession of fire made them unique, distinct among creatures, yet their firepower itself flowed from nature, which inscrutably gave and withheld. Their fire starters were stone, wood, bone; their myths often told how fire leaped out of wood or flint when freed from its bondage by people. So, it seemed, had humans freed flame from nature's fickle thrall and then held it, as best they could, as their own.

This pattern of fire applied and fire withheld changed as people began to manipulate fuel as they did ignition. They could create kindling, on a landscape scale. They could slash, grow, chew and trample with their domesticated beasts, or otherwise cultivate combustibles. Fire is only as powerful as its fuel: now those fuels and their scope expanded. Almost any biomass could serve, if properly minced and dried—woods, scrub, sod, peat, stubble, dung, pine needles, even seaweed. To feed the fires meant searching out new sites for slashing, or allowing old ones to regrow, or in more desperate straits, hauling fuel from elsewhere to the site. In this we find a partial explanation for the practice of fallowing. The abandoned field was not burned as waste, but grown in order to be burned. Even a season's growth of weeds, grasses, forbs, and shrubs could support enough flame for fire to do its ecological

23

duty. Whether the farm cycled through the landscape, as with slash-and-burn cultivation, or whether the landscape in effect cycled through the farm, as with field rotation, the site at some point in its ecological circuit needed fire. And fire needed fuel.

The domain of cultivated fire propagated widely. Fire spread to wherever cultivated plants or domesticated livestock could thrive. Throughout the Holocene, some variety of fire-fallow agriculture propagated across much of the Earth, from African rain forest to Andean plateaus, from grassy steppes to upland peat, from Mediterranean scrub to eucalypt woodlands. Everywhere fire regimes altered, as new practices rearranged the timing, the placing, the intensity, and frequency of burning. Fire existed in places that had not known it previously, and it morphed in places whose previous regimes now throbbed to new rhythms and arrangements. Most of the Earth's open burning today still resides within the dominion of fire-fallow agriculture.

Yet this system of fire use, too, had limits. One could only coax or coerce so much biomass from the land. To burn more fuels than could be regrown was to snuff out cultivated flame, not stoke it. If humanity craved more firepower, it would have to find another source of fuel, which it did in the form of fossil biomass— coal, petroleum, lignite, natural gas. In effect, people excavated whole landscapes from the geologic past in order to kindle a new world of combustion.

Burning unshackled its fuel fetters and became more or less unbounded ecologically, even as it became more intensely confined within special chambers. No longer was combustion limited by its sources (fuels) but by its sinks (the capacity of the environment to absorb its by-products). Throughout human history, the capacity to ignite fire has only been as powerful as the land's capacity to propagate it. Aboriginal burning could not penetrate where nature did not provide abundant fuels. Agricultural burning was predicated on the ability to fashion fuels where nature did not. An appeal to fossil biomass, however, broke that link. The sources of fuel were, for practical purposes, unbounded; so, then, was humanity's firepower. Yet a check appeared from the other side of the equation. The Earth could only absorb so much of the effluent combustion liberated, the gaseous emissions and aerosols, the unshackled chemicals. Industrial fire's by-products threatened to overload the atmosphere and clog ecosystems.

The ecological, economic, and social effects of this upheaval have been enormous. Industrial burning quickly substituted for most domestic hearth and manufacturing furnaces and even agricultural fallow, and then pursued open flame into the bush. Why industrial societies would wish to suppress free-burning fire in sites outside their machines and beyond their cities is unclear; it is just a historical fact that they do. It may be that they simply emulate the example of those nations that preceded them, which, being European, distrusted open flame. Regardless, this transformation, for fire history, is the meaning of the industrial revolution. By 1990 it was estimated that 60 percent of the global emissions from burning derive from industrial fire; and because industrial societies suppress open flame, that proportion must grow as more regions industrialize. By 2003 China exceeded the United States in its combustion of coal, with petroleum and gas likely to follow quickly. The burning of fossil fuels is the deep driver of contemporary combustion, the great biological rearranger of burning, the dark attractor of earthly fire.[3]

The planet has been, and is likely to continue, segregating into two master combustion realms—one fed by living biomass, the other by fossil biomass. The two rarely coexist, and when they do—in places like Mexico and India, where rural villages stubbornly persist next to plentiful reserves of coal and oil—such comingling is likely transitional. Evening satellite photos depict an Earth fissioned into electric lights and fire lights. We have barely begun to understand, in any systematic way, what this means or how industrial fire cascades through whole landscapes. There is some consideration of how the outpouring might affect the atmosphere, particularly how it contributes to greenhouse gases and global warming. But there is no coherent assessment of how industrial fire shapes fire regimes on the surface, or even a general recognition that it shares in a common combustion history with fires feeding on living biomass. The fact is, industrial, anthropogenic, and natural fires compete. Each substitutes for, and evidently seeks to drive off, the others. How they do so may be the most fundamental three-body problem in fire scholarship.

The mechanisms behind this transformation, by which industrial fire arrives and begins shouldering aside anthropogenic fire, are not understood—have scarcely been studied. But we can give it a name, the pyric transition; and we can note that the fire problems of the developed nations are largely those inherited from their passage through the pyric looking glass from open to closed combustion. So, too, knowledge about this passage holds considerable meaning for developing nations as they maneuver through the same transition. What institutions do they need? What policies are useful, which misguided, which irrelevant? Which fire practices should be preserved, at some cost if necessary, and which should be gratefully discarded as a country moves from a context of aboriginal and rural fire to one dominated by industrial fire? Does the pyric transition itself reveal patterns—offer suggestions about how to seize the opportunities and slip through the obstacles?

It does. The primary process seems to be one of technological substitution. Fire as a tool—combustion as a source of heat and light—is amenable to flameless replacements. Domestic fire goes, followed by manufacturing fires and agricultural burning. Yet industrial societies typically extend their reach, the apparatus of contained combustion, into wildlands as well. Here the substitution takes the form of an active suppression, whose consequences are paradoxical and often deleterious.

Within this upheaval, there seems to exist a demographic transition in fire similar to that for humans. The old fire practices remain, while new ones proliferate, with the upshot that the population of fires explodes. Eventually, industrial fire supplants the old versions, and the population fails to replace itself. Early industrializing nations thus have a surplus of fires, including many abusive ones. (Arid lands are an exception because they lack a sufficient background count of biomass fuel. The sudden onset of industrial fire typically arrives through steam transport, which stimulates a burst of livestock herding, which simply crushes flame from the land.) By contrast, mature industrialized nations may lack those burns they need for biotic purposes. During their early industrial evolution, nations seek to suppress the excess fires; later, they try to overcome the shortfall. Fire agencies have little direct control over these processes. Rural fire vanishes, ultimately, because rural populations depart along with the economy that sustained them. Fire did not disappear from much of the United States, for example, because Smokey Bear hectored adults and seduced children. It disappeared because society found combustion alternatives to open fire as a tool and because a rural economy, which had relied on open burning, withered away.

Societies dependent on industrial fire have their combustion maladies. The removal of fire may be as ecologically powerful as its introduction; many such countries suffer a fire deficit within their nature reserves. The urban recolonization of rural landscapes, ardently accompanied by an abolition of open flame, has slammed the wild and the urban together, a collision of environmental matter and antimatter, with frequent explosions. Flame makes little distinction between dried wood bunched together into a thicket and cellulose hammered into a cabin. For whatever reasons, industrial (and industrializing) nations spawn large metropolises, which in turn fling out a sprawl of outlier settlements, still fundamentally urban although they may reside amid former agricultural or wild lands. In fire-prone settings, industrial societies have often discovered they have exchanged an annoying domesticated fire for a demonic feral one. Fire, they have learned, is not simply a tool to be handled or discarded by people at will, like a stone plucked off the ground. It is also an ecological process whose extinction can unhinge whole landscapes, so that even as flame vanishes from everyday life, it reappears in episodic eruptions.

This industrial chapter in fire's narrative explains why the larger story of fire in America is one of fire's disappearance—the sublimation of open flame into chambered combustion. Fire did not vanish because government bureaucracies smothered it and advertising campaigns hoodwinked gullible citizens. It went because better combustion tools evolved, urbanites distrusted flame and loathed smoke, and farming opted for a mechanical menagerie of tractors and a fossil fallow of herbicides and fertilizers. Fire's long-spanning narrative also tells us why, once removed, open burning is so troublesome to restore.

Today, the domain for combustion is peculiar, arrayed within three broad realms. At the cellular level oxidation is carefully confined within molecular machinery. There is no prospect for combustion to propagate wildly through mitochondria and protoplasm. Cellular chemistry breaks fire into its constituent parts and prescriptively channels each into its proper position. Similarly, in the industrial world humanity has fractured combustion into its component processes and confined each within prescribed chambers. Oxygen may be abstracted from air, fuel refined into its most volatile fraction, and the broth mixed in precise proportions within closed chambers. Engineering labors mightily to prevent the reaction from escaping its confinement.

Where fire—fire, in the vernacular sense—flourishes is in that vast realm between the cellular and industrial spheres. It thrives within that largely open cauldron in which the active agents are diffused among earth, air, and life, in which plains and ravines, winds and droughts, layered air masses, and Darwin's "entangled bank" of plants and creatures decide the properties of burning. The power of fire derives from its power to propagate; it spreads, constrained only loosely by gross features of its environment; escapes are common. Interestingly, at the two polar realms—the cellular and the industrial—biological parameters clearly dominate. The character of fire as a feature of the living world is undeniable. (Industrial fire only appears paradoxical in this regard because we so often refuse to see ourselves as fire creatures, as ecological agents who interact with fire rather as moles do with soil or elephants with trees.) Curiously, it is within the middle realm of free-burning flame that fire's biological character gets lost, that fire scientists look to physical parameters of terrain, wind, climate, and lightning as dominant, forgetting the fundamental biological circumstances that allow fire to spread through a biological medium and the biological controls that shape fire's behavior.

When Americans speak of a fire problem, they mean the combustion characteristic of this middle realm. America's fires flare where combustion escapes its technological confinement, in cars and buildings, for example. It thrives in still-rural landscapes, although these are fast imploding. Economic incentives and environmental legislation are rapidly strangling the last pockets of agricultural burning—burning for grass seed, burning wheat and rice stubble, burning decadent pasture, burning prunings and general waste. And fire flashes where modern societies have sought, paradoxically, to create nature preserves in the belief that they might be spared from the corrupting presence of humans. To shield such lands from fire was a compelling argument in their establishment. In practice, often exactly the opposite occurred.

An Imperial Narrative

The thrust of fire's industrialization should have steadily squashed fire from the land, not only where its obvious apparatus such as internal-combustion machines flourish but wherever an industrial society can reach via fire codes, institutions, changing land use, and so on. Fifty years ago suburbanites burned lawns and leaves. Today they bag that debris and have it hauled to landfills. The expectation in a fully industrialized nation like the

United States is that fire would exist only in the cracks of the new order, from arson and accident, as it does in modern cities.

Yet flame—free-burning fire on a scale of millions of acres—continues to blaze across the American scene. Why? It endures, mostly, where it has always been: the South. The southeastern United States dominates every category of open burning—ignitions, acreage burned by wildfire, acreage burned by prescription. The reasons are simple. Its natural setting is primed for fire, and its lingering rural heritage stalled the flame-extinguishing juggernaut of the industrial order. Its fires, however, simply merge into its milieu, like routine flooding and pelagra; with few exceptions, notably Florida, the fires remain invisible beyond the region. Instead everyone understands that the national fire problem lies in the West. America has extensive wildland fires because, in the fire-prone West and Alaska, it has extensive wildlands.

In its fire geography the United States thus stands as a microcosm of the Earth. There are regions where open fire has more or less disappeared, places not disposed to natural fire and which have undergone the industrial transition: the northeastern United States, for example, or Europe north of the Mediterranean. There are vast dominions that are both fire-prone and welded to an agriculture still dependent on periodic burning: vestigial patches of the American South, sub-Saharan Africa, tropical South America, southern Asia. Here, routinely, is where the bulk of the world's burning occurs. And there are swathes, sometimes extensive, that burn under quasi-natural conditions on landscapes reserved as public domain or Crown lands: America's West and Alaska, large chunks of Australia, Canada, and Russia. These are nations that are, paradoxically, both industrial and prone to free-burning combustion and that have created the institutions for coping with wildland conflagration. They are the contemporary Earth's fire powers, the Big Four.

They share a geography disposed to burn—this is obvious. But much of the Earth is prone to burning and does not burn in the same way. What these nations share, more fundamentally, is a common history grounded in European imperialism. The critical factor is not simply an ideology hostile to open burning but a particular pattern of governance based on wholesale settlement. The Big Four are countries that Europeans not only colonized but demographically overran during the nineteenth century. The timing of this process mattered. In each instance, the indigenous populations were removed—by disease and forced relocation—and before the newcomers could repopulate the landscape in numbers, a national or imperial government set aside large estates as public or Crown land and turned over their administration mostly to foresters. The practice worked reasonably well where the lands were kept uninhabited, and not very well where they were not, where indigenous hunters, herders, foragers, and occasional swiddeners continued to pass through the scene. The Big Four are examples of the former; India, Cyprus, and Algeria of the latter.

The story of America's public lands has been written often, but typically as a national peculiarity and in fact as a national disgrace. A New World beckoned: the government, ever greedy and careless, sold off that natural heritage as quickly and mindlessly as it could, and, most obnoxiously, freely lavished its largesse on corrupt railroad companies. Like Esau, the nation sold its priceless inheritance for a bowl of pottage. Eventually sense and shame prevailed—the "Great Barbecue," as V. L. Parrington famously called it, shuttered its booth; what remained from the wreckage the country wisely turned over to scientific experts to administer for the common good, an exemplar of Progressive politics.[4] The implication prevails that a normal country would never have divested its natural wealth so recklessly, that the creation of the public domain was salvage conservation on a continental scale. In 1934 the government closed land sales altogether and amalgamated all the as-yet-unpatented lands, mostly pastoral, into yet another agency, the Bureau of Land Management (BLM). Over the past few decades the nation has found it necessary to buy back, occasionally at fabulous sums, pieces of its estate that it had fatuously thrown away. (The nation paid $187 million in 1968, for example, to purchase 28,432 acres of what became Redwood National Park, including some lands already logged.) Not surprisingly, the chief architects of this narrative of America's public lands have been foresters, or their successors, themselves a principal beneficiary of the public lands.

There is another version possible. It begins with the observation that these kinds of public estates were the peculiar legacy of a Europe that was both Enlightened and imperial. Even as European nations, guided by liberal economics, sought to modernize their economies by dismantling and selling their ancient "commons," they were installing a colonial commons, often immense in scale, beyond the seas. Odder still, the leading proponents of liberal economics, Britain and the United States, were among the most active practitioners. Lord Dalhousie commenced the process in Burma and India amid other modernizing reforms, while the United States began sequestering its public lands during the capitalist excesses of the Gilded Age. The other imperial powers had customs of government intervention on which they could draw. France deferred to *dirigisme*, its tradition of state-controlled political economy, and Russia to Tsarist ownership of acquired territories. Throughout Britain's empire, ownership devolved to "the Crown."

The practice of reserving land, then, occurred globally. The reasons were many, including a lust for revenue, but among the most compelling was a philosophy of conservation, which held that local communities (or places emptied of people) could not resist global political and economic pressures to scalp the land, that the lost resources would cripple the growth of their societies, and that some institution of government with vision and political clout would have to intervene in the name of a greater commonwealth. This was not a matter of arbitrary perception and abstract principle. Colonial contact could be brutal: forest clearing, savage hunting, the loosing of feral animals, the collapse of native cultivation, unfettered capital, all could make a shambles of land. Islands were especially vulnerable, and from Saint Helena to the Antilles, there seemed abundant evidence that contact could shatter native ecosystems.

In good European tradition it was axiomatic that environmental ills were the result of social ills, and hence, that the more thoroughly a landscape was scrubbed of its inhabitants the closer management could hew to right principle. Judged by criteria of administrative efficiency, this was certainly correct; judged by environmental outcomes, less certain. Some human practices were clearly undesirable; some, however, might be valuable in ways not really understood. Regardless, a collateral concept emerged in those colonies most completely depopulated: their vast blocks of bush encouraged a quixotic belief that such lands had always been truly "wild," beyond the historic touch of humans. By the mid-nineteenth century the Trans-Mississippi West seemed such a place, with its relict "nomads" clearly incompetent to have forged landscapes wholesale, as agricultural peoples did elsewhere. This perception reinforced prevailing wisdom that the solution to contact's contamination was to purge both the source and the evidence of contact.

Curiously, one of the most powerful arguments for forest reservations, in particular, was the presumed power of woodlands over climate, a doctrine of "forest influences." A wholesome woods could stabilize climate, dampening the tendencies of wrecked forest lands to career between drought and flooding. The prevalence of forests argued for foresters to administer the reserves. (Britain had none, and recruited its early corps from Germany.) This was a momentous decision. Foresters thus joined that extraordinary throng of western engineers who circulated around the European imperium and built railroads, bridges, dams, mines, and otherwise sought to "rationalize" wild lands and primitive societies. Foresters differed from the rest, however, in that they had to administer the lands under their jurisdiction, not simply advise. They became conservation's proconsuls.

The apparatus used for administering reserved lands first took coherent shape in British India during the 1860s. The early proponents of forest reserves in the United States looked to the British Empire for administrative models, and Gifford Pinchot, founder of the modern U.S. Forest Service, wrote Dietrich Brandis, architect of the Indian Forest Department, that he hoped to accomplish in America something of what Brandis had achieved in India. He also thought American foresters had much to learn from French colleagues in Algeria (other than getting out, it is hard to imagine what exactly he had in mind).[5] Perhaps colonial foresters' clearest commonality was a perceived threat from fire. Their lands seemed overrun with flame, a kind of opiate for a peasantry utterly addicted to burning and indifferent to fire's darker dangers, its long-term subversion of soil, water, and air. From the onset, foresters found themselves in a chronic firefight. Writing a centennial history of the American Forestry Association, Henry Clepper spoke for a global brotherhood when he wrote that "if none of the other reasons for the [conservation] movement had obtained, the fire menace alone would have required that it be started."[6] For foresters, fire was an evil, a taunt, and a challenge.

Foresters quickly established themselves as the engineers and oracles of free-burning fire. Yet forestry made an uneasy overseer. As an academic discipline and a practice, forestry was a graft on the great rootstock of European agronomy. Silviculture meant, literally, the cultivation of trees. But most fires were not in pure forests, certainly not in the forests of temperate Europe, where forestry evolved. They were often in long-fallow woods (the burning jungles of India—"jungle" coming from the Hindi word for uncultivated land). Moreover, foresters knew fire as it threatened their trees, a danger bred by pastoralists, slash-and-burners, travelers, charcoalers, and miscellaneous transients, and those other competitors for the woods, such as gatherers of honey, nuts, and medicinal plants. Foresters feared and detested flame. Thrust into fire-blasted colonies, they became nearly apoplectic with outrage. Nothing could be done about honest forestry until fires were controlled.

Imperial forestry was thus forged in fire. Flames were there at the creation, in the daily life of foresters as fully as malaria, cobras, and timber thieves. The first question posed at the first conference on forestry in British India asked whether it was possible to control fire, and if so, whether it was desirable. While almost everyone thought fire protection admirable, most doubted flame could be contained. Opinions split along the same fissures as in Europe; practitioners thought fire control implausible and unwarranted, officials and intellectuals believed it necessary. The control of fire became colonial foresters' great, indispensable challenge. Berthold Ribbentrop, inspector general of the Indian Forest Service, wrote how, from the onset of the dry season, fires increasingly dominated a forester's working calendar.[7] Revealingly, Rudyard Kipling had Mowgli of *The Jungle Book*, after coming of age in the man-village, serve as a forest guard, where among his prime duties he gave "sure warning" of fire.[8]

For the 1880 census, Charles S. Sargent, Harvard professor and director of the Arnold Arboretum, plotted a map of American forest fires. The United States was then a developing country, a volatile compound of industry and agriculture, churning through its pyric transition. Its rural landscape simmered in smoke, newly hacked stumplands in the North Woods erupted in lethal conflagrations, wildfires gorged on the raw scraps of logging and railroad construction. It was to the world of the 1880s what Brazil seemed in the 1980s. The country's first professional forester, Bernhard Fernow, having emigrated from Prussia, dismissed the American fire scene as one of "bad habits and loose morals." The first native-born Americans to become professional foresters trained in the British imperial model: study in Europe and fieldwork in the colonies, with the *Manual of Forestry*, written by William Schlich, Brandis's successor, as their text. Gifford Pinchot thundered that "the question of forest fires, like the question of slavery, may be shelved for a time, at enormous cost in the end, but sooner or later it must be faced." Henry Graves, Pinchot's collaborator, and later successor as chief of the U.S. Forest Service (after a stint as dean of the Yale School of Forestry, endowed by the Pinchot family), declared that fire protection was 90 percent of American forestry. There could be no forestry—no genuine conservation—without fire control. Rightly or wrongly, state-sponsored forestry around the world declared itself the vanguard of global conservation and accepted that it would succeed or fail most simply according to its capacity to subdue free-burning fire.[9]

From its onset, wildland fire protection was a political act, and more, an imperial invention. The circumstances of colonization made it possible for the state to reserve vast expanses of countryside; administering those lands required an apparatus for fire control. Though most fire remained in rural settings, fire protection focused on the reserved lands, particularly forests, which placed them under the intellectual and institutional influence of forestry. Forestry's proconsuls responded by creating an army of occupation to quell the ecological unrest stirred by their new regime. Our understanding of fire management, of the scope of fire science, of what kinds of fire institutions are appropriate, of the very nature of "fire" as a "problem"—all derive from these peculiar historical circumstances, and especially the appeal to state-sponsored forestry for intellectual authority and practical administration. Today's club of firepowers exists because they shared this common history. America's experience was part of this global project, which helps explain why its fires are in one place and its fire problems in another, and why its national government cares about the one and not the other.

This era is rapidly collapsing. The past fifty years have witnessed the spectacular implosion of Europe's imperium and the fraying, collapse, or rebuilding of the institutions it had created. Large public domains, especially those overseen by foresters, were the outcome of a historical accident. They are recent, the earliest being less than 150 years old; they may be—in fact, are—

segueing into novel forms that will shape fire anew and guide its human handlers. The extreme example is New Zealand, which has disestablished its Forest Service outright, sold off its most commercial woodlands, and tossed the rest into a Department of Conservation. But everywhere such institutions are devolving, privatizing, renegotiating rights with former indigenes, allocating prime sites as themed nature reserves, and otherwise downsizing the imperial model into something closer to local communities and particular needs. Perhaps the most dramatic illustration is the rising role of The Nature Conservancy, not only as an active fire institution in its own right but as a broker between competing interests in public-land fire practices. What the federal government had once done—had insisted it alone could do—is increasingly spread among nongovernmental partners.

This tectonic shift, breaking apart once-hegemonic fire institutions, helps account for the global mismatch between fire problems and proposed fire solutions. The fire problems of the world extend far beyond the berm of public lands left by a receding imperialism. The 1983 fires in Borneo and Ghana, the 1998 fires throughout Mexico, the crippling 2000 fires in Ethiopia, the 2002 fires that smothered Guatemala, the lethal conflagrations that savaged Portugal in 2003, all stand outside the classic institutions devised for vacant public wildlands. While massive fires on their public estates rightly command the attention of the Big Four (America, Canada, Australia, and Russia), and grab the media spotlight, most of the Earth's burning lies elsewhere. By both economic and ecological criteria, the most damaging eruptions are those that are accompanying transmigration schemes in Indonesia and Brazil, that are raking over abandoned agricultural lands in the northern Mediterranean, that are attacking a metastasizing urban fringe, that affect private landholders, that pertain to the maintenance of cultural landscapes, and that are accompanying fitfully industrializing rural economies—those riding out the pyric transition. And industrial combustion, arguably the more profound fire concern, simply sits beyond wildland-fire protection's intellectual reach no less than its institutional grasp. Since 1989, three international conferences on wildland fire have moved between the United States, Canada, and Australia; they are unlikely to be held in Kenya, Thailand, or Germany. While global in ambition, the problems such conferences address are still those characteristic of the imperial era and its legacy.

Behind the global outbreak of burning lay not only climatic pressures but massive shifts in land use, what might be characterized as a suite of contemporary colonizations. There was, for developing nations with large hinterlands, a wave of new colonization, opening lands to fire in often huge ways, especially in the tropics. Brazil and Indonesia are good examples. For the developed nations, two other movements prevailed, however. There was a recolonization of rural landscapes, with older residents gone or hurried to cities and an exurban outmigration reclaiming the sites. And there was a decolonization of public lands. Everywhere, even among the Big Four, state-sponsored forestry is fracturing, either disestablished outright, or forced into partnerships with NGOs and local communities, or broken up and its hands handed over to other agencies. The founding model, in brief, no longer worked even for the founders.

In 2005 the U.S. Forest Service will celebrate its centennial. Loosely modeled on the Indian Forest Department established by imperial Britain, it no longer works as it did in the early twentieth century. At times, it barely seems to work at all, stalled by a combination of bureaucratic sclerosis and competing political interests, mustering support for action only when big fires fill TV screens. One good reason for this condition is that the country lacks consensus on what the national forests should be, although general agreement does exist that the goals and devices of forestry should not direct their administration. Nature protection, biodiversity maintenance, recreation—such purposes, not logging and ranching, have the general sanction of the American electorate. The public lands are moving from an economy of commodity production to an economy of services, and from a command-and-control system of fire suppression to a more community-based suite of negotiated fire practices. No longer does fire protection speak with a single conceptual voice, an exclusive claim of science, or even through a unified institution.

What might this mean? It means that foresters have lost their privileged status as oracles and engineers of fire. It means that the institutions they nurtured and in which they applied their ideas, such as the U.S. Forest Service, are disintegrating, devolving, or otherwise morphing in ways that mean they no longer control the political discourse of fire management. It means that the blood feud between state-sponsored forestry and environmental groups over the proper use or preservation of public lands is becoming an anachronism. The Forest Service as monolith and evil empire has succumbed to a shambolic, shackled Gulliver; and instead of a tidy cold-war polarization between massive blocs, a swarm of competing interests and NGOs—the political equivalent to a black market—is turning the agenda for fire management into a policy bazaar. Arguably, the most successful fire practitioners (those matching fire regimes with land needs) are NGOs like The Nature Conservancy; the arenas most in need of fire treatments are privately owned lands, and boutique burning in niches, or among an archipelago of sites, may be more productive for biological purposes than broadcast treatments of unbounded public estates. The deconstruction of state-sponsored forestry may mean that the public lands themselves will undergo a fundamental metamorphosis into something quite different. They are, after all, a relatively recent invention. At society's pleasure they could change substantially or even disappear.

The irony almost folds upon itself, like a Möbius strip. While early foresters brazenly proclaimed that fire protection was 75 to 90 percent of American forestry, they also dismissed the task as something that serious, science-based administration would leave behind, as though fire were a childhood disease like measles that one outgrew. Fire protection was not forestry, in this view, only a precondition to forestry. Today, some 40 percent of the Forest

Service budget still relates to fire; apart from logging, which has been steadily strangled, fire management is virtually the only task that the public identifies with the agency. Instead of withering away, fire dominates the Forest Service's horizon. Yet foresters, for all their hard-won expertise, still fail to see that fire management may be itself the core mission of the agency, that fire *qua* fire is both a means and an end, that proper fire management may be an index of successful land management. The institution would not be a fire agency once, but forever.

Now, however, the plot begins to thicken. It was the perceived need for fire protection that bolstered state-sponsored forestry, which in turn devised the institutions of modern fire management, including fire research. Fire protection legitimated those institutions, gave them a hard, massive task, and brought in money. That the government assumed this responsibility meant that other competing institutions dried up; no one else, for example, funded fire science because the national government in effect exercised a monopoly over such research, and in the United States the government assigned the job to one agency. Something similar happened with practical expertise about firefighting: the torch passed from common lore to a government agency. What had been common practice, widely diffused among rural communities, increasingly belonged exclusively to an organ of the state. What it did not do itself, it contracted out to others, but the ultimate authority still resided firmly within its hands.

The environmental irony is easily understood. Creating public lands in good part to protect them from fire created instead a protected habitat for fire. Shielding those lands from replacement by industrial fire kept free-burning flame on the land. The premise of course was that the forces of an industrial society could suppress those annoying and occasionally ravenous flames, but the nature of fire-prone public lands encouraged just the opposite reaction. Fire returned, often more feral than before. The attempt to contain those flames, however, built up a vast reservoir of practical knowledge about fire in those institutions with responsibility for administering the public domain. Less well understood is the consequence of dismantling those institutions. The creation of a Fire Learning Network, overseen by The Nature Conservancy, demonstrates both the need for such arrangements and the political vacuum left by forestry's institutional collapse.

As state-sponsored forestry goes, so might the rest of the machinery. That, for example, is what happened when New Zealand disestablished its forest service and South Africa privatized its forest research institutes. The rural fire services of New Zealand disintegrated and had to be reconstructed painfully from the ground up. Basic research shriveled. Science became a service rendered to those who could pay, which meant commercial forests that wanted better techniques to combat fires, not more nuanced insights into fire ecology. Moreover, it is one thing to transfer land, another to transfer knowledge and experience. The transition from public forests to nature reserves could well mean moving from discredited institutions that knew a lot about fire to more politically popular institutions that know little. In recent years the flagship national parks of America, South Africa, and Australia have all realigned their programs away from direct control by the tenets and instruments of state-sponsored forestry—and have burned massively.

The institutional scene remains unsettled. What kind of fire infrastructure should exist? What is the proper role of government? What variety of research is needed, into what kinds of questions, under what range of sponsors? What global arrangements might be desirable? Our times offer an occasion for extensive institution-building in fire management. The issue applies not only to developing countries, and to those new countries from the continued breakup of former empires, but to those nations with an existing apparatus that no longer meets the goals society wishes for its collective commons. The question of fire nation-building, as it were, applies as much to the Big Four as to the former republics of the Soviet Union. It certainly applies to America. Reclassifying public lands from forests to parks, or from logging to recreational use, does not eliminate fire or the need for on-the-ground experience.

The fact is, modern fire protection is a political invention. It is not enough to buy more engines and niftier Nomex jumpsuits and to sponsor scientific studies. The core issues are social and lie outside the realm of science; they involve cultural values and politics, and an honest resolution will demand better values and sounder politics. As yet, however, we have barely begun to understand in any systematic way the politics of fire or the fire institutions that various societies need. This would require, at a minimum, comparative and historical study for which there is scant interest.

The one near certainty is that the era of the imperial model is fast ebbing. With each year, it works less well within nations, and it has declining relevance between nations as an exemplar suitable for export or emulation.

America's Narrative

Fire's narrative explains the larger circumstances for earthly fire of any kind. It explains why fire has, overall, disappeared and why reintroducing it is so tricky. The imperial narrative accounts for the peculiar geography, institutions, and attitudes toward free-burning fire and why America's fire scene, on one hand, differs from that of Latin America and Africa while, on the other, it aligns smartly with that of Canada and Australia. The imperial narrative explains why a club of countries has evolved elaborate institutions for coping with wildland fire; and it lays out a set of management options that is common to all nations with fire-prone public lands.

The actual expression of fire requires a further narrative, however, a national story that tracks how political decisions and cultural choices create distinctive fire practices, policies, and regimes. America's story congeals in the late nineteenth century, when the country was undergoing its pyric transition and when it yet had, within its interior dominion, territories that it could remove from settlement in the name of conservation.

Sargent's 1880 map documented where and how America burned. It did not, however, explain how the country should cope with fire or its still-unsettled lands. Over the next twenty-five years a throng of competing strategies clamored for attention, from laissez-faire colonization to state-sponsored conservation to military rule.

The laissez-faire option held that the problem would take care of itself, that the conflagrations were the product of a tumultuous spasm of settlement that would disappear along with other frontier ephemera as the landscape matured. Wild fires would go the way of wild beasts and wild woods. The riot of flame was simply part and parcel of the violence that accompanied fast-developing frontiers. Fire brigades would assemble out of villagers as needed, called up as though they were fire posses. Like rustlers and rattlers, the fires would vanish as raw forest and prairie settled into farms, fields, and towns. For most of preindustrial America, this is pretty much what happened.

There were variants, as private interests sought to protect their holdings. This, too, had frontier precedents in voluntary associations that, in the absence of government, banded together to create a civil order. Railroads dispatched special trains to fight the innumerable fires started along their tracks. Landowners in the Northwest gathered into timber protective associations, providing collective fire control for member lands. These were not strictly voluntary. They typically had behind them the threat of legislation that would mandate a fire tax or other levy, or some system of government oversight for fire protection. (This strategy, too, was part of an international project; in 1885 Ontario, Canada legislated into existence a tax-funded program of "fire ranging.") In any event, such associations were not, in the United States, conceived as permanent features, but rather as temporary measures to overcome an explosive epoch.

What decided the question of governmental responsibility was the reservation of public lands. The federal government began the process in 1872 when it set aside Yellowstone as the nation's first national park. Other parks followed, almost exclusively amid the monumental scenery of the West. An underfunded and generally toothless civilian administration surrendered in 1886 to the U.S. Cavalry, which assumed direction of Yellowstone and later the other grand western parks, until a civilian agency, the National Park Service, finally replaced it in 1916. (Hence, the origin of the Park Service's familiar grey uniform, epaulettes, and hat, descended from its cavalry antecedents.) The army spent its first summer driving off poachers and vandals, and fighting fires—extinguishing sixty flare-ups in all.

Here lay the ancestral hearth of fire control by the federal government. Creating the reserve mandated a responsibility to protect it, which soon became an exercise in firefighting. Of course the military could hardly entrench and hold against a full-bore crown fire through Yellowstone's lodgepole pine. But the majority of fires, year in and year out, came from people, and by confining the movement of park visitors and drumming in the virtues of fire prevention, the army choked off many fires, some of which would have blown into the canopy. A disciplined force for firefighting, the "moral" power of a military presence, the logic of an infrastructure of roads, trails, and patrols, all contrasted brilliantly with bumbling amateurs, ad hoc crews of transients and townsfolk, the lethal indifference of laissez-faire. The visual metaphor proved powerful: the firefight as battlefield. Eventually the country demanded civilian authority, but for fire protection it would create a civilian facsimile of the cavalry's fire *force majeure*. The specter of wildland firefighting as a paramilitary endeavor haunts the community to this day.

Alternatives were appearing, however. The same summer that the cavalry rode into Yellowstone, the state of New York established its "forever wild" Adirondacks Park, followed by a smaller echo in the Catskills. The arguments were similar to those

44

invoked later for federal reserves (and throughout Europe's imperium). The twist was that a state, not the national government, would oversee fire protection, and that state officials would evolve a system out of existing rural practices, including fire wardens. Early experiments stumbled because the authorities did not recognize (or admit to the political costs) of a full-fledged program. Twice, major fires pushed the park to its limits, and beyond, once in 1903 and again in 1908.

The New York model was widely studied. The arguments hammered out to justify the preserve were later applied to the nation; the governor, Grover Cleveland, later urged similar actions when he became president; Charles Sargent underwrote a study for New York, as he later did for the national forest reserves under the auspices of the National Academy of Sciences. Other states, notably around the Great Lakes, emulated the Empire State's example. Its limitations as a paradigm were political and historical, which is to say, matters of timing. Few eastern states could claim a vast hinterland—their own interior "West," as it were. (Minnesota could, and sought to transfer the model.) Few western states had enough population and clout, and were avid to populate by selling off land, or were as yet still territories.

More powerfully, the thrust of Progressivism and conservation argued for national institutions. The mood of the country, or at least of its educated elites, was to reserve what of the public domain had escaped ruin, to change the character of settlement from unregulated exploitation to efficient utilization ideally under some scientifically informed direction. When the United States committed to vast reservations of public land, it committed, unwittingly, to a vast institution of wildland fire protection.

That process began in 1891 when a clause in the Sundry Civil Appropriations Bill authorized the president, by proclamation, to establish forest reserves out of the unpatented public domain. The announced purpose was to stabilize watersheds and, secondarily, to assure a steady supply of timber. The first reserves were proclaimed around Yellowstone National Park, expanding the pale of protection. The second rimmed the mountains of Southern California in an effort to shield its water supplies. Most centered in the West, in those landscapes where forests flourished; but swatches of public domain still existed east of the Mississippi, and forest reserves appeared in Minnesota, Arkansas, and Florida as well. The process reached its climax under President Theodore Roosevelt. In 1911 the Weeks Act authorized the acquisition, by purchase, of mostly eastern lands for what had come to be called the national forests. The first additions targeted the White Mountains of New England and the southern Appalachians.

Reserving land was one thing; administering it was another. Initially the General Land Office oversaw the estate, without much knowledge or skill. In 1896 the National Academy of Sciences was commissioned to report on the reserves and to recommend suitable policies. Fire and trespass were the two great threats, the Forest Committee observed. For six weeks, through six western states, they were never out of the sight of smoke, and burned landscapes greeted them on all sides. The extravagance of flame became an unanswerable argument for government intervention. It was not simply that the reserves required fire protection but that fire protection demanded reserves. It seemed a task amenable, as an interim measure, for the army, which was already overseeing several national parks. The 1897 Organic Act that resulted, however, left responsibility with the Department of the Interior. Then, in 1905, President Roosevelt transferred the reserves to the Bureau of Forestry in the Department of Agriculture, under Chief Forester Gifford Pinchot.

There were other kinds of reservations. In 1903 Roosevelt proclaimed the first wildlife refuge; in 1906, the Antiquities Act allowed the president to set aside parcels of the public domain as national monuments to protect archeological artifacts and sites of scientific interest. The public domain closed altogether in 1934 with the Taylor Grazing Act, amalgamating the flotsam of settlement into grazing districts and what became the Bureau of Land

Management. But it was the forest reserves—renamed the national forests after the Transfer Act of 1905—that brought American experience into alignment with imperial Europe, that installed foresters as arbiters of public conservation, and that led to a system of fire protection for wildlands.

The Transfer Act resolved the institutional question of who should provide forest fire protection. It left unsettled, however, the precise strategy for controlling fire. While fire's exclusion remained the dream of forestry, a handful of rangers and fire guards could not strangle flame from the western wilds. Excluding people excluded a prominent source of burning, but not all; lightning persisted, in some years and places massively. Paradoxically, excluding people also excluded a primary source of firefighters (and fire wardens)—indeed, the whole process by which settlement itself snuffed fire from the scene. Instead, the proconsuls of the public domain would have to "settle" their wildlands in the name of fire protection. They would have to lay out roads and trails, string telephone lines, erect lookouts and patrol cabins, and staff the backcountry. Each region contributed to this solution in distinctive ways, peculiar to its environmental and social setting.

The most fundamental debate over strategy involved the use of controlled burns. Sentiment was strong among folk frontiersman for widespread, frequent burning as a means of reducing the threat of wildfire and rendering the land more malleable for farming, herding, hunting, and the like; and this preference would linger politically through the 1920s. In the Florida National Forest, ranger Inman Eldredge proposed a plan that combined firefighting with fire lighting.[10] It made ecological sense, he insisted, and would enlist locals' support in ways that simple fire suppression would not. In the West, ranchers, timber owners, settlers, even literary figures and the state engineer of California, among others, argued in favor of "light burning," what the poet Joaquin Miller characterized as the "Indian way" of forest management.[11] Frequent surface firing in brush and open pine forests would scour away the crust of combustibles that powered conflagrations. It would make healthier, less diseased and less pest-ridden woods. Some foresters were willing to consider controlled burning to remove logging slash, and maybe other tasks, but they regarded fire as a necessary evil, at best, an expedient that surer administration and better funding would banish. While the outright abolition of fire might be impossible, it remained a noble goal, a commandment of conservation.

The controversy climaxed in 1910, when the Great Fires of that summer combined with a political firestorm that began with Pinchot's dismissal and culminated in a crisis not only for the Forest Service but for the Taft administration. Fires had broken out steadily throughout the West as a summer drought deepened. By mid-July dry lightning combined with human ignitions to plunge the Northwest, particularly the Northern Rockies, into a rhythm of smoke and flame. As dry cold fronts passed, the smoke cleared while the fires rushed over into new landscapes. When the winds calmed, smoke smothered the valleys. The Forest Service was determined to fight the blazes, invoking every reserve of manpower it could claim in the region and ultimately inducing President Taft to call out the regular army. The climax came with a horrific swath of firestorms that rushed from the west over the Bitterroots, the fabled Big Blowup of August 20–21. More than three million acres burned in the region that summer, perhaps 75 percent during the Big Blowup.

Suddenly the whole apparatus of American fire protection came together: vast acres burned, immense costs incurred, firefighters lost (seventy-eight dead was the official count), the army called up to help staff the lines, timber salvage and replanting operations carried out, fire policy publicly aired. The fires tested the special funding Act of 1908 that allowed the Forest Service to overspend its budget to pay for fire emergencies (almost $1 million in 1910 dollars), thus confirming the peculiar financial arrangements that would make America's military-like fire mobilizations possible. They traumatized a generation of foresters. Until 1940, every chief forester after Graves had personally weathered the fires; each resolved never to allow such burns to happen again. The policy debate became politicized when Pinchot's rival, Secretary of the Interior Richard Ballinger, supported light burning, noting that the Forest Service seemed incapable of effective fire protection. No single event can shape a century; but the Great Fires set the country down a path from which it could not return. They confirmed that the Forest Service would dominate fire policy and programs, and that fire suppression would, as fully as possible, dominate thinking about fire's administration.

A coherent American narrative is possible because the U.S. Forest Service did, until around 1970, enjoy a hegemony over fire programs and policies and continues to furnish a thematic axis around which the other fire institutions revolve. Still, even that history is complex, far more so than implied by today's received version, which holds that the whole affair began from bad ideas and poor intentions later sold to a brainwashed public by Smokey Bear. Several alternatives are possible, each pertinent to a particular theme.

One might, for example, profitably view America's national history as a loose confederation of regional histories. Each has its own distinctive evolution, adjusted by climate, local biota, settlement experience, fire practices, and maturing institutions. Some regions have little basis for natural fire, some experience it annually—the Northeast and Southeast, respectively, for example. Some have undergone exhaustive land clearing and logging as a prelude to farming, others leaped more or less instantly into the public domain—the Lake States and Intermountain regions, in turn. Fire exclusion originated, for the Southwest, with massive overgrazing and the removal of indigenous firebrands, followed by the establishment of public lands and state-sponsored fire suppression. Fire protection arrived in the Northwest amid cooperative fire protection by timber companies and an abundance of forest already lodged in the public domain.

Similarly, different regions have become nationally prominent at various times and for various reasons. In the early decades of the Forest Service, the Northern Rockies loomed over the agency, confirming a determination not to allow a repetition of the 1910 holocaust. In the postwar era, California surged into preeminence. Southern California's explosive growth sucked in almost a quarter of the national fire armory, while advertising the intermix fire problem defined by Los Angeles's famed sprawl into the San Gabriel Mountains. Northern California reopened the debate over prescribed burning on terms that sounded remarkably similar; what had changed was their context. This time the controversy focused not on high-value timber lands but on ecologically valued and culturally honored national parks. And this time the light burners won, so much so that even the Northern Rockies began accepting natural fires under prescriptions. More recently, one could argue that the Southeast, notably Florida, has become the gravitational center for contemporary fire concerns—fighting fires, lighting them, hosting training academies, coping with the wildland-urban fringe fire scene, and pioneering legislation for fuel cleanup and private burning.

Still other concepts could shape a narrative. One could craft separate institutional histories, those of the federal agencies, those of the states, and those of alliances between agencies. One could focus on technology, or on ideas and science. One could embed fire within the epoch of American settlement and land use: it was part of the environmental shock wave of pioneering, which a maturing nation suppressed. The choice of narrative driver depends on what question one intends to answer.

The options are many. But especially useful as an organizing conceit are three historical rhythms, cycles of significance to American fire that beat in sixty-, thirty-, and twenty-year cadences. They help weigh the relative prominence of the many events that crowd into fire's American chronicle. They help identify the significant events from the common, and those fires that are important from those that are merely big.

The sixty-year rhythm has two sources. It coincides roughly with the pyric transition by which old rural burning habits grudgingly give way to an industrial order and open burning expires. But the rhythm also blocks out a common cycle in the administration of public lands by which a preliminary determination to exclude fire gradually surrenders to a compromise with controlled burning. Both are expressions of industrializing societies. The paradox is that, for inhabited lands, the fires do vanish, while for uninhabited lands, they must be reinstated.

The first of the imperial era's grand experiments, British India, set the pattern. "Light burning" was here known as "early burning," since the fires were kindled early in the dry season. Their primary purpose was to establish fuelbreaks or otherwise eliminate excess grassy combustibles in advance of the major fire season. If we date the onset of full-grade administration with the Indian Forest Law of 1865 (especially as amended in 1878), with its admonition to eliminate fire, then the 1926 forest manual, with its formal (if reluctant) concession to early burning, brings us within the crude sixty-year cycle.

In America, a good test of the pyric transition is the conifer-forested Lake States—Michigan, Wisconsin, Minnesota—where railroads punched north in the late 1860s. Big fires commenced shortly afterward, in 1869–1871; they continued through the severe droughts of the early 1930s, a roughly sixty-year era. When they began, nothing better than the laissez-faire assumption that wild fires would go when wild country did guided the response. When they ended, all levels of government, from local to national, had fire-protection programs and the means to implement them. A similar long rhythm characterizes fire policy on the federal lands. If we take 1910 as the originating moment, when suppression became the announced ambition, reform arrives between 1968 and 1978, more or less within the sixty-year range. While the reasons are murky, it seems to take this long for the policy to undergo transformation.

51

Viewed this way, the history of fire policy divides in half. The United States spent about sixty-plus years trying to suppress fire and is nearly thirty years along in the effort to restore it. The value in this analysis is that it urges us to think in longer historical horizons than normal, and it reminds us that the nation is well advanced in its second phase. The issue is not that we have failed to cross that divide, but that we have so little to show for having breached it decades ago.

The shorter-cycle thirty- and twenty-year rhythms so intertwine that it will be simpler (and less repetitious) to relate a stripped-down version of their common story and afterwards pluck out their separate cadences.

Begin with the Transfer Act of 1905, which brought the forest reserves to the Forest Service, followed by the Great Fires of 1910, the ur-fire of modern American experience and the source of the originating narrative that would guide national understanding of wildland fire throughout the rest of the century. The fires were great not because they were large, although big they certainly were (five million acres on the national forests alone), but because they burst out of the political fissure between Chief Forester Pinchot and Secretary of the Interior Ballinger, a fissure both personal and ideological concerning the proper role of government in the public domain, a rift that would help sunder the Taft administration. The 1910 fires ignited the first great firefight by the Forest Service, sparked the first national discourse on fire policy, and welded wildland firefighting to a national thirst for a "life of strenuous endeavor," as Teddy Roosevelt put it, or for what William James urged as a "moral equivalent of war."[12]

Firefighting embodied such sentiments exactly, so that in intellectual circles, no less than in the field, firefighting attached itself to the prevailing culture. Out of the Great Fires' ashes arose the 1911 Weeks Act that crafted the basis for cooperative fire protection between the states and federal government and that allowed the national forests to expand by purchase. All these threads the standard story of the Great Fires knotted together into a master narrative—a story of fire control, the firefight as the basis for our relationship to wildland fire—that for decades guided the Forest Service and, through it, the other federal agencies and the Service's state cooperators.

The challenges were many, clustering around what might be termed the issue of frontier fire—the promiscuous burning that characterized settlement, a spectacle worsened by the pyric transition. The intellectual challenge was to defeat the arguments in favor of light burning; the practical challenge, to establish "systematic" fire protection in the frontcountry; and the political challenge, to ensure that foresters (and the Forest Service) held the torch. Success came during the regime of William Greeley, a veteran of 1910. Light burning was condemned by a tribunal of foresters in 1923, while the Clarke-McNary Act of 1924 magnified the Weeks Act, expanding federal-state cooperative programs in fire control and enlarging the national forest system. "Cooperative fire" was a magnificent means by which to leverage Forest Service programs beyond the national forests. In an effort to reduce duplication and save money, the Coolidge administration chartered a Forest Protection Board in 1927 to oversee all the forestry programs of the federal government. Mostly, this meant fire protection. Inevitably, the Forest Service dominated the board.

Yet fire protection in reality could not go everywhere. It could not, without obscene costs, pursue large fires into the untracked backcountry. The problem with such fires was not simply practical, the thirst for better roads and pumps; fire practices needed surer intellectual justification as well. In truth, critics abounded, the old refusing to fade away, while new voices restated the arguments in fresh terms. They were waved aside, again and again, dismissed with the patronizing tone one might use with obsessed autodidacts or urban legends. Mostly, critics lingered in the South, where locals argued for fire's necessity in the management of the southern pines—for grazing, for wildlife, for fuel abatement, for control of bluespot fungus. When the Forest Service's own research (in the ever-exceptional South) agreed with some of these arguments, it was, to the agency's shame, suppressed. It was considered politically dangerous, particularly threatening to the shaky alliances with state forestry bureaus. But it was also considered illogical, surely the result of experimental error. There could be no real vindication for fire. The first break in the ranks of professional foresters came only at the 1935 annual meeting of the Society for American Foresters, when H. H. Chapman, an academic from Yale, oversaw a panel on the value of burning in southern pineries.

Nature added its indifferent voice in the form of shattering droughts in the early 1930s that powered monstrous burns—signature fires for their regions—that erupted beyond the grasp of the agency and its collaborators: Matilija in 1932, Tillamook in 1933, Selway in 1934. The Forest Service worried that its paltry presence in the backcountry, symbolized by towering convective columns, like the dirt-clogged clouds of the Dust Bowl, would be used to claim the agency could not perform the most elementary task demanded of it.

In particular, the 1934 fires that savaged the Northern Rockies forced the Forest Service into a soul-searching review of what it had accomplished, or failed to accomplish, since 1910. Assembled in Missoula, the Service's fire authorities agreed on three options for the backcountry: Keep every acre green. Leave it alone. Or muddle along with some compromise between all-out suppression and letting fires burn. Everyone agreed that compromise was meaningless. It solved nothing. Between the extremes, the corps of forester bureaucrats opted for control. As one participant observed, agencies and professions simply don't walk away from such challenges (actually the British in Burma had, abandoning a failed fire-suppression program to laissez-faire native practices). Other, more slippery arguments arose out of the proceedings, particularly from Elers Koch, another veteran of 1910. Not only had fire control not worked, he insisted, the stubborn effort to install it—punching roads ever more deeply into the backcountry—was destroying some of the natural and cultural values that the agency had pledged to protect. These were hard choices for an agency still proud of its frontline legacy in American conservation. Even so the Forest Service could only pursue ends for which it had sufficient means. That changed with the advent of the New Deal, which installed a gentleman-forester as president and disbursed the vast bounty of the Civilian Conservation Corps and other emergency conservation programs.

What really decided the matter was politics: the Franklin D. Roosevelt administration was eager to pair the rehabilitation of America's Depression economy with that of its wrecked lands. The CCC, in particular, placed the resources to rework fire practices into the hands of those who had the power to decide goals. Suddenly, a civilian army existed to build roads, string phone lines, cut corridors through snag fields, construct enormous fuelbreaks, and fight fire. Almost overnight, an infrastructure for fire protection appeared. The magnitude of New-Deal means clearly argued for a similar inflation of Forest Service ends. The windfall addressed the question of how far one could justify aggressive fire control. The answer was, everywhere.

Three decades after the Transfer Act, Chief Forester Gus Silcox, another veteran of the 1910 fires, promulgated the 10 AM policy, announcing as an experiment on a continent scale a program of all-out fire control. Officers should plan to control every fire by 10 AM the day following its report; and failing that, to plan for control by 10 AM the next day; and so on, ad infinitum. Fire protection swarmed over the backcountry. The administrative orders inspired new programs to supplement the lone smokechaser. In 1939, two took the field: smokejumpers (parachute-equipped smokechasers), adept at attacking snag fires in remote hinterlands, and "shock-troop" crews of forty men, specially trained for large, campaign fires. The 10 AM policy became both symbol and goal, soon acquiring the authority of a papal encyclical. Here was a more intense and lavish story of fire protection, though one that shot out of the rifled narrative bore of the Great Fires.

Here, too, was an ideal program for a country entering a world war and the hot conflicts of the early cold war. Forest defense—fire control—became explicitly identified with national defense. (In 1945 Japan did launch balloons outfitted with incendiaries in the hopes that they might start crippling conflagrations. The Strategic Bombing Survey documented the power, if not always the precision, of aerial firebombing. And the war, after all, ended with two atomic-kindled holocausts.) The war years were filled with fiery images. Not accidentally, the two national fire-prevention campaigns, Keep America Green and Smokey Bear, both began during World War II, the latter under the auspices of the Wartime Advertising Council. It was amidst the war, too, that Disney Studios released *Bambi*, which climaxes in a horrific wildfire. The original story says nothing about fires: that was inserted for an American audience that inevitably associated forests with fires. The movie sent a powerful antifire message to children, especially, because the people who kill Bambi's mother are the ones who start the fire that threatens Bambi and his father. As the country moved further from its rural roots, its sensitivity to open fire changed as swiftly as suburban demographics.

By 1950, while another war heated up, interest shifted to the ways and means of controlling large fires, the kind started by military conflict or their civilian analogues, what technocrats trying to downplay journalist hyperbole over "firestorms" began to call "mass fire." (Two weeks after a forest fire overran a crew of smokejumpers at Mann Gulch in the Northern Rockies in August 1949, the Soviet Union exploded its first atomic bomb. That was the blowup fire that got the government's attention.) The next war, authorities agreed, would be a fire war. Meanwhile, civil defense became a permanent institution. The Forest Service assumed oversight for a rudimentary rural fire defense. Big science came to fire research in the form of military contracts, three national laboratories under Forest Service administration, and a National Academy of Science Committee on Fire

Research. The United States embarked on a two-decade cold war on fire. The 10 AM policy remained in effect.[13]

Fire suppression's problems seemed technical: force enough, fast enough—getting sufficient crews and equipment to a still small fire quickly. After the Korean conflict, an immense storehouse of war-surplus equipment became available, to which the Forest Service and its collaborators had priority access. Its sudden mechanization, most spectacularly with aircraft, allowed fire suppression to extend its reach over the countryside; its reliance on military hardware reinforced the metaphor of firefighting as a moral equivalent of war; and the implicit association between fire control and national defense lent a patriotic cast to the endeavor. "Conflagration control" dominated planning. A one-year field experiment, Operation Firestop, explored ways to transfer war-surplus hardware to fire protection. It was a golden age for equipment development and for scientific research. And it ended in quagmire.

A reckoning came during the 1960s. There were internal strains. Costs were escalating, crowding against the point of diminishing returns. Suppression was demanding more of everything—crews, research, equipment, outlays for actual firefighting. There were mounting environmental costs as well. An efflorescence in biological science confirmed a vital role for fire in many biotas. The ecology of fire exclusion made clear that fire's removal had penalties. When old criticisms revived, including that living dead of fire policy, light burning, they did so in the garb of ecology. And in the giant sequoias, fire ecology found its poster child, a charismatic megaflora deemed in desperate need of remedial fire. But mostly there was a vision of The Wild, and the need to bend fire suppression to its will.

The precipitating factors, that is, were cultural—a passion for wilderness and parks. In 1963 the Leopold Report for the Park Service argued for parks as "vignettes of Primitive America."[14] A year later Congress passed the Wilderness Act. For such places it was fire suppression, not fire, that threatened fundamental values. The era redirected the national discourse away from keeping bad fires out and instead turned to the problem of putting good fires back in. Agencies ceased to demonize "wild" fire, and instead began to celebrate it. An institutional midwife appeared in the Tall Timbers Research Station, a private Florida corporation that in 1962 commenced a series of annual conferences in "fire ecology," openly contemptuous of official policy, and that became a forum for opinions outside not only the Forest Service but the entire federal establishment. Fire suppression had, it appeared, become the self-defeating ogre its early critics had predicted. A fire counterculture flourished.

It was a heady time, full of frothy philosophy and the politics of protest. The era became one of wide experimentation, under a growing conviction that because fire was "natural" it was also good; and that the best remedy for past interventions was not to intervene at all, that natural fire was the ideal vehicle of restoration, and prescribed fire a less desirable if necessary surrogate. All could agree, however, that untrammeled firefighting had to cease. Suppression needed ecological shackles. Free-burning fire needed to reclaim its wild heritage, to achieve its self-actualizing nature. The reformation spread from ideas to institutions. The Forest Service—hammered on any number of wilderness and environmental issues, of which fire was but one—lost control over its agenda and, with remarkable swiftness, its hegemony over fire management.

The 10 AM policy collapsed. A cascade of institutional reforms followed. The Park Service broke ranks first, installing a new policy over the winter of 1967–68. A year later, under pressure from the Department of the Interior, the Interagency Fire Center opened in Boise, a site for shared dispatching and collective response, eventually on a national basis. The push continued with a doctrine of total mobility that sought to remove differences that prevented instantaneous transfers of crews and equipment among agencies. Then the detente between the Departments of Agriculture and the Interior culminated in 1976 with the establishment of a National Wildfire Coordinating Group to achieve consensus on training, certification, equipment standards, and the like. Two years later, after several temporizing measures, the Forest Service formally abandoned the 10 AM policy in favor of a mixed-response strategy (a policy of fire by prescription). In less than a decade, Forest Service domination over fire—its policy, its science, its equipment and crews—had crumbled. Across the country a hundred flowers of fire experimentation bloomed. A euphoria for heavy equipment gave way to one for prescribed burning. Ideas triumphed over gadgets, and ideals over raw power.

As always, however, principle was easier than practice. It proved simpler to denounce the culture of suppression than to invent a working successor. Prescribed fire's narrative never fully replaced suppression's, and in striking ways, never established itself on its own terms. Its narrative grew around suppression's like a bean vine around a maize stalk. Its accomplishments were ofttimes more symbolic than practical. Its logic proved often garbled, its execution frequently faulty. There were plenty of poorly publicized failures—breakdowns in execution, escapes that bolted beyond prescriptions, an inability to get sufficient acres burned on the ground or burned in the right way. When stressed enough, the master narrative defaulted to the firefight. Power still came out of the nozzle of a fire hose. Controlled burning rested, finally, on the ability to control fire.

The vision of fire by prescription was exhilarating. Its blunders could be dismissed, for a good while, as part of the grim side effects of a necessary national detox program from suppression. An escaped "natural" fire, the Ouzel in Rocky Mountain National Park in 1978, nearly incinerated the town of Allenspark, and the Park Service sought to reclaim some central control over its fire program by issuing national guidelines the next year, even as the Forest Service was scrapping the last vestiges of its 10 AM policy. The Ouzel fire, however, proved but a dress rehearsal for the mammoth burns that swept over Yellowstone National Park in 1988. The era ended with Wagnerian flourish in Yellowstone's *Götterdämmerung*.

Since then, as its problem of choice, the fire community has latched most fiercely to the question of fire on the urban fringe, that ecological omelet of wildland and exurban fragments, a variously named fractal geography of fire. (Call it, for simplicity, the intermix fire.) America is recolonizing its rural countryside but doing so with an urban outmigration, crafting a landscape to satisfy urban ambitions and esthetics. The compound is proving metastable, easily provoked into explosion. Annually, wildfires gnaw into communities. In recent years, powered by drought and drought's collateral damages such as beetle infestations, the flames have moved beyond the realm of trophy homes and trailer parks. Fire is no longer a spectacle of the wild, a curiosity—however majestic—of remote places. The feral fire has literally turned on the domestic.

Yellowstone's 1988 fire potlatch did remarkably little to reshape federal policy. The fires were a mixed bag—some started by lightning, some by people; some burned into the park, some out of it; but all fell loosely under the aegis of a permissive policy of fire tolerance. The park was avid for large fires. The federal government footed the staggering bill (in excess of $130 million; this was a national election year). The fire community rallied to defend the conviction of its new principles, deflecting public debate into the question of whether fire belonged in Yellowstone, not how it should belong. The conflagrations did, however, alert the public to flame's environmental character, and they introduced an era of celebrity fires.

But as the intermix scene relocated fire's geographic frontier, so Norman Maclean's 1992 best seller, *Young Men and Fire*, a meditation on the 1949 Mann Gulch fire, repositioned western flames in the national consciousness. It made fire in the West something worth contemplating, something other than a freak of regional violence, the western equivalent of a southern lynching. Fire, Maclean demonstrated, merited intellectual attention. Two years later the South Canyon fire outside Glenwood Springs, Colorado, recapitulated the Mann Gulch story. The media now had a prism by which to interpret this updated Rocky Mountain tragedy, a drama full of journalistic human interest in ways that abstract concepts of wilderness could not match. However grisly the sinews, America's free-burning fires were reconnected with their sustaining culture.

The 1994 season was an *annus horribilis*—deadly, costly, futile. This time reforms targeted the actual practice of fire management, not simply its philosophy. By December 1995 the federal land agencies merged their various fire practices into a common policy. Meanwhile, the Long Drought settled over the West, and near-record fire seasons burst forth. More studies, more reforms—fire was becoming politicized in ways not true since the New Deal. Agencies began to restate policy the way post-Enron corporations did profits. In 1998 a Joint Fire Science Program, overseen by both the Forest Service and the Department of the Interior, sought to consolidated federal research, and pump into it the kind of money not seen for decades. In 2000 a National Fire Plan (NFP) proposed a major investment in the fire establishment, while (yet another) review of federal policy (again) confirmed its core precepts. In particular, the NFP and its successors sought to break out of a hopeless cycle of flame and suppression by attacking the underlying causes, particularly exuberant fuels. To ensure compliance, a Wildland Fire Leadership Council convened among the agencies.

Since the media, with stirring oversimplification, usually identified "fire suppression" as the source of a land overgrown with combustibles, fire's grand narrative became publicly ironic. Suppression had yielded a public domain that for all the billions expended was less secure. (Irony might not matter much to the literate public since it had become modernism's default setting, but it had not yet infected fire protection's public persona.) The upshot was that no single story line could triumph. Even as suppression was called upon to save fast-incinerating fringe communities, it was denounced as the source of America's wildland-fire problem. This complicated, too, honoring those firefighters who fell in the line of duty. The nature of their duty had become murky, and how they might be remembered unclear. Those who were presumably protecting society were also responsible for corrupting its lands; and those crews were eager to say so. (Hotshots were only too eager to explain to journalists that they, the "shots," were not putting fires out, only putting them off.) Away from housing developments, the fallen more resembled trekkers lost on Everest than defenders of the national estate, as though firefighting had metamorphosed from an exercise in national security into an extreme sport.

The public was rightly confused. What ought to be done? The answer was simple in principle: a lot of things in a lot of places, different things in divers places. Instead of being a model for society, an inspiration for other institutions, a template of moral clarity, fire management had apparently joined the crowd. It was as complex, muddled, and quarrelsome as everything else, with the quirk that it could occasionally turn deadly.

How might one tease out of this tangle historical patterns?

A twenty-year rhythm is fairly easy to detect. Every two decades the fire community seems to identify a new "problem" fire, which then commands inordinate money and staffing and which appears to inform the establishment overall. (One can trace this odd phenomenon back to the creation of the earliest forest reserves by presidential proclamation in 1891, though it makes more sense to launch the sequence with the 1910 fires.) Not only does each era have its distinguishing problem, it also tries to solve it by appeal to distinctive institutional abundances that become available.

The sequence plays out like this. From 1910 to 1932 the critical issue was the frontier fire, the cumulative practices of settlement. The task was to create an infrastructure in the frontcountry, fight off light burning, and rely on the emergency fire fund to staff firefights. With the advent of the New Deal, fire protection moved boldly into the backcountry (1933–1949); new emergency monies and the CCC, especially, made this surge possible, perhaps irresistible. Then came an era informed by what we might call the mass fire (1950–1969) during which the United States commenced a cold war on fire. Fire protection folded readily into the ambitions of a national-security state; war-surplus equipment replaced the CCC as a source of institutional inspiration, and lab-based fire research sought to apply science to the task. This gave way to an era of wilderness fire (1970–1989), bracketed by the removal of the 10 AM policy and the Yellowstone fires. The outpouring of research suggested that knowledge could substitute for brute power, that prescriptions were a kind of control. Around 1990 the era of the intermix fire arrived.

A thirty-year rhythm tracks deeper shifts in the goals and, if you will, the narrative of fire management. Begin with the 1905 Transfer Act, followed by the Great Fires of 1910. That combination inaugurated a program of systematic fire protection, but one self-constrained by weak resources and a belief that the costs of fire control should not exceed the values it sought to protect. Thirty years later that perspective came under boisterous review, but despite determined criticism yielded the 10 AM policy. This carried through until the Seismic Sixties, when wilderness, a culture of protest, and a fervor for prescribed fire sparked policy reforms. The next wave hit roughly thirty years later, symbolized by the consolidated 1995 Federal Wildland Fire Management Policy and the 2000 National Fire Plan. Together they completed the most comprehensive overhaul of fire practices since the New Deal.

Restated, those phases run like this: The first wave devised a rude program of fire protection for wildlands. The second wave promulgated a doctrine of universal, unconditional fire suppression. The third wave promoted fire's restoration, largely through prescribed burning. The fourth wave, underway but still finding its sea legs, appears destined to focus on modifying landscape fuels. Even so, these bold storms characterize only America's fire narrative. The deep currents and bottom waters belong with fire's grand narrative and with vast shifts in land use, notably the status of public lands.

Rhythms and Reasons

Such rhythms are merely an aid to insight, not an exercise in historical astrology. They are like lattices when the real chronicle is the tangle of vines weaving through and among them. There is much more to the story, or stories, of course. But an exuberance of facts may be considered bureaucratic foam, the routine froth that accompanies any large undertaking. This three-stranded scheme—fire's narrative, the imperial narrative, and America's narrative—should be enough to bear the weight of the analysis to follow.

What do the three suggest for the United States? First, that we are well into a second phase of the sixty-year rhythm, one without precedents, with the only discernible trend a fuller global commitment to industrial combustion and, in developed countries, a per capita reduction in carbon release. Second, that we have just witnessed the formative onset of another thirty-year rhythm, one that will probably involve wholesale fuel modifications in some way or another. Third, that we have crested the most recent twenty-year rhythm—the attempt to grapple with the intermix fire, however unobvious that may appear—and ought to begin contemplating fire's next new thing.

They suggest, in brief, different levels of crisis and response. With regard to the intermix fire scene, we may be riding the crest of that wave and ought to begin searching the near horizon for its successor. For major federal policy reforms the revolution has passed, and the future is likely to mean working through its practical implications. This may consume considerable effort, however. The current policy, one of "appropriate response," is as generic as its 10 AM predecessor was emphatic. Today's lacks the rigor, the specific rules of engagement, that tell on-the-ground personnel just what to do and in what order. Its ecumenism forces a constant discourse about goals, and muddles what is for participants a concrete truth, that the different agencies exist because they have different missions.

With respect to the deep-current chronicle of global combustion, the United States is at one place and most of the world at another. Some of America's visible problems it shares with other nations. All industrial nations seem afflicted by some variant of the intermix fire, as their rural landscapes unravel. Those nations with vast public domains find themselves suffering from larger, more costly wildfires and stumble as they try to restore some fraction of the burning that those protected biotas crave. But most of Earth's fires lie outside the pale of industrialization. They burn in sub-Saharan Africa, South America, south and southeast Asia, and those unsettled outbacks of the more developed nations. America's fire obsessions have little to say about such concerns. Nor has the American fire community seriously considered the relationship between industrial fire and landscape burning, between the closed combustion of fossil biomass and the open flame of free-burning fire through living biomass. Yet the hand turning the lever will ultimately direct the hand holding the torch.

So why are America's fires out of control? The reasons are many and layered.

The most immediate cause is ignition. Even the worst briar patch of fuels does not combust spontaneously. Something has to kindle it. Horrific mounds of combustibles avoid burning all the time—big fires are the exception, not the norm. Unimaginably awful fuel dumps routinely escape kindling. Often they burn because a fire started elsewhere blasts into them, but otherwise the burden of ignition falls to lightning or, in some way, to people. A large fraction of fire starts, even in nominally uninhabited places, continue to emanate from people, and a goodly percentage of those appear to be deliberate. Two of the biggest began as signal fires set by lost hikers (Cedar fire, and Chediski, which merged with the Rodeo fire). While lightning typically burns the most area (in remote sites), human ignition burns the most houses. For many fire-prone landscapes, fire in principle might be inevitable, but a particular fire is not.

The reason ignitions of any sort spread, however, is that the environment can propagate them, and this is mostly a consequence of short-term weather. Regional-scale bouts of drying and wind associated with the arrival and breakdown of high-pressure systems, events ranging from five to fourteen days, underwrite most of North America's extensive burns and explosive runs. The largest fires undergo this pattern of calm and conflagration over and over. Meanwhile, seasons full of large fires track the spiky oscillations of El Niño–La Niña. A deep-wave drought set in around 1985, moderating briefly from 1989 to 1992, before strengthening; and as long as it persists, so will a succession of big-fire seasons.

Behind that cause of fire's resurgence is fuel. These reside in public lands, and they reflect everything we have done, and not done, over the past century and a half. The amount of biomass has increased virtually everywhere; but biomass is not the same as available fuel. Only a fraction of the vegetation is of a character that can burn (the percentage can be high for a prairie, low for a mature forest; even a so-called stand-replacing fire, one that obliterates an existing forest and makes possible a wholesale replacement, incinerates only the needles and fine branches and merely scorches the trunks). What matters is the amount and arrangement of fine fuels—grasses, needles, brush, particles with a high proportion of surface to their volume, landscapes stuffed with fine-particled forests, shrubs, understories. There are legitimate reasons to believe that the amount of combustibles suitable for burning has increased over the past century. Even so, the fraction that is actually available for combustion also depends on a particle's internal moisture. Green or wet wood will not burn, no matter how thickly congested. A few soggy years (like that in the early 1980s) and the "fire problem" will fade from public consciousness like yesterday's smoke.

The deeper drivers are land use and industrial combustion. The habitat for free-burning fire centers mostly in the public lands, or in fire-prone places where widespread abandonment by agriculture has encouraged a tumult of vegetation, which can then sustain a riot of flame. These respond to economic and political forces, themselves buffeted about by demographic storms and global economic winds. The mass migration of people, the movement of land into and out of agriculture, the shift from a commodity to a service economy, the tidal flows of capital to make such changes, the collapse of governments or revolutions in political economy—all so seemingly removed from fire's front—in fact alter what is available to burn and how fire is applied and withheld. Again, fire is a sensitive synthesizer of all around it. And beyond the realm of open flame lies the proximate prime mover of contemporary fire, the burning of fossil biomass.

The cause of the West's fires? Dry lightning storms; inept or malicious people; overgrazing that scrapes away the grassy fuels that make light fires possible; high-grade logging that upsets the structure of fire-adapted forests; programs of fire suppression; a dry cold front that stirs up embers into flame; a national forest or park that, as a matter of policy, seeks to replace one fire regime with another; the eccentric cadences of warm waters in the Pacific, altering the balance of wetting and drying; the cars we drive, and other implements of industrial combustion; a transcendental longing for wilderness with its implied change in fire regimes; an esthetic for woodlands that discourages active management of landscapes; coal-fired power plants contributing to global warming; exurban patches amid overgrown conifers; misplaced prescribed fire, either bolting out of control or not doing the burning demanded; exotic pyrophytes like cheatgrass that rapidly remake landscapes in ways that promote undesired fire regimes; the hard-environmentalist ethos of the religious left, unwilling to allow human agency in fire management; timber slash that provides points for fire infection; a loss of everyday lore regarding burning such that the public has no firsthand understanding of how fire behaves; an atmosphere choked with combustion effluent, nudging global climate into patterns that may make wildfires more common and ferocious for a few decades— take your pick. Or better, pick them all.

To focus on the fire plague of the past two decades, however, is to mistake an opening lead for a topic sentence. The fundamental American story is not fire's savage, quickening assault on western woods and exurbs, but its overall disappearance. America has gone from a fire-flushed country to a fire-starved one. That is what has unhinged its lands.

CHAPTER TWO

Torch and Shovel

🖎 *The Means of Fire Management*

THERE ARE PUBLIC lands that are not fire-prone, and there are fire-prone lands that are not in the public domain. But the "fire problem" that has grabbed the body politic by its lapels is that of the American West, where abundant public lands and a fire-kindling climate overlap.

On these landscapes four options exist for fire management. They are the four elements out of which all the compounded practices of fire management come, as true in Gippsland and the Siberian taiga as the Sierra Anchas of Arizona and the boreal forest of the Canadian Shield. Simply put: You can do nothing, and leave the fires to God and nature. You can try to exclude fires and to suppress those that do break out. You can do the burning yourself. Or you can change the combustibility of the landscape such that fires, whether from accident, arson, lightning, or prescription behave in ways you favor.

The lesson of the past century is that none of these strategies can succeed by itself. We can't cut our way out of the problem. We can't burn our way out. We can't suppress. And we can't walk away. Proper fire management requires bits of each, mixed to proportions suitable to the taste of particular sites. That is not a romantic vision, primed to enflame the hearts and souls of a confused public. There is no conversion experience awaiting fire policy, washing away the errors of the past, affirming a straight-and-narrow path to salvation. There is instead a drabber story of redemption by faith, good works, and long-patient commitment. That's what makes our pact with fire a relationship.

Option 1. Let Burn

Let burn has many attractions. If fire is "natural," good, and useful, then in wildlands why not just stand aside and let nature's fires solve nature's fire problems? If people have mucked up America's fire regimes, then it should follow that removing people will allow those lands to rebound back to their former state. Not least, letting it all burn has to be cheaper than any other alternative. Besides, let burn has a long history, for unless a fire threatened life or property it was, until relatively recently, left alone. The source of the fire did not matter, only its remoteness from what society valued. No community had either the resources or the will (or the urgency) to fight it. The fires free burned. They might burn for all of a season, alternately creeping and sweeping, smoldering and blowing up as winds, woods, and terrain warranted.

This laissez-faire regime ended with the creation of public lands because governments felt responsible, or were made to feel responsible by their agencies and critics, for fires on lands within their writ, however remote. Yet practical considerations—poor access, small staffs, the sheer risk—argued for letting distant fires flame and puff where they were. In the early years of the Forest Service, rangers considered "let burning" and "loose herding" as valid strategies for coping with difficult fires in the backcountry. Most such fires expired while small. The big ones could not be stopped. Let burning made a virtue out of necessity.

Long-loitering fires, however, have a way of looking for trouble. They can smoke in valleys and settlements even several ridges away, sometimes for months. They can break out of their hinterlands. (One of the major reasons why large fires have become fewer is that small fires are no longer allowed to linger on the landscape, with the increasing likelihood that they might dry out and catch winds and swell into conflagrations.) Moreover, experience taught that it was far cheaper to hit fires when they were small than after they had become large. Attacking every fire, even smoking snags on talus slopes, avoided having to guess which such ignitions might, eventually and through unforeseen means, become problems. The expense of even a single large fire could be so exorbitant that it made the cumulative cost of suppressing many tiny ones trivial in comparison. If one could reach such fires, it was better to attack them than to trust to weather and luck.

Besides, public institutions had politics looking over their shoulder. The Forest Service from its inception had argued that the surest, most scientifically justified policy for conservation was systematic fire protection. A let-burn strategy challenged that doctrine in the backcountry, as light burning challenged it in the frontcountry. If let burning was okay in the mountains, then why wasn't light burning okay in the foothills? Worse, if foresters were wrong about fire, which was so fundamental to their administration, then could they not be wrong also about other matters, many of which riled local settlers? Not least, letting fires ramble sent an awkward political message: If an agency did nothing, then why did it exist? If the Forest Service (or Park Service, or a state lands bureau) was unable or unwilling to control fires, then why was it entrusted to oversee so vast an estate?

These were arguments grounded in economics and politics and the rude state of early-days fire protection. They assumed that less fire was better than more fire, and that the purpose of fire protection was to shield valuable sites from the waste and ruin of flame. Fire protection was an investment: forests that seemed remote today would be needed tomorrow, and future generations would not be pleased to find blackened snags instead of robust timber. Let burning happened because no agency had the money

71

and manpower to stop every fire. This fitful debate ended conclusively with the New Deal, which made available the means and the mandate to pursue fires into the backcountry. No longer could let burning be winked away as a virtue made from a vice.

A reconsideration came with the Great Cultural Revolution of the 1960s. Its epicenter was a rupture in values, and fire management shared that tectonic shift. There emerged a passion for the wild; for parks that could preserve, or where necessary, recreate "vignettes of Primitive America"; for outright wilderness, preserved by statute; for the creatures and storms and untrammeled ecological might that such sacred places held; for fires unrestrained by human technology and bureaucratic ambition. Ecological science added its voice. Fire was natural, fire was a legitimate disturbance to which ecosystems had adapted, fire's removal could lead to damaging side effects. Fire was useful, its restoration was urgent. And a widespread revulsion had developed against paramilitary programs like elk culling at Yellowstone and firefighting in the wilds—bulldozers ripping up what fire control had promised to protect. The Vietnam War had seemingly come home. Americans were fighting their very land.

The insurgents seized the high ground: it was fire's suppression that was wrong; it was suppression, not free-burning flame, that needed shackles. Revealingly, the winter of 1967–68, when the National Park Service revised its fire policy, was the same season that *Star Trek* began its TV run. Both accepted the same prime directive, a doctrine of noninterference, with allowances for corrections. If, for example, something had intervened in the natural evolution of a people or ecosystem, it was acceptable under the prime directive (in fact, obligatory) to intervene further in such a way as to return it to its original path. This is an apt characterization of the reformed fire philosophy at the time. Leave it to nature, but where human meddling has upset the process (say, with fire suppression), deliberately reintroduce fire until the system returns to something like its former state, and then withdraw. The move to restore natural fire was, in a sense, Star Fleet's mission to Earth.

One upshot was to revive let burning as a competing doctrine of fire management. The reasons were both practical and philosophical. Fighting fire in the wild was costly, dangerous, and often damaging, particularly where tracked vehicles smashed forests and rutted soils. Letting fires burn, which was their "natural" state, had to be less expensive. (Anything short of invading a foreign country had to be cheaper than a campaign fire.) Surely, this was a case where economics and environmentalism agreed. But the metaphysics mattered too, because it tapped into the zeitgeist: nature knew best; humans were invariably stupid, selfish, and clumsy, forever doing the wrong thing; the optimal strategy was to stand aside and let nature's fires run wild and free. While deliberate burning was useful, the ultimate goal should be to let fire free-range as fully as grizzly bears and bighorn sheep. Natural regulation was intrinsically superior to anything humans could contrive.

Still, let burning had regrettable connotations. It was the function of an agency to manage, or appear to manage, and beyond the politics of perception there were issues of liability and financing. If a fire misbehaved, the government could be sued. When a "natural" fire blew up in Rocky Mountain National Park, Boulder County famously sued the park for violation of air-quality regulations. Instead of fire crews, let burns would confront a phalanx of lawyers. If even 2 to 3 percent of let burns ran amok, the court costs could run into real money, and the suppression expenses would shred any pretense of let burning being fire protection on the cheap.

The ingenious response was to devise two techniques for granting fire more room on the ground. Each sought to sponsor fires that were both wild yet unfree. One, a specialty of the National Park Service, was the prescribed natural fire (PNF). This was a fire set by nature but managed by fire officers according to a plan that specified where and under what conditions such fires could occur. (The search for a usable expression began with "let-burn fire," coined in 1968 at Sequoia–Kings Canyon National Park, before undergoing several bureaucratic metamorphoses into "natural prescribed fire" and eventually "prescribed natural fire.")[1] The other was the confinement fire, one of several options available under prevailing concepts of suppression. In effect, the standards for suppression loosened to allow for different degrees of control.

The PNF was always a policy platypus. It was an attempt to have wildfire yet keep it bottled up. In practice it meant that the ability to forecast fire behavior could replace the force of muscle and machine. It meant, if done properly, having trained teams of fire monitors camped at the site to measure environmental conditions, observe actual fire behavior, and report. In effect, the new regime substituted monitors for the smokechasers who had traditionally made a first attack. (Particularly with the Park Service, the new era tried to create a fire organization for prescribed fire in parallel to that for suppression.) The differences mattered, however. Monitors might be on the scene for a long time, or if the fire smoldered in a remote site, they might leave and the fire might be monitored by aircraft as part of general reconnaissances. If a fire burned beyond its prescribed borders or outside its designated zone, suppression would beat it back into its paper cage; and if that failed, the fire was declared wild, to be hunted down and shot.

The other, parallel approach was to broaden the standards for control. Instead of meaning only extinguishment, unrelenting unto the last smoke, suppression could be construed to mean a suite of options, the (for the public confusing) Three Cs. One could "control" in the traditional sense of direct attack, an effort to stop and put out every fraction of the fire. Or one could "contain," which meant to halt a fire's perimeter spread, leaving the interior to burn out. Or one could "confine," which meant to keep a fire within a given area under acceptable conditions. Credible fire plans specified what those places and circumstances should be. While, in the field, a confinement fire might be indistinguishable from a prescribed natural fire, the bureaucratic and cultural distinctions were real. The PNF had more philosophical clout in that it celebrated naturalness; it brought the transcendental wild to center stage. The confinement fire had the advantage that emergency fire accounts paid for it, since it was, technically, a fire being "suppressed." By contrast, the PNF had to operate, like other prescribed burns, within a budget set well in advance of fire season.

The let-burn strategy had its triumphs and its debacles. The effects of both linger today.

The successes, beginning in 1968 but flourishing during the 1970s, were sometimes spectacular. A determination to repudiate the culture of suppression could have no more majestic symbolism than to stand aside and let a large fire ramble through the landscape. Lightning-kindled fires burned in Grand Teton and Sequoia–Kings Canyon National Parks, in Yellowstone, in the White Cap Wilderness, and elsewhere, and agencies rejoiced in fire's liberation and used the events to argue their case before a public they assumed would be skeptical if not implacably hostile. There was an element of countercultural theater at work, mocking an establishment that seemed (to the insurgents) intent on suppressing novelty and spontaneity and only able to appeal to authority or to call out troops. Suppression was recklessly, mindlessly intervening in affairs that were, at bottom, only an internal quarrel of nature's.

It was relatively simple to dismiss the critics of the new ways (and one could always find some idiot, writing to the editor of a local paper, whose ignorance and prejudice could make him a straw man for an imaginary public too ossified to comprehend anything beyond their Winnebago windows). When smoke from the Waterfalls Canyon fire obscured Jackson Hole, the Park Service shrugged off complaints. The smoke was a nuisance, well worth the annoyance, like having an eagle or wolf take an occasional lamb. Nature was restoring nature's balance. The agencies were finally doing what they should have done from the beginning. Instead of a threat, the agency informed its visiting public that such fires were a scenic marvel, at least equal to bison sightings and geysers. And rather than unremitting hostility, chunks of the public, certainly the literate public, quickly grasped the essence of the experiment. They appreciated the ethos of natural fire and even threatened to subvert fire's avant-garde by endorsing it.

Once the philosophical euphoria wore off, however, the difficulties were no longer irritants but genuine problems. Monitoring proved boring, and not all parks and forests did the hard labor of scrutinizing a fire, particularly if it smoldered over a season. Prolonged smoke could be tolerated, like an errant bear rooting through a garbage dump; but if it persisted for weeks, it segued from a nuisance into a public-health menace. More worryingly, the ability to forecast fire behavior proved poorer than the proliferation of agency-issued nomograms and hand calculators would suggest. (Fire monitors wore TI-59 calculators from their belts as earlier smokechasers had Buck knives and compasses.) The economics proved tricky, too. For small fires, there was no savings in money, and often more expense as monitors remained for days while a fire smoldered on to burn out instead of the hours it would have taken to knock it cold. If the fire became big, it was almost by definition out of control, and hence had to be fought, so its expenses became huge. Budgeting a PNF program was no more predictable than budgeting any other fire program: one could never forecast what the actual needs would be. After a few slow seasons, the temptation was irresistible to siphon unused PNF money off for something that had a real need, now. By contrast, one did not have to pay for a confinement fire until it happened, and then by using emergency funds. There was a limit to how much symbolism a program could afford.

The big-fire question went to the pragmatic heart of a natural-fire strategy: the PNF worked beautifully on innocuous snag fires and flames that flickered over the surface, but broke down on the monster burns that had prompted the let-burn argument in the first place. Such fires were uncontrolled; they were immensely expensive; and they tended to occur precisely when large fires broke out over a region, which is to say, they further overloaded a suppression organization. The latter mattered because, if an agency decided the prescribed fire needed to be controlled, it might not have the firefighting resources to do the job. What had evolved as a compromise position had become laissez-faire fire loitering, which only confirmed what fire agencies had learned by hard experience: small fires left alone led to big fires. For a decade some of the country's largest, most expensive, and damaging fires were prescribed natural fires that went bad. When that happened, they became reclassified as wildfires, and the public knew them as such. The fire community was not anxious to advertise its breakdowns.

Still, if the issues had remained strictly practical, they might have succumbed to steady, technological fixes. More troubling were deeper matters of ecology and of philosophy. The first called into question the presumption that the new policies were science-based in ways that the suppression strategy was not. Fire ecology might inform programs no better than its forestry-based predecessors. Science might, for example, explain that sequoia seedlings would not regenerate in dense duff but would do nicely in the thick ash left by intense burning. But that did not argue for the necessary reintroduction of lightning fire into the groves, or for free-burning prescribed fire to scour away the organic matting beneath the Big Trees; one might achieve a good seedbed by walking around with a blowtorch. The insistence on a "natural" solution stemmed from cultural values, not from scientific data. The appeal to ecology subtly highlighted how the nominally neutral science really masked a metaphysics of nature. If the science disagreed with those fundamental values, would not contemporary managers dismiss it or send their researchers back for another look, much as foresters had earlier done? The new science could demonstrate the flaws of a suppression program. It could not say what, precisely, should replace it.

Ecological analysis, moreover, posed a practical problem, a question of scale, that administrators could not resolve. The fact is, large-area, often high-intensity fires do much of the biological work demanded of burning—and most of it in northern conifer forests and in chaparral. A program that banned such burns was a biological sham, yet almost invariably such fires exceeded their prescriptions because they were beyond the ability of an agency to control them. They shattered the planning premise that, should a fire blow up or bolt beyond its designated habitat, the fire organization could beat it back into containment. Many programs, that is, denied precisely those fires that were most needed. Besides, it goes without saying that such fires were impossible in small parks and wildernesses. A legal wilderness could be as small as 5,000 acres. A conflagration could burn it clean in a couple of hours. Fire science could offer no solution.

Thus the significance of the second issue, that of philosophy, the values and worldviews that underwrote both science and institutions and all the rest of what a fire program had to engage. The reformation had not begun from hard evidence but from beliefs, from a faith that the wild, the free-burning, the natural, and the ecological formed a whole and a better way. That inchoate belief motivated and sustained through the daily, grinding, bureaucratic slog to bring fire to the land. Eventually, it faltered, as the higher criticism that had subverted suppression also turned on let burning.

One could tolerate glitches and the occasional collapse if the cause was right and just. But as "natural fire" went from philosophy to policy to practice, fissures appeared in the premises behind it, like expansion cracks in an aging highway. It was not obvious, for example, how "natural" these fires were, and doubts increased as fire-history studies documented the pervasive shifts that had accompanied not only settlement but the internal development of the reserved lands themselves. Creating national forests and parks had not removed such lands from history, but had set into motion new histories, perhaps far different from what they had known over millennia. In general, fuel loads had intensified; fires burned hotter and more broadly.

But the dilemma involved more than human-heaped fuels. The record hinted that lightning-kindled fires could not be wholly natural today because they acted on lands shaped by human finagling for eons. There were far fewer fires and less area burned at the end of the twentieth century than at its onset—everyone agreed on that. Probably, though, those missing fires were not fires nature had set and suppression squashed but the fires people no longer set. The ancient fire regimes had, in fact, been a medley of natural and anthropogenic burns, which meant that the aftermath of "restored" lightning-kindled fires might or might not "restore" the site to an earlier condition. "Natural" fires might, rather, fashion a landscape that had never before existed. And the attempt to reinstate them might kindle fires of unprecedented ferocity, which is to say, they might be natural in the sense of transcending human control but not in the sense of being a restoration to past times.

What such fires had done is highlight the potential differences among environmental values. In particular, the wild might be at odds with other ecological goods—with air quality, biodiversity, ecological integrity, historic scenes, and the like. The wild simply required the absence of overt human agency. It was a cultural construct, not the immanence of nature. (But then so were all the other values.) It clashed most directly where historic ecosystems had likewise been cultural landscapes, if only through the medium of anthropogenic fire. Nor could one evade the conundrum by replacing the preservation of historic scenes with the preservation of ecological processes because human land use, including burning, had likely contributed to those processes. As fires probed and poked, blustered and blew up, they forced fire agencies to choose among competing environmental values. It was not simply ecology against economics, but clean air against biodiversity, and wilderness against ecological integrity.

At this point the intellectualizing behind natural fire begins to look like real work. It is easy to mock the PNF as an oxymoron, a bureaucratic sleight of hand, or as a prime directive better left to Hollywood's backlots than the nation's backcountry. The core concept, however, is very much a modernist paradox, of a piece with Heisenberg's principle, Russell's paradox, and Gödel's proof, all of which revolve around the enigma of including an observer within the system observed. The problem was, wilderness fire had no place for people. There was no way to insert ourselves into the land as fire agents. We could only observe. If we acted, we violated the premise behind the wild. Yet if we did not act, we probably upset the ecological workings of the reserve. The assumption that fire was simply a part of nature and that, if left alone, free-burning fire and the wild would quickly reconcile themselves proved untrue. Both showed themselves to be variables, not constants. Fire was a hybrid of nature and culture, and wilderness, as it turned out, was less an immutable condition than a continually evolving state of mind amidst a continually evolving state of nature.

The PNF, then, was not simply a contradiction or an exercise in irony but a paradox, with no logical resolution. It took the peculiar form it did because wilderness, not fire, defined the context. (Had wilderness been considered a subset of fire, the paradox's stresses would have expressed themselves in other ways.) Like reintroduced wolves, the numbers of PNFs were finally few, though huge in their symbolism. That symbolism mattered, however. There would have been little let burning, prescribed or otherwise, without a wilderness sanction, and almost certainly prescribed burning of any kind would have struggled without the implicit belief that its surrogate flames were spreading the goodness of the wild to other lands.

Foresters, especially, might celebrate fire as a tool but the public—and what of the intelligentsia concerned itself with fire—accepted fire's exuberant return because they associated it with the wild and the natural. In the end, however, the PNF would flourish or perish according to what happened on the ground, by how agencies practiced what they philosophized.

The experiment ended with the Yellowstone fires of 1988. For many Americans those conflagrations became a tutorial in fire's ecology. They learned the intrinsic value of flame in certain biotas; they understood that wildfires, even those of high intensity, belonged in wildlands, even if they remained skeptical about these particular fires. Their skepticism was warranted. Although Yellowstone appealed to Park Service guidelines that allowed for natural fires, the park did not have a PNF program because it categorically disallowed any prescriptions. Decisions about any particular ignition resided wholly with the judgment of an internal fire committee. No public document outlined under what conditions the park might accept or reject a fire, save for some areas along the park borders. The fire plan was not an operational document but a statement of philosophy. Yellowstone had, in truth, a let-burn program, and was proud of the purity of that fact.

Apologists for the park and the daring fire strategies of the new era quickly deflected public discussion onto the issue of whether fire belonged in Yellowstone. Of course it belonged. The real conversation concerned *how* it should belong. The park deserved censure not for allowing fire but for how it allowed it, and behind that, for bad faith, for violating the social compact that promoted natural fires under the auspices of a plan that specified, open to public inspection, a suite of prescriptions. Instead, Yellowstone accepted every fire that came to it; 60 percent of the area burned occurred from fires started outside the park or from human causes. (Only one national forest outside Yellowstone proper experienced a large fire.) The park continued to embrace new starts until, in the middle of July 1988, the secretary of the interior ordered it to stop. The fires were now too large to contain. Despite a national mobilization—Yellowstone became a black hole for suppression resources—the fires blazed on, assisted by repeated, failed attempts at backfiring. Suppression costs exceeded an obscene $130 million. Much of the landscape regenerated, as predicted, though the scale of the fires probably accounted for a century's burning in a single season. To its shame, dazzled by media limelights and the auroral glow of wilderness philosophy, the fire community rallied mindlessly to support the premises of natural fire, ignoring the deep flaws by which Yellowstone had administered and abused its privilege. Solipsistic Yellowstone escaped a holocaust, either biotic or bureaucratic.

The real ecological impact of the fires occurred off-site. Yellowstone's fires could not be confined to Yellowstone because they rippled through fire institutions and splashed across journals and other venues of information, throughout the United States and the Earth. Every federal agency had to revert to a policy of suppression until the plans of each unit could be reviewed individually according to new guidelines. The cost of prescribed burning rocketed upward. Yellowstone's fires thus reached to Florida and Minnesota and New Mexico, with generally negative consequences. This impact went unobserved as an expression of fire's ecology because there was no way by which to include people within the conceptual framework of ecological fire science. People stayed on the sidelines, as tourists, motel operators, summer-home residents. The inability to incorporate people as fire agents was a contributing cause to the fiasco, by urging the park to rely only on lightning ignitions and to shun deliberate burning, while the inability to incorporate people as institutions and purveyors of ideas contributed to a feeble appreciation of what the fires had meant. The community most affected by Yellowstone's summer of fire was the fire community, and through it those ecological communities they administered.

In the end, the threat was that one fire absolutism, that fire was bad and came at the hands of people, might be replaced by a mirror-image absolutism, that fire was good and came from nature. Fire paid little heed to either thesis. The national agenda moved on.

After Yellowstone, the federal agencies shunted the PNF to a policy hospice where it could expire quietly. The Three Cs of suppression soon joined it. Another problem fire loomed, the intermix fire scene, this one gratefully not encumbered by metaphysics. The country could ill-afford another such fire potlatch. What endured was the conviction, now so fundamental that it was unquestioned, an axiom like Euclid's postulates, that fire needed to return, and that it might be possible to let existing fires do part of that work. The search continued for a philosophically fat-free PNF.

Quietly, without idealistic fanfare, the PNF "transitioned," as the agencies were wont to put it, into the concept of wildland fire use while the confinement fire slid into the general suite of options available under a policy of "appropriate management response," a marvelously generic phrase that apparently meant whatever its user intended. A subtle distinction between the two fire types endured, however; conceptual birthmarks from their different origins. Wildland fire use applied to fires with tangible "resource benefits." That is, it was accepted because it enhanced the mission of the agency, be it timber or range or wildlife habitat. A confinement fire, because it was technically being suppressed, had no overt resource benefits. This was a discrimination often lost on working fire crews, and no doubt on the general public. The practical difference was the method of financing each. Thus, a hard residue of understanding and practice did survive from the let-burning experiment. Mostly, it meant backing off from *mano a mano* firefighting where the risks to firefighters were high, the threat to property and life low, and the land remote.

In June 2003, for example, Arizona commanded the national fire scene. There were two large fires of special interest to the public and a smaller one, which it more or less ignored. Lightning-set, the small one burned on Powell Plateau, an obscure mesa in the western Grand Canyon, within the path of scenic flights but otherwise beyond both the vision and ken of the touring public. Park fire officers let it wend through pine and juniper until it finally expired.

Of the large fires, the Thomas fire started by lightning in the Blue Primitive Area of the Apache-Sitgreaves National Forest. It was rugged country, desperately parched, fluffed with long-unburned brush and patches of conifers. With dry winds from the southwest driving the flames up twisting ravines, it was dangerous only to firefighters who might seek to work close to the flanks. The nearest hamlet lay a dozen miles north. The solution was to burn out along the existing roads, letting a fire that had run to 1,500 acres swell to 10,500.

The other, kindled by people, began in the lower stretches of the Santa Catalina Mountains, which skirted the northern limits of Tucson. The Aspen fire, as it came to be named, blasted upslope and fried more than two hundred homes at Summerhaven. Along the eastern flank, the flames burned out when they struck the still-blackened perimeter of the Bullock fire that had roared over the mountain only the year previously. At night the flames were visible from the town, like the sinuous flow of lava down a volcano. Powerful winds pushed the flames northward until they expired amid the sparse brush of the Sonoran Desert. Crews worked to clear around structures still sited on the summit, including the University of Arizona observatory complex. But the Aspen fire was deemed too dangerous to fight directly. It became clear that the extreme conditions and rugged terrain meant the fire would burn until monsoon rains extinguished it or until, as along the northern flank, it worked its way downslope into the flimsy fuels of the desert foothills. More than another hundred structures burned during a flare-up. Eventually, with a perimeter more or less secured, crews burned out, setting fires along the fire line and letting those flames rip upward, doing quickly what the wildfire might have taken weeks to do. Then it rained.

This was not really let burning, though neither was it all-out suppression. It looked rather like the old art of loose herding, holding where it was easy, firing where it was not. Fire fundamentalists might sneer that it was a muddle. Yet it got some fire back into the land. And fire, being unschooled in the rhetoric of discourse, did the job required of it. The strategy worked best where there were few people and a lot of room. Even for the pioneering Park Service, 87 percent of all wildland fire use from 1989 to 1999 occurred in only seven parks (as did 80 percent of all prescribed burns, although 40 percent of that number came from one unit, Big Cypress National Preserve). The loose-herding strategy could be normative in Alaska, optional in the Northern Rockies, High Sierras, and Mimbres Mountains, and closely shepherded where flame and smoke might wash against the outer pale of settlement. Symbolic fires would burn, their smoke rising like incense, on islands and canyon mesas and in isolated cirque valleys. On such sites, remote and sacred, like hilltop altars, the practical and the metaphysical could merge.

Letting such flames burn was sensible firefighting, sound ecology, and defensible philosophy. The brief on their behalf was less that they were wild than that they were remote, and less that they posed no threat than that they were biologically useful. Shackled symbols they might be—like reintroduced wolves with radio collars—but their power lay not in the size of their burned lands but the size of their significance. They were America's vestal flames. The hard burning would have to come from other sources.

Option 2. Suppress

Suppression is the classic approach to fire protection: prevent fires from starting, and where that proves impossible, rapidly attack and extinguish any blaze that breaks out. This is how cities respond to fire. It is what the European oracles of academic forestry urged, and what colonial foresters put into practice. It can work, brilliantly. It can also be expensive, dangerous, ecologically damaging, and self-defeating.

Everywhere it has been tried, the strategy has prompted a rapid plunge in burned area. Removing people and their fires, installing a first-order firefighting system, swatting out fires in a previously fire-flushed (and hence lightly fueled) landscape—these methods can be enormously robust for a time. The question is whether they can be sustained, and at what cost. Part of that cost is monetary, and part environmental. Here the story gets interesting.

The case for fire exclusion works well where there is no natural basis for fire. In such settings fire exists because people have put it there, sometimes inserting it violently. Thus flame follows the wreckage of slashing and maybe grazing into rain forests or shade forests. Remove those insults and the biota will regenerate. Exclude fire and you exclude much of the human-caused havoc.

A variant is the case of temperate Europe. Natural fire is rare (Europeans consider it a freak of nature like a monstrous birth). While open fire has been abundant, it has existed because people made it happen, and historically they did so by crunching up the shade forest into combustible tinder or draining and digging up organic soils like peat. Then they burned as part of herding and fallowing. This was a cultivated, constructed world; fire burned within the landscape as it did on candles and within stoves. Fire was an instrument of the European garden, part of a tool kit that included axes, rakes, spades, and plows. When other tools became available, they replaced flame, and as open fire vanished, there was little urgency to put it back.

Town and country thus shared a similar fire sentiment. Fire belonged in hearth and forge, or in paddock and fallow, but only under strict control by its human minders. Strict control, too, was possible over fuels—those in the landscape and those in the city. Wildfires broke out when that order collapsed, when famine, plague, war, or insurrection left the garden untended and overrun with weeds, when poverty and crime sprouted into slums overgrown with hovels of wood and thatch, when human firebrands scattered sparks on that sullen tinder beyond what the normal instruments for order could handle. Fires blazed within the context of human violence—wars, peasant revolts, urban riots. European intellectuals, residing in cities, have thus viewed flame as an index of social unrest. Both society and landscape would be better off without it.

Temperate Europe is but a small patch of the planet. But from the Enlightenment onward, it has held the Earth's major industrial, economic, political, scientific, and imperial powers. It has accepted its own circumstances as normative. It believes that, if wanton fire were banished, the land would restore itself to its true, fire-immune state. What Europe found in the rest of the world— places far more prone to fire—it condemned as unruly and primitive, and in need of rationalization on the European model. Beyond the Garden, however, colonizers could control little—not the climate, not ignition, not the arrangement of fuels on the landscape. Of all earthly exemplars possible for fire, Europe's became the best known and the least usable outside its formative hearth.

Early American efforts at fire control followed Europe's lead. Most emanated from New England, the most European of America's fire provinces. Here, fire tracked social movements; the seasons followed temperature, not precipitation; ignition was almost exclusively human. When large fires, sometimes catastrophic, occurred, they followed from massive land clearing or logging with its mountains of slash, droughty Indian-summer autumns, and reckless ignition from residents. All this could cease—would cease—as the society matured. The experience had little relevance for the rest of the country.

Other regions, by contrast, know some kind of a wetting and drying cycle, if not annually, then over decadal rhythms of drought and deluge. Most experienced the chronic unrest of settlement or resettlement, with fuels heaped and reheaped. In principle such places might contain their flames, following the example of frontier towns that eventually ceased to burn down once they passed through their wildest, most haphazard phase; began to build out of brick and stone; and created firefighting brigades. Most landscapes eventually followed a similar scenario, as the pyric transition purged flame. But not all. The process plied slowly in the rural South, and nearly a third of the country, including its most fire-prone lands, went into the public domain. Here, even in principle, the European model lost its meaning. There could be only partial control over ignition, and little control over fuel. The land would stay wild. Fires would happen.

Universally, officials seek first to prevent as many ignitions as possible. Fire codes were thus among the earliest of public-land legislation, however feeble their enforcement. They sought to control the activities of people, not as permanent residents but as transients. Prevention meant educating, exhorting, hectoring, browbeating, fining, or otherwise seeking to instill a greater sense of care with fire. Few visitors sought to broadcast burn (sheepherders and prospectors being an exception); most simply littered with fire, from unwatched campfires, rifle wadding, or stray matches. Prevention also meant sequestering American Indians onto reservations. It meant, in extreme cases, closing the public lands to access altogether during the period of emergency. Even with perfect control over people, however, dry lightning could blast mountains and plateaus, sometimes saturating a region with fire.

That put the burden of fire protection on active suppression. The fires had to be fought. The firefighting ranger and the seasonal fireguard are among the forgotten frontiersmen of the American West. They explored, they "settled," they imposed order on a lawless land. In the classic formula of pioneering, they brought civilization to the wilderness, and found that by so doing they had destroyed their pioneering world. The glories of fire suppression are those of the frontier; its damages are those wrought by other frontier harvesters of wood, water, forage, and game; its ironies are those it shares with the westward movement overall.

Yet suppression, in its heroic age, was crude—men and horses and hand tools, and a vast domain of mountains and tall forests. In 1910 a ranger patrolled, on average, between 450 and 670 square miles. That fire control was even attempted under such circumstances is astonishing—one could ask no finer testimony as to the convictions of such rangers. They understood, moreover, that fire protection was a long-term investment, that it was a precondition to proper forestry, and that it would open up the public domain to other purposes. They knew that they could only succeed if the land was rightly developed, by which they meant that it have suitable roads, trails, observation points, tool caches, telephone lines, fuelbreaks, and crews.

Their technology was simple. If a fire was small, it was extinguished much as one would put out a campfire. They scraped out a break in the fuels around the flaming perimeter so that the fire could not spread; then they doused the flames with water (from stream-filled buckets) or with dirt. They broke up the larger pieces or let them burn out. Even one smokechaser could tackle quite a lot of fire in a day, provided it was still in a snag or if on the ground, creeping and not galloping. But if it was much beyond an acre or if it was "blowin'-and-goin'," then the scene called for a more indirect attack. Instead of swarming over the entire fire, crews concentrated on the running flanks. Their fire lines needed to be larger, so were situated on ridgetops or along rivers or lakes. Since it could take several days to construct such a "trail" or "trench," they had to locate the line some distance from the fire or risk having it overrun before they could complete the barrier. Then they would burn out from their line when conditions were favorable and hope that they could contain their backfire while it devoured the fuels that would otherwise feed the wildfire. After that they would patrol their line and let the interior burn itself out, perhaps over weeks. These two strategies of attack, the direct and the indirect, remain fundamental. What modern technology has done is to allow for a more powerful assault on small fires and a closer flanking of large ones. What modern thinking has added is the concept of prescription control, that in addition to direct extinguishment or perimeter control, one can contain a fire by predicting its behavior. Such was the premise that transformed laissez-faire let burning into scientific prescribed burning.

The early politics, too, were simple: use it or lose it. If the land was not used, that is, occupied, it would be lost. Fire control was the typical means by which an agency could first establish an administrative presence. Nothing else could justify the cost, which could be mind-boggling. The Forest Service was being asked to do with public money begrudgingly appropriated what the private sector had achieved over many decades at huge expense, and that by stripping environmental assets like woods and soils. The Forest Service had to plead and pry its funds from a parsimonious Congress that saw little opportunity for either patronage or pork. Unsurprisingly, the agency concentrated on frontcountry lands. From the onset, however, it had access to another pot of money for actual firefighting. A law enacted in May 1908 allowed it to borrow from other budgeted funds during bona fide fire emergencies, with the understanding that Congress would make up the deficit. The reasoning was simple: no one could predict what an upcoming fire season might bring. Initial outlays ran from $30,000 to $40,000. In 1910 emergency costs blew up to nearly a million dollars. After tough political infighting, Congress upheld the 1908 act. Fire protection grew around that funding source like crystals on a string.

The federal fire agencies would never have all the money they believed necessary to prepare their lands for proper fire protection, but they would have all the money they needed to actually fight fire. It was as though a national health-care system had unlimited funds for emergency responses but little for education, vaccinations, and routine checkups. The outcome would be a spectacular display of crisis medicine—medevac helicopters and high-tech ambulances, emergency room surgery, abundant EMTs, rapid reactions to outbreaks of contagious disease—the stuff of TV drama and telegenic news. It would do little, however, to improve inoculations for childhood diseases, address adult obesity, pry out the environmental causes of cancer, and the rest. Yet the 1908 act made fire management what it became: the agency went with the money. It did what it was paid to do, which was suppression, a mandate that seemed, for a public institution, the cheapest solution for conserving the public's domain. Implicit was the belief that fire control would be an ephemeral enterprise. The extraordinary costs of fighting fires would fade as protection progressively tamed the land.

The basis of this strategy was common knowledge. The essence was to attack a new fire as quickly as possible. This required the means to spot a fresh start, to report it, and to dispatch someone to extinguish it. The sooner the fire was hit, the smaller it would be and hence the less force it would require and the less money it would extort. In 1914 California's regional forester Coert duBois translated the project into the language of Taylorism, breaking down every component of the larger task into smaller units and assigning numerical values for each. Eventually *Systematic Fire Protection in the California Forests* became the conceptual foundation for organized firefighting throughout the national forests. The necessary infrastructure lagged until the New Deal, when it appeared, suddenly, everywhere, as if by magic. The CCC provided, for the first time, a standing militia for fire and inspired techniques for organizing such crews. The 10 AM policy codified the credo in nonnegotiable terms. In 1939 the logic of fire-dedicated crews led to the smoke-jumpers and the forty-man crew. After the Korean conflict, war-surplus equipment inspired the mechanization of fire control.

Each advance brought greater force to bear more quickly on fires, however remote or seemingly benign. The ability to fight encouraged the desire to fight. Fire control became more aggressive, more able to crowd fire along its flanks. The older methods that involved pulling back to a ridge or a river or the nearest road and burning out gave way to clanking assaults with bulldozers and close-support aircraft that cut a line as near to the flames as possible and that quenched flaming fronts with retardant. There was less burning out, so the average size of fires continued to shrink, with fewer acres burned overall. By the late 1950s burned area nationally had reached a quantum minimum. There it seemed likely to stay, perhaps an irreducible presence in nature's economy like some base level of unemployment.

If the only problem before it had remained ignition, systematic fire protection could probably have succeeded. Even against lightning and arson, it could have met blow with blow. One could build up initial attack forces for even extreme events (as fire brigades proved in London and elsewhere during the firebombings of World War II). It is not ignition but the capacity of the land to spread those kindled fires that matters. The power of fire lies in its power to propagate, which is to say, the availability of combustibles. Ultimately fire suppression, too, is only as powerful as the fire-proneness of the land it protects.

To control fuels—this was the ultimate logic of the European exemplar, and the urban fire analogue. Even in Mediterranean Europe, where fire was a permanent fixture, its subjugation depended on close cultivation. Yet this was precisely what American foresters could not do, certainly not with the intensity the scene demanded. The European model would not work because natural conditions kept sparking fires, and because the creation of a public domain prevented precisely the kind of meticulous gardening that made conflagrations unlikely. In truth, western American fires spiraled out of control because the people who had organized the old burning were banished and because the fuels had become a fast shambles.

The wrecking of western fire regimes began well before the first fireguard arrived at a mountain lookout. For most of the arid West it commenced with overgrazing, first by sheep, then by cattle. The herds cropped off the grasses that had carried the spring-flush of routine fire. What should have fed the fast-combustion of flame fed the slow-combustion of metabolizing livestock. With little to stoke them, the fires expired. Elsewhere, as rail access became possible, logging broke the structure of the woods, plucking out the fire-immune big timber and leaving the fire-provoking scrub. Promiscuous, mindless fires sprang up from prospectors, hunters, tourists, whoever roamed heedlessly over otherwise hale wildlands. Much of this happened before the forests were reserved, before anyone could imagine a juggernaut of fire suppression.

This was the scene that greeted intellectuals and officials, that Charles Sargent recorded for his 1880 map, that V. L. Parrington labeled the Great Barbecue. Educated observers saw landscapes wracked by the logger's ax and herder's hooves and wanton blazes and demanded that it all stop. Sorting out the various types of fire seemed an exercise in scholasticism. Stop the fires and the land could recover. The most direct way to halt the riotous fires was to send in a constabulary. In some places, serious fire exclusion only began with fire suppression; but mostly, fire suppression only confirmed what was already underway.

American foresters welcomed the challenge. They knew they had a fire threat unlike anything in forestry's European hearth, and they considered their struggle to contain the menace an essential and distinctive contribution to conservation. They conceived the problem as one of means—imagining new concepts to guide fire protection planning, inventing better tools for firefighting, devising better techniques to detect and hit fires quickly. What one could not prevent, one had to suppress. But, matching these arguments stride for stride, others on the American scene questioned the very premises of suppression. For them the issue was not whether fire control was practical, but whether it was desirable, and they decided against both. They regarded fire suppression as quixotic and wrongheaded. They urged instead that forest protection be based not on fire control but on controlled burning.

The debate was bitter, public, and tenacious. The controversy flared into the national media during the Big Blowup of 1910; it split the Departments of Agriculture and the Interior; it pitted West against East, those who lived off the land with the educated elite who lived in cities, those who favored local control over natural resources against those who wanted national control for a higher good. Light burning, as it was called, likely had the backing of the vast majority of the American public. It was far from inevitable that suppression would triumph as the dominant strategy of fire protection. The best explanation for its institutional victory is that those who supported it did so with immense conviction and that suppression captured the sentiment of the nation at large. The Progressive Era favored activist government, federal institutions, a doctrine of conservation based on national goals and scientific advisors. Still, suppression did not prevail until the 1920s, and then only by cooperation and compromise. No single agency could do the whole job, and no one argued that suppression was more than a means, not an end in itself, that control was justified only to the extent that its costs did not exceed those of the lands under protection. Hegemony came only with the 10 AM policy and the New Deal's limitless resources.

Suppression's detractors had plenty of bite. Even amid the Big Blowup of 1910, critics questioned the very essence of the fire-exclusion argument by proposing that the strategy could never succeed by itself, that it was in truth self-defeating, for it blighted the land and created conditions beyond suppression's capacity to control. The principle behind fire exclusion was bogus because it could never be successfully practiced. Without light burning's routine flushing away of combustibles, fuels would pile up. The early, easy firefighting only made for a later, intractable firefighting. Instead of the virtuous circle promised by forestry, in which fire's exclusion would create conditions that would make further fire increasingly difficult, a vicious circle would arise, in which fire's exclusion would only promote conditions that would make further suppression impossible. The argument turned the premises of academic forestry on their heads. And there was worse to come. More damaging was the recognition that there were forests for which fires might be good.

This was not an altogether new thesis. It had sounded brazenly through the aboriginal debates from British India. The first question asked in the 1871 Indian forest conference was whether fire control was possible and if possible, desirable. The concerned community immediately divided. Academic foresters and administrators argued for exclusion's virtuous circle; field men, for its vicious. Officials could further argue, plausibly, that fire protection under such conditions had never really been tried, that the nominal failures happened because administration in the field had been sloppy or incomplete, that the war against fire suffered from too many slackers and conscientious objectors. As G. K. Chesterton said of Christianity, it had not been tried and found wanting, but tried and found difficult, and hence not really tried at all. Within thirty years of the formative forestry conference, however, the conservator of forests for Burma in 1906 declared a truce and walked away from aggressive suppression. It was the very time the light-burning controversy was sweeping the western United States.

In America the counterargument was again that serious suppression had not been truly attempted, that professional foresters—as disinterested civil servants—could properly answer the flaks and flakes who fronted for light burning and who spoke—either from cunning or naïveté—for timber barons, railway companies, fire-careless frontiersmen, poets and novelists, and other technical incompetents. Light burners belonged with circle-squarers and perpetual-motion mechanics. Besides, an increase in the woods was precisely what a country needed that was otherwise headed for a dire and imminent timber famine. Light burners thought only of protecting existing old timber. Fire protectionists labored for the future, aptly symbolized by the young reproduction that light burners dismissed as "brush" and sought to purge.

Throughout, there was plenty of rhetorical misdirection. Light burning focused on frequently fired pineries, places laden with ponderosa and sugar pine, for example. Most lay in montane landscapes, far enough up the mountain slopes to capture ample moisture for woods but not so elevated that they segued into soggy, fire-rare biotas like spruce and fir. Yet these settings were confused

95

with others, for which fire protection could do little damage and much good. Moreover, how soon a landscape might feel the effects of fire control varied. For tallgrass prairies a change to woody scrub might occur in a handful of years. For cutover lands, subsequently burned for pasture, a decade or two of fire protection could allow the straggling reproduction to take hold. For ponderosa pine forests the worsening problem became apparent only after random heavy-seeding years. For coastal Douglas–fir forests, the internal consequences of decades of fire exclusion were minor; what changed was the coarse mosaic of green and gashed patches where infrequent fires ripped. Each side chose examples to suit its own principles, just as more recent advocates have also done. There was, in the early years, no simple, one-to-one correspondence between aggressive suppression and uncontrollable fuels; too many variables intervened, from wind, drought, browsers, whatever. That remains true today. Unlike oily rags piled in a corner, the worst heaped fuel does not spontaneously combust. Against the argument that more fuels meant tougher firefighting, the agencies could reply that the country needed those woods and that better suppression could counter any putative increase in hazard. Both sides might argue that there was no fuel like an old fuel.

The public agencies readily accepted their strategy as a novel invention, a contribution by Americans to the global scholarship of practical conservation. Coert duBois exulted that, in fire protection, America could instruct Europe.[2] Suppression's advocates were confident the outcome would prove their point; they held the science, while their critics huffed with folk wisdom and puffed with pulp litterateurs. Suppression lacked only the practical means to prove its principles. When it could bring its full force to bear, it would sweep its critics off the field. In announcing the 10 AM policy, Chief Forester Gus Silcox boldly labeled it "an experiment on a continental scale."

By 1970, however, it was an experiment no longer. The evidence mounted with every dog-hair thicket of pine, every matting of southern rough, every grassland replaced by woody scrub.

Worse, as the light burners had predicted, the overgrown forests were decaying from beetles, blights, and simple thirst. An old argument; but it was a thesis now recast in ecological terms and sited in a society skeptical of big government and sensitive to environmental disorders. The charge was not simply that fire suppression had piled fuels like a squirrel stocking a winter midden. The issue was that fire's exclusion had started an ecological shock wave that was slowly shattering the biotas it had sought to protect. Biodiversity smothered under a pavement of pine needles and the gloom of woody shade. The landscape's quilt of niches, patches, and biotic embroidery was unraveling. Trees were dying. Weeds flourished. Textured habitats had become green smudges. As drought gripped the West, the collateral damages of fire exclusion erupted, like ecological boils, into beetle plagues and mistletoe infestations and outright dehydration. A simple strategy of suppression had proved self-ruinous, not merely in practice, but in principle. It was not overlooked, however, that those wrecked landscapes became more tinder for more fire.

The costs of suppression had become, if not unbearable, then open to widespread skepticism. The base budget had risen. More tellingly, as part of the 10 AM policy, the Forest Service had enlarged the scope of the emergency accounts to accommodate *pre*suppression activities, such as hiring extra fire lookouts, cleaning up debris, or contracting for standby crews during high fire danger. A little extra money spent during extreme conditions would, it was argued, reduce even greater expenses during the crisis of a large fire. In fact, neither a swelling base budget nor the presuppression slush fund made the slightest difference in emergency expenditures. All costs rose, well above the rising tide of inflation. The system had built out; the easy work was done.

The cost in firefighter lives had also persisted, despite better training, better equipment, elaborate research programs, and hard-won organizational skills. The three decades that boasted the final plunge in burned area also witnessed a dark litany of burned-over crews: the years from the 1937 Blackwater fire in the

97

Northern Rockies to the Decker fire of 1968 in Southern California marked the worst era for fire fatalities since the Great Fires of 1910. Of 465 firefighters who have died from burns, these three decades claimed 227, or 49 percent. (Drop the fatalities of 1910 and the 1933 Griffiths Park fire, and those years of aggressive suppression—a third of fire protection's tenure—claim 88 percent of its fire-induced fatalities.) Still, fatalities continued, if less from flame than from workplace hazards and transportation accidents. The charred bodies of the 1994 South Canyon fire, in particular however, mocked the presumption that fire control was improving or that, more unsettlingly, it was even effective.[3]

But these losses could yet be explained or rationalized as indicative of what further engineering might remedy. What could not be blustered away was the alarming—now undeniable—increase in fuels. The woods that foresters had predicted would thrive in the absence of fire had in fact flourished, and they were now so congested that they stoked fires that demanded more and more force to contain them. It was not that big trees had grown bigger, but that scrub, brush, reproduction, and windfall had swollen into a bloated understory of fine fuels that could transport flame from the dead-needled floor to the green-needled canopy, and from treetop to treetop. The once vacant strata between the soiled surface and the forest ceiling was often stuffed with combustibles. The old patches that dappled the canopy now blurred into a solid smear. A full-bore fire in such a setting was unstoppable.

When reform arrived around 1970, critics within the agency as well as without regarded fire control as a runaway engine, stoked by the bottomless reserves of the emergency fire fund. It was accountable to no one, and now threatened everyone. It seemed to rule the federal land agencies like a military junta. Reformers struggled strenuously to subordinate it to agency goals (fire protection had never been accepted officially or doctrinally as an end in itself). They redefined "fire control" as "fire management" and they sought to integrate fire management with land management. They scrapped the 10 AM policy, along with the emergency presuppression fund. Instead, they proposed (in a kind of policy doppelgänger of earlier thinking) that if we only start fires, the land would recover. Moreover, they demanded a change of mind, not merely of behavior. Critics observed that early fire prevention campaigns had demonized fire, which was, they reasoned, why society had blindly tolerated suppression. Now they demonized suppression. It symbolized all that was wrong with the American way of fire.

After the 1988 Yellowstone debacle, however, that critique's intellectual clarity became murky. Wilderness surrendered the high ground, much of which, in any event, was becoming overrun with car-powered sprawl. As exurban villages began to burn, suppression reasserted its necessity, and with the threat of terrorist attacks, firefighting seems destined to fold into a milieu of homeland security, with the possibility that control over large fires might be removed from the land agencies and handed over to an institution like the Federal Emergency Management Agency (FEMA). Certainly the development of the incident command system made fire control into a flexible, all-purpose emergency response. (When NOVA broadcast a two-hour special on American fire, the nuances of fire ecology and suppression's many maladies melted away as the film crew followed the Arrowhead Hotshots through the 2000 fire season. A complex narrative defaulted to the genre of a war movie, the fate of a platoon through a long campaign, and the outcome was appropriately titled *Fire Wars*.)

No one believed that suppression alone could extirpate fire, but when the flames struck, no one wanted to be without those crews, and engines, and helitankers. At such times the fire pacifists shrank from sight. In the end, as prescribed fire faltered, as drought sparked mammoth fire seasons in the West, and as exurban sprawl collided with flames, suppression returned as the default setting for fire management. Wild fires demanded action. Suppression acted.

Nonetheless the era of reform had changed how suppression did its work. In 1967 it was acceptable—unquestioned—that fire bosses might order a phalanx of bulldozers to gouge firelines through Glacier National Park. In 1968 a lightning fire on a remote butte within the Grand Canyon could unleash a B-17 to drop retardant, while crews wended over deer trails and scrambled up limestone cliffs to reach another. Twenty years later, incident commanders might appeal to dozers at Yellowstone, but selectively, and only after written authorization from the secretary of the interior; and not many years afterward, it was censorious to dispatch crews into hazardous locales and honorable for crews to refuse such assignments. Having a tool did not mean suppression could use it.

The culture of firefighting shifted into a kinder, gentler suppression, like the national thirst for whiskey into a taste for wine. Commanders were less likely to hurl tracked vehicles into delicate environments. Crews practiced "coyote" tactics—more backpacker than woods worker. They adopted a light-hand-on-the-land philosophy, routing fire lines where they would erode less and even etching water bars into those lines that slashed across slopes. They factored rehabilitation into shift plans. They practiced more indirect attack, pulling back to natural breaks or existing roads and burning out. Firefighting had become, if far from a profession, a genuine craft, worthy of its own proud guild. (The time had long passed when a raw crew could be told, as in the 1930s, "Stay with your foreman. He has been to many fires and is still alive.") Still, even Suppression Lite was an inherently rough act. It met one form of violence with another.

Within the fire community, though, the crisis arrived in 1994 when the South Canyon fire blew up and burned over a suppression force that blended smokejumpers, hotshots, helitackers, and others. The military metaphor was trotted out—again. But the real interpretive prism came from Maclean's 1992 bestseller, *Young Men and Fire*. It seemed outrageous that "young men" should still die like this. The fire acted on the suppression community as the Mogadishu ambush of American rangers did on the American military—there was a profound reluctance to put more lives in harm's way. That changed, for the military, with the war on terror and the invasion of Afghanistan. It has not yet changed for fire suppression. Paradoxically, this has left suppression with an ambiguous identity. If fire control is no longer to be a misplaced exercise in national defense, then it risks being no more than a government-sponsored extreme sport. The portrayal of hotshot crews in Sebastian Junger's *Fire* suggests as much. The public might rightly ask why the fallen should be mourned any differently from white-water kayakers lost in Borneo. The uncertainty over how to honor those who have died in the public service reflected confusion over what public service fire protection is rendering. What, and to what ends, exactly, is fire management managing that is worth the lives of its practitioners?

Fire suppression will not go away, any more than will fire. In neither case would we wish it to. Yet it has limits and should never have been made to carry the full burden of fire management, for it was never possible to remove every fire, and this would not be desirable even if it could be done. Complete prevention is chimerical—accidents, arson, lightning, something will start a blaze. This shifts the burden of protection to rapid detection and initial attack. By any measure, small fires are easier, cheaper, and safer to control than large ones. But here, too, complete control is impossible. Even the best systems will lose 2 to 3 percent of starts under extreme conditions, and these fires may sweep widely. (During the 2002 season, initial attack caught 99.2 percent of all starts—and lost 7.2 million acres.) That is the rub: no one has discovered a way to prevent the big fire or the big fire season, the colossal crash that will instantly wipe out all the slow gains of many years. Moreover, the mere attempt to abolish burning can destabilize a landscape.

Suppression is akin to policing, and a big firefight, to a declaration of martial law. It is useful, and often necessary, to quell an environmental rebellion. It is not a means by which to govern a landscape. Each nominal success only ratchets up the cost of future suppression. In brief, no system of fire management will succeed without the capacity to fight fires; yet none can succeed with only that capacity. This means rethinking the strategic uses of suppression. The integration of fire control with land management remains an unmet promise. (It is also an American oddity; the international norm is to leave fire protection as a stand-alone operation, rather like urban fire services but dirtier.) It means thinking about where suppression can be effective, and where not. Firefighting cannot by itself rebuild wrecked landscapes, any more than a military force can rebuild a failed country. A few corollaries might follow: If you want to suppress, do it early. If you want suppression to be effective, do it on your terms, so far as possible, which means crafting an environment that yields controllable fires.

It also means reexamining suppression's tactics. There are ample reasons to distrust the military analogy when applied to firefighting. In its logistics and field operations, however, the similarities are often suggestive. The recent effort to "transform the military" from heavy-armor, heavy-artillery columns to a nimbler, mixed force that can appeal to high-tech for information, precision, and mobility—this, the American firefighting machine could well emulate. Unlimited money has too often sustained limited thought. Crews pile on crews; fire camps become administrative entities in themselves. A serious alternative to the classic campaign fire would go a long way toward integrating fire control into fire management.

But that is not a decision fire suppression can make on its own. It serves land management agencies, which serve the public, which is understandably confused about what is happening and contradictory about what it wants. What the public needs to know is that suppression cannot make wildland fire go away. Suppression has forcibly revealed this reality. What suppression needs to know is which fires to extinguish and which to encourage, and to what purposes. These directives the public has not yet decided upon. Until it does, the public will call for suppression to contain not only rogue wildfires but its own uncertainties—ambiguities and apathies that may be every bit as dangerous to crews as a toppling snag or a blowup fire in a box canyon.

Option 3. Prescribe Burn

If we cannot fight fires, then perhaps we could light them. If fire is inevitable, and desirable, then we should set it ourselves. Better fires of choice than fires of chance. That, in brief, is the case for replacing a bloated and battered strategy of suppression with a policy of prescribed burning.

The issue involves more than fire's control; it engages equally the matter of fire's necessity. One could argue that the tragedy of American fire history is not that wildfires were suppressed, but that controlled fires were no longer set. If, then, fire control is the problem, it ought to follow that controlled fire is the solution. In principle, restoring fire can enhance suppression, enrich ecological values, and pay penance for past sins against nature. The doctrine of prescribed fire offers the country a chance to revisit the light-burning controversy and this time to pick the road not taken.

History, however, has resisted. Putting fire back into the land is not the simple reverse of taking it out. Fire synthesizes its surroundings. Those surroundings have changed dramatically over the long decades since controlled burning has been squeezed from the land—and not just controlled fire, but all the other practices that flame catalyzed and that, in turn, helped shape fire's context. Setting new fires does not necessarily kindle flames like those of the past. Promoting prescribed fire means more than standing suppression on its head. Restoring fire is instead more akin to reinstating a lost species. That light burning had been unfairly denounced in the early days does not mean prescribed fire might not be unfairly boosted today. By itself prescribed fire is no more a comprehensive strategy than suppression.

Return again to that formative controversy. The early arguments against suppression were, in fact, arguments in favor of controlled burning. If let burning was the left hand of suppression's critics, then light burning was their right. In those landscapes that had routinely experienced surface burns, advocates urged regular "light" burns as a means of culling out combustibles and generally promoting healthier forests. It was, they insisted, the "Indian way" of forest protection, the means by which long centuries of indigenous use had yielded the majestic woods that Americans now longed to protect. (Foresters dismissed the prospect as "Paiute forestry.") Suppression had for its spokesperson professional forestry, a homogenous (and hegemonic) crowd. Light burners were, by contrast, a herd of cats, finding voices in the poet Joaquin Miller, the novelist Stewart Edward White, California's state engineer William Hall, timber baron T. B. Walker, and the Southern Pacific Railroad, not to mention Secretary of the Interior Richard Ballinger. During the Big Blowup of 1910, *Sunset* magazine ran an article that accurately predicted what the consequences of a suppression-only policy would be and proposed with tongue only slightly in cheek that the army be called out to do the burning necessary to protect private landholders from federal malfeasance.[4]

The light-burning argument, though, had a long pedigree, tracing back to the earliest exploitation of fire by humans. The ability to fight fires head-on, matching force with counterforce, is a modern invention and its purpose a recent conceit. Most societies protected themselves against wildfire by preemptively burning the sites they sought to shield. Protection, however, was often a collateral benefit; the primary purpose of burning was to render the landscape habitable. People burned in order to hunt, forage, fish, open vistas, prevent ambushes, stimulate basket twig–producing shrubs; the list is endless. A reduction in fuels was but one benefit among many.

The expulsion of the indigenes, the sequestering of a permanent public domain, the exchange of a rural for an industrial economy—

all eroded the landscape arguments for burning. What remained was simple protection. The suppression crowd could make a plausible case, it seemed, for systematic fire protection as a modern alternative to primitive practices. That fire was natural was irrelevant; so was smallpox. That indigenes had burned was beside the point; a new society and a modern economy now ruled North America. Folk burning was a dangerous holdover from a past best left behind. Woods burning had no more place in modern America than witch burning.

While the crisis over self-amassing fuels contributed to the Great Reforms launched in the 1960s, the debate was largely about principles and philosophies of nature. It pitted competing confessions against one another and created a schism within the fire community. The propositions, recall, were creedal: fire was natural and belonged on the land, fire suppression had had its day and failed, the remedy to fire's exclusion was fire's restoration. This philosophical disputation the fire radicals readily won.

It was, in retrospect, fire's Old Testament era, full of prophetic voices from the wilderness thundering out denunciations of their generation's stupid ways and the promised terrors of ecology's righteous retribution. It was an age of protest, and fire threw out its own bold dissenters against the Establishment. Unsurprisingly a large fraction came from California; students of Harold Biswell and Starker Leopold, trained in ecology and wildlife, not forestry, hired by parks not national forests. The most consistent countervoice to officialdom was the Tall Timbers Research Station, outside Tallahassee, Florida, under the leadership of E. V. Komarek (protégé to an earlier dissenter, Herbert Stoddard, another wildlife biologist). Their charter encompassed the globe, and their annual fire-ecology conferences constructed an overwhelming case for the potential virtues of burning. It is no accident that, when the Forest Service abjured its old ways, it did so within the overflowing tent of a Tall Timbers conference. By the early 1970s the fire community had converted wholesale.

Policy followed on the heels of philosophy. Fire's official renaissance commenced more than three decades ago. The real difficulty lay not only in conception, however, but in practice, for it proved surprisingly tough to burn instead of extinguish. The reasons were many, though the essence may boil down to two. First, the fire establishment's infrastructure existed to fight fires, not light them. Society, too, sought fire protection, and considered prescribed burning a token gesture in select sites. The big money still went to suppression. The second reason is that no one really knew what prescriptions were appropriate or how, other than scattering fire over a setting like the ashes of a burnt offering, a restored landscape might happen. To their discredit, and the public's confusion, the agencies began calling every kind of semicontrolled burn a "prescribed fire," whether set in logging slash or the sedges of a wildlife refuge. And so it went. One grand exercise in experimentation, suppression, yielded to another, prescribed fire.

Eventually a parallel establishment arose. Prescribed fire came to have its own training manuals, its own job-qualification rating system, its own national awards (in mimicry of the gold and silver Smokey Awards, a kind of shadow Oscars), its own prescribed-fire training academy, its own dedicated line budget, and the rest. Prescribed burns became set pieces, transposing the order of suppression.[5] The dual organization emerged most powerfully in the National Park Service, such that fire's army seemed ruled by dual tribunes, like ancient Rome's and with similar outcomes.

One effect was to perpetuate the false rivalry between lighting and fighting. Failures were dismissed by appealing to prescribed fire's country-cousin status relative to suppression. Prescribed burning lacked the money, particularly the carte blanche of emergency funds. It was starved for sufficient staffing and equipment, and agency commitment. It lacked the telegenic grandeur of the firefight. Most of all, its apologists argued, it lacked public understanding. Criticisms from outside the community, proponents dismissed as false consciousness—the public had been duped by the suppression industry, gulled by Smokey Bear, deceived from ecology's gospel. At bottom, the quarrel remained one of wrong ideas and faulty metaphysics. As that founding generation aged, even as they became themselves the new Establishment, they continued, like Civil War reenactors, to replay the Good Fight against Smokey, suppression, and a timorous, straw-man public. They recycled the old jeremiads. The only dissent allowed was the now-domesticated dissent of their youth. No one questioned the premises behind prescribed fire as they had once criticized suppression. Many continued as though the revolution had just happened, as though prescribed fire remained yet a bold novelty.

It was not. By the 2003 season thirty-five years had passed for the Park Service and twenty-five for the Forest Service, with the restoration of fire as an agency goal. For the Park Service this was a longer period of time than it had operated under the 10 AM policy. For the Forest Service this was as long as the period from the 1910 fires to the 1934 review that laid out, with brutal candor, its fire-policy options. Beyond those agencies, prescribed fire had been used by commercial forests in the southeast, by wildlife refuges, by prairie restorationists, by ranchers, and others, often for decades. Prescribed fire was not a startling innovation desperate for public acceptance and agency application. It was not a brash fire rookie beaten down by a bullying suppression organization. It had, rather, become the agencies' treatment of choice. If it has not fulfilled the ambitions of its advocates, the reasons lie elsewhere.

They lie, first, in practice. The set-piece model of prescribed burning works well in simple-fuel landscapes like prairie, slash, or the pine-strawed understory of commercial pulp plantations. It works poorly in complex forest environments with layered fuel arrays and mottled caches of moisture. The resulting fires are too varied, too likely to linger, too mixed in their results. Conditions that would work for a carpet of pine needles might not work for large dead logs, for example. The premise of prescribed burning is that each prescription leads to a specified output, like a gene programming for a specific protein. In reality, a fire shape-shifts into whatever its conditions allow for it. It is unrealistic to expect a precise match between a kindled flame and a particular outcome, and unnecessary; but it is also unrealistic to cast flame about as though it were ecological pixie dust, as if its mere touch could transform the bad and the ugly into the good and the beautiful.

Instead, prescribed burning requires a rack of techniques. It needs precision flame—boutique burning or bonsai burning, as it were. It needs the capacity to spot-burn in the woods as people once burned leaves and lawns. It also needs fire foraging, the ability to follow the fuels as they become available, which is how aboriginal societies burned. One could track the snow line up a mountain, or work down a valley, as the dry season gradually leached moisture away from springs and streams. This can take months; it requires that crews effectively live on the site and trail fuels as they might gather maturing berries; it means a lot of burning some years, and little in others. Prescribed burning needs a fiscal and operational flexibility beyond set-piece prescriptions. Perhaps most audaciously, it needs the ability to set prescribed crown fires, which is prescribed fire's version of the big-fire dilemma. It needs controlled fires that can incinerate select landscapes in the self-immolating way some forests require.

Ironically, the environmental movement that helped sustain criticism of a suppression strategy has ofttimes worked against prescribed burning. In principle, the restoration of fire is fine. But many do not want to see handheld torches in wilderness, and no one wants flames in his or her backyard. The burgeoning legislation and rulings that govern what happens on public lands have made it harder to burn, because lighting up is an act that has an agent. The National Environmental Policy Act, the Endangered Species Act, the Clean Air and Clean Water Acts, the Wilderness Act, the Archeological Resources Protection Act—all are intended to prevent the federal agencies from doing something some constituency dislikes. The only way not to offend someone is to offend no one, which is to say, do nothing. Add to this the traditional nervousness over liability for an escaped fire or other collateral damages (smoky roads and car accidents, for example) and normal bureaucratic caution over anything that might annoy the public. (The prescribed natural fire was attractive in good measure because it had no culpable agent. No one could be sued, fired, or made to stand in front of a minicam and stammer to the ambush journalists of Action News. If it blew up, the fire belonged with wild nature or an inscrutable deity.) The upshot is paralysis.

The prescribed-fire model requires that all the preapproved boxes be checked off before one can light up. Those boxes keep multiplying. Any one unchecked item can shut the operation down. This is a formula for continual regression; it is easy to postpone a burn, very onerous to make one up. Burning outside the prescriptions is often too hazardous, both for control and liability— which is why the prescriptions look the way they do. The risks keep ratcheting up what is required before one ignites. No one in the fire community doubts that fire belongs. The issue is where and how and at what costs to reinstate it.

The above roster makes prescribed fire difficult. What it does not address are the outright failures. Prescribed fires have escaped; prescribed fires have killed; their smoke has obscured views, led to car crashes, and compromised human health; prescribed burns have failed to do the work demanded. In its ceaseless contrast to suppression, prescribed burning is said to be safer, easier, and cheaper. It is, inherently, none of these. Many of its costs are hidden because suppression still supplies the fundamental infrastructure, and if a fire escapes, it is reclassified as a wildfire and hence financed by emergency funds. As more burning gets done, more lives are being lost. Interestingly, the percentage of fires that escape prescription is estimated at approximately 2 to 3 percent, roughly the same as those that escape initial attack. Suppression and prescribed fire thus share a similar failure-to-control rate.

Some of the largest fires of the past two decades have been prescribed burns that bolted out of control. Prescribed natural fires that have fled their prescription leashes belong in this category (the Yellowstone fires among them). More overt are those set burns that slipped past their minders. In the spring of 2000 the National Park Service set and lost fires under extreme conditions that, respectively, forced the evacuation of the North Rim of Grand Canyon National Park and blasted out of Bandelier National Monument and incinerated part of Los Alamos. That the same organization lost two fires in two separate states testifies to the theological power that prescribed burning holds in the community. They would force those fires down nature's throat if necessary.

The more serious failures, though, are those fires, or botched burns, that simply do not accomplish the ecological tasks expected—fires that do not burn, fires that yield more small fuels than before, fires that do not shake and bake sufficiently to act as ecological catalysts. Critics of suppression are quick to point out that not every acre blackened by wildfire is "destroyed," as breathless journalists often announce. Yet the same criticism can apply to prescribed burning. Not every acre blackened has been enhanced. Controlled burns may be as patchy as wildfires. A tally of what a prescribed burn has achieved is as complicated, and perhaps as ineffable, as a tally of a wildfire's damages.

And that—the continued comparison with suppression—may account for the deeper dilemma. Prescribed fire's promoters had claimed that such burning could remake fire control into fire management; that controlled burning could replace wildfire with a fire both tamer and more natural; that fire by prescription could become, by itself, the basis for fire protection. Prescribed fire could inspire an alternative institution. It could even challenge suppression on its own grounds, as a means of fire control: prescribed fire could reduce fuels, while suppression could only inflate them.

Yet this is where prescribed fire has faltered in practice and where, even in theory, it remains most vulnerable. Fuel reduction is a complex undertaking. One cannot burn off unwanted combustibles as one can flare off natural gas at an oil derrick. Moreover, prescribed burning for fuel reduction is not a one-off event, like an inoculation; it requires, typically, a sequence of burnings, followed by endless maintenance. Getting that first burn right is often both tough and delicate. The burn is prescribed because the place often has unruly fuels, which make the use of fire tricky. Successive burning rekindles all the legal, political, social, and cultural controversies; over and over again.

Despite bombast about fire being a tool, it is an odd sort of biotechnology. It is a biochemical reaction, an interactive event, whose properties derive from its setting. A controlled burn is less a tool, like a blowtorch or a hammer, than a domesticated species like a sheep dog or a milk cow, or in the context of wildlands, a captured ecological process like an elephant trained to haul logs or a grizzly bear taught to dance. It behaves as its surroundings tell it. Messed-up forests only yield messed-up fires. If it is a tool, it has to compete with other tools; open burning is not uniquely suited for the task, and it carries considerable liabilities. Industrial combustion offers a lot of alternatives, which society for the most part prefers. Defining prescribed fire primarily as a tool defines its value in the same utilitarian terms as suppression. The fire-and-fuel thesis, that is, binds prescription burning to suppression. Again.

What truly matters is fire's ecological role. Combustion does what nothing else does environmentally, and where the biological values warrant, fire has to belong—unique, indispensable, obligatory. There is no alternative; the smoke, the escapes, the sloppiness, the surprises, the bureaucratic awkwardness, all must be tolerated because the proper fire does ecological work without which the biota will decay. The issue is not to use fire to manipulate fuel, but to manipulate fuel to get the right fire. The pith of the problem is not to control fire or to set controlled fires, deciding with Manichaean rigor between one or the other, but to fashion the right fire regime. If suppression is failing because of excess fuels, so also prescribed fire is suffering because of unsuitable fuels.

This analysis takes us beyond both strategies. It is not enough to invert one or the other but to turn both inside-out, as it were. Fire management does not consist of a spectrum, with suppression at one end and let burning on the other, and prescribed fire as a middle-ground compromise. It more resembles a constellation of techniques, reconfigured according to needs. Those needs, rightly conceived, will be ecological. The lack of criticism within the fire community regarding the failures and fallibilities of prescribed fire is one of its great lost opportunities, maybe its disgrace. This critical vacuum happens, in part, because many of those in power are true believers, their identity indelibly tinted by the fire revolution of the 1960s, much as many of their contemporaries are by other Sixties movements. They are unable to imagine beyond that reformation as it was first announced.

But it happens, too, because the larger argument is framed such that the only alternative to prescribed fire of one kind or another is suppression of one kind of another. Better to push on, however dismaying the task, than to return to the failed philosophy of the past. Of course, this is not the case. It never was. What fire requires, being a creature of context, is the right circumstances to behave as it should. Rather, the future of prescribed burning will depend on whether the proper habitats exist for what its handlers want. The success of controlled burning will not rely on manipulating prescriptions alone but on remaking the environments to support particular fires. The debate over burning needs to shift from tedious dialectics about ignition, over starting and stopping, and into a discussion about suitable settings, over modifying the combustibility of fire's environment. Fire is what its setting makes it. Describe its circumstances and you describe fire. Control those circumstances and you control fire. Fire's setting is its prescription.

If prescribed burning has achieved less than it promised, it can still point to genuine accomplishments. Across the country fire officers have kindled a thousand points of light to drive back the ecological darkness. Some snuffed out, some blew up, but many at least put a daub of fire back into the land and gave fire agencies some capacity for maneuvering beyond knee-jerk suppression.

The premise that prescribed burning can, unaided, redeem degraded wildlands has proved overblown, however; and the belief that, through prescribed burning, free-burning fire might recover its old dominion has proved hyperbolic. Fire will no more reclaim those acres than free-range bison will reclaim the Great Plains. Such results will happen only in places, selectively. Most of prescribed fire remains where it has always been, in the Southeast (80 percent of acres burned nationally). The enduring political legacy of the prescribed-fire era is the near-universal attempt to incorporate burning into any and every environment. Even official statements about the intermix landscape insist, in cumbersome bureaucratese, that the presence of houses should not deny the presence of fire as a natural and necessary process.

Such declarations point to what may be the truest legacy of the era, which is doctrinal. The stormy decade of policy reformation was a kind of Council of Nicaea, out of which emerged a creed of American fire, for which a triumvirate of natural fire, suppression, and prescribed burning was fundamental dogma. To question prescribed fire was an act of heresy, akin to doubting the Divinity of the Son, that might well result in excommunication. No new prophets could arise. The American fire community threatened to become a confessional community, complete with catechism. Such was the extraordinary legacy of prescription burning—its power and its glory, and its limitations.

Option 4. Change Combustibility

Like the rediscovery of controlled burning, the rediscovery that fire can be manipulated by manipulating the fuels it consumes only appears novel. Combustion can only occur if there is something to combust. The kind of fire one has depends upon the kind of fuels available: change the fuels and you change the fire. This is obvious to anyone who has ever scrounged for kindling, nurtured a flame in a hearth or campfire, or burned out an irrigation ditch. The strategy of changing a landscape's combustibility as a way of containing fire has, since forever, intertwined with fire management, like paired strands of DNA.

What it means in contemporary America varies with context. Changing combustibility might mean raking up pine needles around a cabin, or sending slash through a woodchipper, or crushing brush, or thinning dense thickets of conifer saplings, or opening up intergrown canopies. It might mean restoring grass, where the loss of a grass- and forbs-rich surface makes controllable fire impossible. Or it might mean expunging flash-fuel grasses, like the exotic cheatgrass, that infest much of the Intermountain West. It should mean fashioning an environment in which we can better control the fires we do not want and promote those we do. Changing the combustibility of a landscape should dampen the prospects for damaging conflagrations where they do not belong, while allowing for prescribed fires that will behave as they should.

And that is the rub. The creation of a public domain dedicated to wildlands prohibited the strict application of a European model in which fire burned within a landscape that was not merely cultural but cultivated. What few practices were allowed in the West—commercial logging, ranching, mining—tended to worsen the fuel complex. Even where left alone (save for fire protection), fuels thickened, again transmuting the fire regime into something different from its historic identity. Instead of an integrated program of fuel and fire, the fuels simply stockpiled, and fire suppression was expected to bar the gate against the flames that sought them out. When that endeavor faltered, fire protection picked up the other end of the stick and attempted prescribed burning. Both strategies broke down because the fuel complex spawned the wrong kind of fires. The West's fire regimes became increasingly unstable, full of booms and busts, as though nature's economy had adopted the New York Stock Exchange as a mentor.

An idea so old it was almost prelapsarian revived: control the fires by controlling the fuels that stoke them. This conception, however, has threatened to kindle a political firestorm. The Forest Service estimates that perhaps 190 million acres need treatment. This will take years, and will cost billions, all for wildlands that, because they are fundamentally uninhabited, hold few voters. A constituency has emerged because TV screens show wildfires savaging communities; a few wet years, with those flames off the tube, and that constituency will likely prefer those billions spent on issues of human not forest health. One generation made a fuel bed that later generations had no option but to lie on. Given a choice, the public would likely go elsewhere.

More, the proposal has bred a debate over just what "treatments" might be appropriate where. What the fire community calls "fuel," most people recognize as living landscapes. Forest thinning, for example, does not mean simply shunting blocks of carbon bullion around a warehouse. It means radical surgery that can alter the existing character of the public estate on a vast scale. Apart from fire, much of the public likes those places well enough as they are, and is wary of intervention. A significant fraction do not want open-air zoos and manorial gardens but (at least the illusion of) pristine nature. The agencies that have created the mess have asked the public for a second chance to set it right. But once bitten, the public is twice shy. It is one thing for lightning to kindle a fire that rips over tens of thousands of acres; it is another to turn that task over to a government bureaucracy. How will the work be done? Who will pay for it? What criteria will decide if the program is working? Who will judge its outcome?

The nuclear issue, that is, is one of values and politics. Just what should those lands be? And who should decide? Wildfire has flushed these vexatious matters out of their covert. Environmental groups fret that the 2003 Healthy Forests Restoration Act will revive the axes of evil. Commercial interests ponder a chance to revive a moribund forest products industry. Rural communities envision a jobs program. Each sees in the wave of flame a threat and an opportunity. Fire, however, sees only stuff to burn and places in which to do the burning.

Can a wholesale program of landscape reform help contain fire? In principle, yes. But as in all topics pertaining to fire, principle matters less than practice. The devil is very much in the duffy details.

The prototype program emerged around Flagstaff, Arizona. Here the Ecological Restoration Institute affiliated with Northern Arizona University devised some demonstration plots amid the ponderosa pine of the Fort Valley Experimental Forest. The regional etiology of ruin is more or less understood. It began with massive overgrazing in the mid-1870s and the simultaneous removal of the fire-wielding indigenes (though lightning remained, a prodigious source of ignition). This stripped off the grasses that had fueled frequent surface fires and deleted a source of many of those burns. That old fire regime had suited the ponderosa perfectly. The pine had thrived in small patches of large trees amid a veritable savanna, which was, not coincidentally, an ideal arrangement for surviving the region's frequent and occasionally savage droughts. When the grasses and torches went, so did the fires, which had routinely abraded the woody brush, including ponderosa seedlings. Here and there, loggers high-graded the old timber, leaving the land to scrubby second growth. Unpredictable cone years flooded the land with seedlings. A dense woods began to spread over the landscape. A program of aggressive fire protection by the Forest Service confirmed and institutionalized the pattern. By the mid-twentieth century a regimen of small, frequent fires was giving way to a regimen of large, high-intensity fires that soared through a contiguous canopy. The proposed solution was to restore the regime that predated the onset of settlement, and this meant those pine jungles had to go.[6]

While fire was the immediate threat, the Institute devised a scheme to improve forest health overall. Thinning out the tiny, stunted pines was the start. Crews spared the old growth and cleared out the small stuff that had sprouted since the upheaval of the late nineteenth century (most of the poles dated from 1919). That restored the forest structure. As soon as possible, they prescribe burned; this revived its ecological dynamics. Grasses and forbs returned, along with weeds. But a cycle of burning and a stout fence to keep out grazers allowed the native species to survive and gradually overtake the exotics. Biodiversity brightened— mostly due to flowers and insects, previously smothered under the blanket of woody debris. Aged ponderosas improved their vitality, as measured, for example, by the flow of sap. Vistas opened. Most visitors preferred the sculpted site to its untreated neighbors. Still, this was an intensive operation, and costly. As the project matured, it became less about silvicultural prescriptions than about political process—endless conversations, adaptive research, ceaseless negotiations. Once field trials began, proponents declared that something similar might be done for other profoundly disturbed woods that have also evolved into unhealthy fire traps. The larger debate began.

Critics piled on their objections. The formula was too rigid, not even adequate for ponderosa pine throughout the West, much less for other fire-perverted forests. The cost was abominable (although what that meant compared to the $130 million for a one-year let-burn program at Yellowstone or to the $631 million doled out to clean up the postburn wreckage at Los Alamos was not obvious). To defray that expense, one would have to allow commercial cutting. To guarantee an adequate supply of wood, the "emergency" restoration program would evolve into a permanent forest-products industry, complete with roading network. That would destroy utterly the prospects for wilderness or deep-ecology landscapes and undermine the thicket of legal procedures that have allowed small organizations (or anyone with an envelope and a postage stamp) to leverage their influence. Environmental groups had struggled for decades to expunge human finagling from the public lands. Now, under the aegis of a fire crisis, the meddlers and tinkerers would return. Fire management would be a wedge that would crack open the land for other, more unsavory doings; outright logging, trailer parks, and casinos couldn't be far behind. Even if the scheme held the conflagrations at bay, its own havoc would destroy any values worth protecting. A holocaust by ax would replace a holocaust by fire. The wild in wildlands would vanish forever. Better to have the fires than this.

And so it goes. Proponents argue that the crisis is upon us: another twenty years, and there will be no forests, either overgrown or old growth, to save. Besides, it is not simply fire that threatens America's wildlands. Mismanagement and lack of management are subverting their ecological integrity. Thinning, burning—these are first-aid measures to prevent a very ill patient from expiring on the way to the hospital. The monster fires, moreover, have cast environmental obstructionists into the same category as extreme civil libertarians after the terrorist attacks of 9/11. In return, critics dismiss the fire threat as alarmist and the response as excessive. Large fires have occurred in the past; fires are natural; even the largest conflagrations have not "destroyed" the biota. Critics can always find some niche that had burned fiercely in the past, or has never burned. They can list the number of landscapes for which the Flagstaff prototype will not apply. They quibble over the diameter of trees to be thinned. They want an exemption for this site or that. They want a further study. There is always some reason to delay and some means to stall.

With fire, however, there is no neutral position possible. It forces us to act. Gradually, a compromise is evolving that allows for thinning in very select forests (such as ponderosa) and where such forests interlock with communities. Such a compromise will tolerate a certain streamlining of bureaucratic decisions, so that *Jarndyce v. Jarndyce*–like stalemates will not endlessly choke any chance of improvement. This would quell the most outrageous spectacle, of mass evacuations and blazing houses.

But it would not of course resolve the more profound problem, the bulk of the public domain. By seeking to limit the zone of defensible space to 200 feet or so, the compromise might not even protect wildland hamlets.

It is not clear how a wholesale fuels strategy will mature. Of the other options, we have a record. We know the power and cost of let burning, suppressing, and prescribing fire. We do not yet understand what deliberately changing the land's combustibility can do on its own, and more, how it will mesh with the other strategies, as it must. The principle only has meaning in its practice. Already, however, a few propositions seem apparent.

Thinning—or whatever removes or rearranges the vegetation—must be site-specific. What works at 3,000 feet may not at 8,000. What works on a south-facing slope may be worthless on a north-facing. What would improve a piñon-juniper woodland may damage a lodgepole pine forest. The greater the detail, the better the prospects for success.

Thinning is not logging, not in the vernacular sense. Rather, it is a kind of woody weeding, and if done right, has more in common with landscaping than land clearing. A critical fact is that not all biomass is fuel: only the small stuff matters. Heavy cutting alone will not clean out fire, and if not mopped up properly, will only smother the land with combustibles. What would not burn before, now may. The technology exists to replace the ruder, brutal slashing of the past with a kinder, gentler culling. One can thin without scalping. Low-impact vehicles, multipurpose fellers, portable mills and biomass energy plants—these can exploit small-diameter wood without clear-cuts and heavy roading. Forest industry would more resemble truck gardens than factories. The outcome can be, for many folks, esthetically pleasing, if not metaphysically satisfying.

Logging is the third rail of American environmentalism. The Bush administration's original Healthy Forests Initiative (2002) stumbled because it sought to link the National Fire Plan—with limited targets for thinning in select forests—to the Northwest Forest Plan, which might revive serious logging in places most Americans do not want it. That coupling proved toxic, like tacking an abortion rider to an appropriations bill. While the shortest distance between two ideological points may be a spectrum, most of the options we want will not lie on any party line. That fire management is simply logging in sheep's clothing is the Big Lie of extreme environmentalists. That a revived forest industry can cure forest ills is the Big Lie of cutting's extreme partisans. The sensible solution is to remove the language and prospects of big-timber logging altogether from what is putatively a forum about fire. Proposals to revive logging may make a political statement, but they are not speaking to fire.

The same holds for parallel proposals such as building roads into yet-unroaded backcountry. The evidence of their contribution to fire protection is ambiguous. Roads increase access for firefighters, but also increase fire starts from travelers; and they lead to other landscape modifications, which may or may not dampen fire. There are cases of roads helping to strangle fire from the land; northern Europe is the best example. But roads are only part of a European equation that includes a fire-intolerant climate, few pyrophytic weeds, and intensive silviculture. Swedish roads, for example, make possible a tree farming so obsessive it scrubs away dead wood—and much of a site's biodiversity. There are equally cases of the opposite outcomes, tropical forests among them. Here, roads lead to logging, which litters the land with fire-gorging slash, introduces a lot of human ignitions, allows pastoralism to further tweak the land into a more fire-prone state, and generally encourages roadside weeds that become fuses for fire. Which of these models applies to the American West? More the latter than the former. If Russian statistics are a guide (and they probably are), most fires hug roadways; a road starts more fires than it helps control. If what is wanted is faster access to fires, then initial attack by air—helitack, rappelling, aerial tankers—is a better and cheaper solution. Besides, how did fire management come to be a job for suburban commuters, with crews driving back and forth daily, punching a clock set with scant regard for fire's chronometer? Like a rugby team continually shunting the ball to the flanks, what should be a discussion about fire gets tossed to one fleeing outlier after another. Proxy fights replace firefights.

Thinning is only one method among many for altering combustibility and is of limited value by itself, just as surgery is but a small part of medicine—essential for some remedies, unnecessary and dangerous for others. It works best as part of a cocktail of treatments—the fire equivalent of operations, chemotherapy, radiation, diet, and the like. Anything that alters the amount and arrangement of the fuel will alter the type and power of combustion. In brief, fire protection belongs more with models of integrated biological control than with urban firefighting. Instead of simply spraying to control pests (or dumping retardants to control fire), one shapes the biotic conditions that make a major contagion possible, identifying those pressure points where biological controls are possible. Targeted treatments are better than broadcast ones. The true task is to make a habitat friendly to the fires we want and hostile to those we don't.

This same logic applies also to the flame-threatened fringe of communities, where an evolving compromise is pointing to thinning-driven fuelbreaks as a means of protection. Is this sensible? It is, if it addresses the particulars of how a house actually burns.

Consider the three mechanisms of heat transfer: conduction, radiation, and convection. Conduction burns structures when flame makes contact. Clearing away the space immediately around a house will break the continuity that allows the transfer. Radiation kindles by immersing combustible material in heat. The distance needed to shield a structure depends on how intense the source flame is and how readily the object ignites. (The intensity varies with the square of the distance, such that small changes can yield big differences, which is why it is so hard to find the right seating distance around a campfire.) Crown-fire experiments in Canada recommend 100 to 200 feet as a minimum distance, which is probably a maximum required distance anywhere.[7] This range refers only to a tree-enveloping sheet of flame blasting its heat against a wooden structure. Radiant heat from smaller caches of fuel will shrink the zone of danger. Planting weakly flammable vegetation and eliminating flaky decoration or needle-drenched roofs will expand the zone of safety. Similarly, the proximity of houses one to another matters. One house can radiate against a too-proximate other, spreading the fire directly from house to house.

The greater problem is convection and more broadly, wind, because it carries sparks. Over short stretches, ember showers can saturate a site with new starts. But firebrands can also travel long distances, and they blow about well after the flaming front has passed, which means someone has to be there to swat them out. This argues for protection not only at the house but over broad areas as well as over time. Studies in both the United States and Australia have shown that many houses have burned not in the thermal wave of a fire tsunami, but later, from small flames that crept to a flammable deck or porch, from sparks that found tiny points of tinder.[8] Had someone been on the scene they could have stopped these latecomers with a squirt gun and a whisk broom.

All parties agree that house protection begins with the house itself. A wooden roof is lethal. Other features like eaves can either cache or discourage combustibles and sparks. The arrangement of houses matters, the fire flaming from one to another or from roof to roof without resort to ground vegetation, leading to the curious spectacle of burned houses amid green landscapes. (Investigations into the 2003 Aspen fire's rampage suggest that most crown burning was the result of ignition from burning houses, not vice versa, while between houses, fire spread on surface debris.) In wildlands, the zone of protection must extend outward into an area known as defensible space. Near landscaping need not be stripped, only sculpted to dampen fire's ability to creep into, radiate toward, or hurl embers at the house. All parties agree that this is properly the duty of a homeowner, not only to himself but to his neighbors. The shouting begins when defensible space is expanded to the community itself, particularly when a hamlet abuts against public land, because it effectively extends the influence of private landholdings into the public domain and becomes subject to national politics.

Regarding fuelbreaks, America has considerable experience, with mixed lessons for community protection. The core reason for ambiguity is that large fires are large events; they can swallow whole swathes of landscapes. Slivers of thinned fuels—the fuelbreak as moat—will not halt the big fire that most threatens a reserve or hamlet. Fuelbreaks work best when they are built into the design of landscapes, not retrofitted. They function nicely in pine or teak plantations, for example, when constructed as part of the original layout. They work poorly when imposed on mature forests. They are temporary features; they reduce an immediate hazard, but cannot hold forever. Broad corridors (and roads) slashed through Oregon's Tillamook burn helped break the continuity of fire-killed snags, but only until the cycle of reburns ceased and the mountains were replanted. Plowed and fired fuelbreaks through the Nebraska Sandhills helped shatter the near-annual flow of prairie fires, but overgrew after the pine plantations ripened. Fuelbreaks require maintenance, and once the crisis has passed, reluctance toward the expense and labor of annually weeding, cutting, and burning overwhelms the project. (Clearing fuelbreaks was one of the early uses of Agent Orange.) Fuelbreaks are, that is, transient devices that work best at the onset of a project for lands of considerable value.

Several grand experiments have attempted to install truly massive arrays of fuelbreaks; interestingly, all have been in California. The Ponderosa Way was a 650-mile-long fuelbreak that spanned the entire west slope of the Sierra Nevada. Built with bottomless CCC labor, it sought to segregate permanently the lower-elevation chaparral from the higher-level conifers, a Maginot Line of fire protection (and a weird counterpart to the New Deal's Shelterbelt tree-planting scheme on the Plains). When the CCC camps left, the Way went with them. Later, several experiments in conflagration control designed broader fuelbreaks, along ridgelines, both in the dense-conifered Sierras and in the chaparral-clothed mountains of Southern California. The conifer model involved selective thinning (not scalping). These fuelbreaks proved expensive, however, and failed during the extreme events that they were intended to staunch. After the 1970 fires, a network of fuelbreaks was constructed along the mountains of the Los Angeles Basin, swinging from ridge to ridge like a Great Wall. While they have their value for access, the control of minor fires, and firefighter safety, they cannot alone halt a major fire. They still have to work with suppression forces, and an all-out conflagration will fling sparks across the barrier as readily as over rock outcrops.

What the intermix scene demands is a much broader scope for defensible space, though it need not be to the same standards as those required adjacent to a house. What the scene needs, considered on a landscape scale, is not a fuelbreak but a fire greenbelt. It needs something on the scale of a golf course, not a moat. The width and character of such a greenbelt will depend on the properties of large fires in each setting, but probably anything less than a mile will prove doubtful, and a mile and a half is a more reasonable scale. The purpose is to break the momentum of a crown fire and the saltation of spotting, the process by which windblown sparks rekindle new fires well in advance of the nominal front. The scheme is less a seawall than a series of speed bumps. No one enters a residential neighborhood from an interstate freeway, braking from 75 to 25 miles per hour within 200 feet. The exit occurs in a graduated series of slowing speeds. So it should be with fire greenbelts.

The intensity of the landscaping would increase as it approaches the village. There is no reason to nuke the woods; the purpose is not to stop fire cold, by paving a surrounding lagoon of asphalt, but to force the flames out of the canopy and onto ground and then, by offering only lightly textured combustibles, to tame the fire into something controllable. There will be fire; there will be a need for firefighters; there may well be some houses lost, the outcome of poor housekeeping or bad luck. But firefighters could stand against such flames, and the community would enjoy a reasonable degree of protection. The greenbelts could well become recreational sites or wildland parks, suitable for picnics and nature walks; they could be regularly maintained by burning, at least in some locales; in places where the existing forest is a shambles, they might well improve biotic health and biodiversity.

Such a program will be neither cheap nor simple. Probably, though, we could come to some consensus, community by community, about how to do it. All sides, however, quickly look beyond that penumbral border. The deeper problem will not end at the hamlet's shadow. Sooner or later we will have to pursue it into the backcountry—not everywhere, but in enough critical sites to matter. Advocates of a changing-the-combustibility strategy will see in the fire greenbelts a demonstration of how that projection might be done, and why. Critics will worry that, once launched, those fidgeting hands and conniving minds will not exercise the same level of care and planning and will blast recklessly into the land beyond. The concept of a fire greenbelt, that is, may prove a tough nut, not because the projects are intrinsically hard but because of what, to various imaginations, they represent for the future.

Flawed fuelbreaks remind us that the core concern is not about trees and thinning but about the overall character of the land. In many of the most wrecked western landscapes, for example, the crisis began with the loss of grass. One could sensibly argue that the urgent task in ponderosa forests is to reinstate those lost surface fuels, which had made the old fire regime possible. The wrangling should not be about cutting trees but restoring Muhley, fescue, and forbs. A recovering grassland demands control over grazing, whether by livestock or wildlife. It probably means getting fire back into that grass, which means smoke into towns or maybe metropolitan areas.

Arguing exclusively over "thinning"—a code word for whatever a group wants it to mean—tends only to recycle the blood feud over state-sponsored forestry. This serves the interests of foresters and a forest industry, which want a second chance, and it appeals to environmental groups, who are happy to replay their triumph over them. But it removes the jabbering still further from fire. In fact, the issue isn't trees, or grass, or elk, or Hereford cattle, or red-cockaded woodpeckers. It's about them all. It's about making all the parts of fire management mesh. It's about synchronizing fire practices with the land.

It's ultimately about the biology of fire, and about ourselves as fire agents. Throughout the whole hierarchy of combustion, from mitochondria to landscapes to the Earth itself, biological controls exist. By conceiving of fire as a physical disturbance, akin to floods, windstorms, or mudslides, we are apt to propose physical measures to counter it—to oppose force with force. But conceiving fire as an event propagated through a biotic medium, something akin to a viral infection, we are likely to search out ecological countermeasures. Fire's ecology is not restricted to fire's "effects," but to the very properties that make open combustion possible. The issue is not about reducing fuel but reshaping fire's essential environment. That should be fire management's reply to deep ecology.

There is nothing sinister about changing the combustibility of the land: it changes all the time, with or without people. Currently, to accommodate the West's Long Drought, nature is ruthlessly culling the woods through beetles and burning on a scale unimaginable for a government agency. One reason the western fire scene seems such a wreck is because its combustibility has changed in ways unfavorable to our interests and the interests of the prevailing biota, as we understand them. Presently, the near future promises to look like the near past.

Our task is to somehow change that setting into something better than what it is. This is an experiment we have barely begun. We know some practices that do not work, and some that might, and have hardly explored the range of *ecological* manipulations—most of them indirect—that will probably suit us best. The whole sphere of biological controls remains largely unexplored. But this goes to the pith of the problem. Without the capacity to change combustibility, the rest of fire-management strategy is engaged in an endless game of rock-scissors-paper.

The trick is to remember that not all biomass is fuel, and that all fuels are parts of a biota. Fire is more than a tool, like a candle, or a process, like a flood: it is an ecological catalyst, a kind of biotic defibrillator. A flood or earthquake can occur without a molecule of life present. A fire cannot. We are not hammering and sawing fuel beds; we are massaging ecosystems. We are creating a habitat for fire. And if we get fire right, we will probably get much of the rest of the mission right as well.

The Elements Compounded

Let burn, suppress, prescribe burn, change combustibility—each of these strategies can point to a characteristic landscape in which it works brilliantly. Let burning can look to Alaska, prescribed fire to prairie preserves, suppression to the urban fringe, changing combustibility to restoration projects. Each is tempted to proclaim for itself a universal standing: if it works here, it can work everywhere. In reality, the techniques often transfer poorly.

In reality, each strategy is most effective arguing against what just preceded it. Each alone, or each embedded in a mosaic of separate landscapes, fails. What the situation demands is a compound of treatments. Every land will likely demand a bit of every approach, the exact proportion adapted to the special character of individual sites. That's not a formula for simple cures. If the fire-

and-fuel crisis is a kind of ecological cancer, then like cancer it takes many forms that require quite different remedies. Some are easy, some hard. Some are incurable.

A few themes recur, however. Fire suppression could stand a modernizing transformation in how it operates in the field. Prescribed fire needs to think beyond its drip torch. Fire institutions remain ripe for reform, despite a decade of vigorous reexamination; probably the most effective prescribed-fire organization in the United States is not a federal agency at all but The Nature Conservancy. The epoch of big-government fire protection has ended, and we need to concoct ways that allow us to achieve political consensus about *something* and to let local communities have more say in how lands are protected—and to hand over to them more obligations to do it. But those communities may not be people residing next to wildlands; they may be NGOs or seasonal visitors or commercial operators. The fire guild needs to acknowledge that the educated public appreciates the merit of ecological fire, that it remains legitimately vexed over the choice among fire's elastic regimes, and that the political confusion may not reflect the public's inability to understand so much as the guild's inability to explain. And looming over every strategy and proposal is the specter of the Big Fire—compromising let burns, voiding suppression, mocking prescribed burning, overwhelming efforts to sculpt landscape.

Whatever is done and whoever does it, however, the task will require intensive management. The era of blanket solutions should end, and is. We can no longer pretend we can carpet bomb fire into submission or believe that we can broadcast purgatives throughout the biota in the hopes that they will somehow cure the malady. Simply calling a burn "natural" becomes a kind of ecological faith healing. Fire management, done right, is intensive management. That does not mean more fussy hands, axes, and bulldozers; it means better knowledge and more targeted techniques, more wits than widgets. It means moving fire protection out of its traditional commodity-style economy into a service-style economy. It probably means fewer skid roads and more automated sensors. More engines and hotshot crews will be no better than the strategy that guides them and the detailed information that informs that strategy.

Whatever is proposed, it will undoubtedly be presented as cheaper than the current arrangement. No one can watch a campaign fire (or better, a complex of campaign fires) and not shudder over the economics. The firefight can suck money the way a firestorm sucks oxygen. In 2003 large fires even had cost-containment teams assigned to them. This missed the point. During smaller fires and slack seasons, it is entirely possible to squeeze savings out of suppression and preparations. Then the big fire vaporizes that nominal economizing in a colossal potlatch. Surely, however, it must be possible to dampen that outlay. Better prevention programs, sharper initial attack, more modern equipment, good fuels treatment, widespread prescribed burning—all should translate into suppression savings.

Don't believe it. The best one can hope for is that the aggregate expenses (including those ballistic budgets from the whopper fire seasons) will remain constant. The assertion that more money up front will reduce the costs of the firefight has repeatedly, decade by decade, incident by incident, proved false. Good intentions and oversight exercises have little to do with the problem; wildfire reckons by nature's economy, has its own ledgers for balancing its accounts. The fact is, America has never paid more than a fraction of what a genuine fire program should cost. It fosters a program of emergency response, not a program of fire tending. Instead, fire funding is a kind of casino, a gamble against weather and ignition. Congress allocates as little money as possible. In slow seasons it must add only a little. In bad seasons, nature sells short and the bills become huge.

This legislative reasoning, however, targets only the mammoth costs of suppression: it seeks to minimize the costs of controlling fire, while ignoring the requirement to get fire of the right sort into the land. An explanation is simple enough. The federal fire agencies are political institutions, not economic ones; their funding reflects political calculations, not the real economics of fire activities, much less a fire program integrated with genuine ecological management. Yet intensive fire management will demand more money, in good part because it will be labor-intensive, not with ever-mounting brigades of hotshots but with researchers, monitors, and analysts. The public lands are a public trust, overall a revenue sink. Fuel-management projects are attractive now because, in part, they provide work for neighboring communities (translate: voters). The true costs of a fire program would probably terrify Congress and not a small fraction of the electorate, which would rather see federal monies spent on deficit reduction than on fuel reduction. The cost of fire is only a portion of the cost of administering the public domain.

Fire and those public lands cannot be segregated, but the struggle to integrate them will continue to be onerous because we cannot agree on what we want those lands to be. Wilderness issues can unhinge discussion as much as abortion concerns can derail social programs, in both cases driven by the most fanatical partisans. The Endangered Species Act has become a kind of RICO for environmentalism, an all-purpose blunt instrument. America's federal fire policy, appropriate management response (AMR)—doing what local conditions call for—is ideally suited to such circumstances, almost completely unprescriptive, and for that very reason difficult to implement, especially under emergency conditions as a glowering wildfire blasts across TV screens and exurbs. AMR represents the end point in repudiating the 10 AM policy, better at excusing what we should not have to do than explaining what we should. It might be worth recalling that the most specific goals, paradoxically, have inspired the greatest innovations. (The contrast is striking with respect to Parks Canada, which has legislated that each park should see that at least 50 percent of the historic burned area gets burned.)

Not all this sponginess can be laid at the feet of the agencies. Their uncertainties, or misplaced convictions, reflect those of

American society. The deeper institutional bankruptcy lies with a fire scholarship that has largely failed to imagine flame beyond the lab. The critical issues in fire's tending are cultural, institutional, conceptual; the failure of imagination lies less in fire's science than in fire's poetry. The most crippling quarrels are fights over values. The endless squabbles over means are, finally, fights over ends. Professional skeptics will quickly chorus that decisions about what is "good" or "bad" about fire and what lands are "healthy" or "ill" are cultural choices. They come not from nature but from a fallible humanity. For some, this makes them not only suspect but illegitimate.

Such critics miss the mark because we *are* the point. Because beyond the burning hamlets, the botched burns, and the bungled slashings, beyond the heroic firefights and the skillful torchings lies the most basic question of all: ourselves as fire creatures. On that, ultimately, everything else turns.

CHAPTER THREE

Sparks and Embers

Ideas in the Wind

NO ONE MUCH LIKES the American fire scene. Their reasons why differ, and are often incompatible. But since the mess seems especially lodged in the public domain, it is easy to bash the federal bureaucracies. Suddenly a crisis that smoldered for decades has burst into flames, while the agencies responsible apparently fiddled, staged palace coups, and did whatever bureaucracies do—or in this case, declined to do. Most of the public became aware of an "issue" during the 1988 season that sent fires blasting through Yellowstone. But from 1993 onward, recurring blazes have kept the West in a state of near permanent emergency.

That perception of institutional cluelessness is wrong. The revolution in philosophy, and policy, within the federal bureaucracy occurred during the Seismic Sixties and its aftermath. The national Wildland-Urban Fire Interface Initiative commenced in 1985. Over the last decade, but with a quickening sense of urgency since the 1994 season, the fire community has sought fixes. A virtual cascade of studies, from organizations as diverse as the Western Governors Association to the GAO, have pondered the implications of what the agencies had long declared to be a creeping crisis. Increasingly sophisticated studies on everything from rephrasing the Ten Standard Firefighting Orders to the loss of field expertise due to early retirement have coursed through the federal institutions; the reports could stock a new wing of the Library of Congress. This outpouring was not the result of a sudden political epiphany but the reckoning of a thirty-year cultural war over fire. If anything, the agencies were too aware, and could be accused not of ignoring policy but of believing that brute policy could reform the awful facts on the ground. To the practical limitations of the other options for managing fire—cutting, burning, fighting—we can add the limitations of studying, discoursing, and administering. We cannot talk, research, or legislate our way through the quagmire any more than we can slash and burn our way out.

The failure lies less in policy than in practice and poetry. There is, if anything, an overabundance of studies, and perhaps of policy wonking, and too little of what might actually make a difference on the ground. Policy by itself is no more than a handle. What matters is the combination of practice and poetry that a policy handle must swing, pulaski-like, at its end. What matters is devising ways to make a difference in the duff. And what matters, no less, is explaining why the larger culture should care.

Ideas of what to do and not do are thick as fireflies. What follows are a handful that I would like to throw out into the night. They begin with the central conundrum of fire management, the big fire. Then they explore a proposal to recharter the technological foundation of wildland fire programs. That leads to a consideration of fire as cultural enterprise—the need to connect to its sustaining society, particularly its intellectuals—and finally to an inquiry into the shifting composition of the fire community.

The Big Fire

Sooner or later, it happens. A let burn boils over, a prescribed fire bolts beyond its paper barriers, a snag fire escapes initial attack—a small burn becomes huge, and more than simply large, fierce. The variants are many yet all the same, and they haunt fire management like a troop of Tolkien's ring wraiths. The big fires do the most damage; they rack up the most stratospheric costs; they draft crews, aircraft, hardware, and supervisors from regular jobs and from around the country, and even from beyond national borders, like a bureaucratic black hole. They wipe out, in days or sometimes hours, the painstaking labor of decades. Years of successful protection and meticulous prescriptions burn away like trash. Efforts to contain suppression costs, successful on small and medium fires, dissolve in the maelstrom of the big fire. Within every ignition—natural, accidental, or deliberate—lies the specter of the big fire, beckoning like the ring of Sauron.

That big fires occur is not for lack of trying to stop them. The thrust of aggressive fire suppression is to prevent the big fire by smashing, as quickly as possible, all the small ones before they develop further. The most serious check on let burning or natural fire programs is the prospect that, one day or another, a fire will kick its way out of its administrative corral and dash wherever it wishes. It does not take many lost prescribed burns (and tort claims) to dampen enthusiasm, either within an agency or its larger society. The big fire is the ancestral curse of wildland fire management.

What makes it a conundrum is that big fires are also necessary. The rub is not just that we cannot control all big burns but that we need some. There are places where big burns would be useful, blazing over large areas, adjusting their intensity to the ecological work required, doing genuine landscape burning economically and efficiently. Equally, there are regimes that require intense fires, which by the nature of the circumstances are usually large in area. Shutting down every fire that might blow-and-go through the canopies of chaparral and dense-crowned conifers would throttle those biota and only create conditions that will make a large fire even more damaging and intractable when it inevitably comes. The only places where big burns can be excluded are those where such fires never occur naturally, when they happen only after human land clearing and torching.

The problem of the big fire, then, is the central problem of fire management, but intensified—the stakes huger, the costs worse, the fallout from failure more daunting. A solution must look to the same suite of options discussed previously, with even more big fires the penalty for not getting it right. A solution requires better preventive measures and initial attack during extreme conditions; controlled fire, of one sort or another, where those flames can substitute for wildfire; and a landscape full of buffers and barriers to untrammeled spread. All that fire protection seeks to do to stop big fires, it could do better, and with collective synchronization could probably reduce the number of conflagrations. Maybe.

A century of trying, however, suggests that this strategy might shrink the number of big fires but not their aggregate size. The big fires would just get bigger. Worse, it does nothing to reintroduce high-intensity fires where the land begs for them. What nature does not get by cajoling, it will extort by force. The traditional scheme assumes that we can coax the flaming genie back into its bottle, that we can bring fire to ground, that even where we believe fire belongs it can be kept on the surface, under a prescription blanket. That is where the big fire diverges, however, from the rest of fire strategy. Sooner or later, the big fire must be addressed as itself, not as a breakdown of other practices.

Perhaps the time has come to pick up the other end of the firestick: to assume that big fires (and big fire seasons) will happen, that some big fires are necessary, that they may be the central, informing phenomenon of fire management around which everything else should revolve. What conclusions follow?

The first is that big fires will be less damaging and costly if they occur within an environment that is otherwise well managed, one that has robust prevention programs and good suppression capability, that does its routine prescribed burning, that arranges its fuels on a landscape scale. The outcome should be to eliminate free-ranging fires that inflict severe damages. They may erupt here and there but will not be able to ramble at will. While the area burned during a major bust may be large, it should be possible to staunch the worst outbreaks without stripping the organization clean, losing houses, and immolating nature preserves. One decouples large-area fires from high-intensity fires.

But some sites need to burn—need to have flame rush through their crown as well as wash over their surface litter. Seeds may lie dormant in duff or waxy cones until released by a pulse of flame; they regenerate best in the ashy aftermath of intense fire that wipes out competitors; they grow in gregarious throngs that set the conditions for the next burn decades or centuries hence. The obvious solution is to kindle those fires under our own terms. We need to prescribe crown fires. The trick is to burn in patches and to turn wind, fuel, and terrain against the flames such that a high-intensity fire would not become an uncontrolled large-area fire.

The proposal depends on our capacity to predict the behavior of fires that are normally off the scale of laboratory modeling. Here our conventional understanding of crown fires can help design suitable settings, ignition patterns, and containment barriers. In fact, prescription crown fires already exist. The high winds that drive such fires can be used to control them, for example, by burning against those winds. The backing flames torch trees and reach up to the canopies but cannot run freely with the wind because that only points them to an already burned patch, the towering sheet of flame irradiating ash and scorched bark. (This tactic has been employed successfully to sanitize beetle-infested lodgepole.) Canada has pioneered a number of techniques—burning summit forests while snow lies on the ground, for instance, by kindling the desiccated canopies with a helitorch, letting the wind blow through the crowns, without connecting to a surface fire and without permitting unwanted spot fires from starting in advance of the front; or letting crown fires rip up steep slopes in Banff, allowing the terrain to control the progress of the flames, permitting rocky crestlines to halt their spread.

Surprisingly, perhaps, high-intensity fires have become the stuff of experimental science. Since 1997, an International Crown Fire Modeling Experiment has sparked a score of full-bore crown fires in the boreal forest outside Fort Providence in Canada's Northwest Territories. Roughly in tandem, Project Vesta has kindled high-intensity fires in the jarrah forest of Western Australia, documenting how precisely they burn and how their ember clouds propagate with the wind. Such knowledge could well be used to prescribe operational fires.

This is an extreme science, and admittedly a spooky scheme. But when big fires dominate the American scene, when fire agencies have concluded that they can no longer thrust crews into the perimeter of such conflagrations, and when some fire regimes pivot on the unavoidable appearance of such burns, the time has come to consider the big fire not as an epiphenomenon of small fires or a breakdown in the capacity to light and fight surface burns, but as an object in its own right—not an outlier in the spectrum of combustion, not a rogue flame that better administration can cage, but for some places, the very essence of what the biota is all about.

We can leave that task to lightning, arson, and accident, or we can take up the torch ourselves.

Firestop II and Firestart I

In 1954 the Forest Service led a pack of its California-based fire collaborators into a year-long experiment to adapt the technologies that had emerged to fight wars and redirect them to the fighting of fire. The timing was right: the United Stated had hard-won expertise in mobilizing and maneuvering corps of men in rough terrain, it had mountains of military-surplus hardware rusting away, and it knew the sharp success of mustering applied science. Operation Firestop proposed to turn all this to civilian purposes, not unlike the way the International Geophysical Year soon afterward redirected the cold war into a global swarm of scientific expeditions. In truth, Operation Firestop did not blossom instantly into new gadgets and machines for fire control, though some devices did spill out quickly. Instead, it did something more enduring: it launched a golden age of equipment development. Air tankers, for one, soon followed.

Since then, nothing like it has occurred. Compared to its usual peers (Canada, for example), the United States has fallen behind, especially in sophisticated initial attack; the U.S. fire community is stuck with lumbering tactics, outdated aircraft, and sentimental relics like smokejumping. This circumstance is an oddity of the American way of fire suppression—undoubtedly a by-product of its system of emergency funding—that new technology rarely replaces old. Instead the new stuff gets added to the mix. Over the past couple of decades quite a lot has poured in without inducing major shifts in the way the job gets done.

To a startling extent, much of the old technology and tactics remain. A firefight today rather looks like one fifty years ago. Crews function in much the same way, though outfitted with niftier clothing and smaller radios. Some of the same planes that flew in the aftermath of Operation Firestop are still flying (more or less).[1] Fire engines lay hose in the same ways to the same ends. A few things have changed, for example, the need for housing protection, since the intermix scene had not yet sprawled into prominence. It may be that this is just how fire protection must work. Or maybe not.

The time has come to restage Firestop—call it Firestop II—to recharter the technological basis for suppression, to render it nimbler, cheaper, more precise. The program ought to extend over at least two full field seasons. It ought to explore not only machines and materials but information technology, of which there is more and more on the fire lines without being completely integrated with the business end of shovels and pulaskis. Everything about how we fight fire ought to be on the table. In effect, the call for a transformation of the military ought to be extended to fire control. There is a need for smaller, better outfitted crews, for example, that live on-site and are able to tap electronic intelligence on demand and call upon precision aerial ignition as needed. It would have been ideal to stage such a project on the fiftieth anniversary of Firestop and conclude it a year later with the one hundredth anniversary of the Forest Service. (But that is the wistful thinking of a historian.)

The flip side should be prescribed burning, an Operation Firestart I. Controlled burning works well in stripped-down systems—simple ecosystems of homogeneous fuels; simple political systems with single, identifiable goals and clear ownership. If it is to achieve what it should, those charged with prescribed burning need much greater power and flexibility.

They should be able to conduct boutique burns—small-size, single-mission, surgical fires. They should also be able to fire forage, that is, to trek across a landscape and burn fuels as they emerge from behind retreating snowfields or drying woodlands, for example. They should, not least, be able to prescribe high-intensity fires. Prescribed burns should be integrated with ecological restoration strategies—as a recurring practice and a broad-spectrum catalyst doing a variety of ecological chores instead of used as one-off solutions, a magic potion. We might in addition explore ways to get fire back into the vernacular landscape, not just the monumental—lawns, golf courses, city parks, the niche habitats that will prove important for biodiversity, something of the landscapes of everyday life. Along with such techniques should come usable field metrics to decide if such practices are meeting the goals set for them.

Such changes require more than a bigger torch. They would involve redesigning crews, equipment, labor practices, and liability laws. Work hours would have to be as opportunistic as fuel availability; crews, for example, would probably have to live in the field for weeks at a time. Burners would need some relief from nuisance suits over flame and smoke. Reforms of this sort would mean a serious integration of technology, particularly IT, with field practice, such that smaller crews could do more work by more precise interventions. Analyses of the current system too often reveal a serious digital divide between high-tech modeling

and what actually happens in the woods; those in charge of prescribed fire need to span that chasm.

The trick, though, is to do it on the ground. Prescribe burning
needs a high-visibility arena in the form of dedicated field experiments in which to explore and advertise the results. Trying to
experiment *sub rosa* during normal fire seasons will likely only
compromise existing programs and frustrate the innovative ones.
Give the trial at least two good seasons, with six reconstituted
crews operating over three regions. Let them compete against one
another instead of against suppression.

Fire in the Mind

Toward dusk on a July day in 2000, a panel of fire authorities convened by invitation at the Taylor Wildlife Refuge, a private holding in Montana's Bitterroot Valley. Earlier, dry lightning had
crackled over the surrounding mountains; by the time the speak-
ers shuffled into the barn cum auditorium to present their
thoughts on wildland fire, the sky was abuzz with helicopters fer-
rying smokechasers to newly started blazes, while air tankers
rumbled up and down the valley delivering retardant and the
highway filled with mobilized crews headed to fires that had
already escaped initial attack. The noise was more than a distrac-
tion: it symbolized perfectly how the need to act so often trumps
the need to contemplate. The culture of fire is one of doing.

Yet the scene should remind us, too, that action follows choice,
and choice follows from the complex understandings we call culture. For too long there has been a disconnect between America's
vernacular culture of fire and America's high culture, between
what gets done "out there" and what gets examined by scholarship. Partly this reflects a failure of intellectuals to see anything
significant in the flames. They see what their disciplines have
trained them to see and fail to hear fire even as it cries out for philosophy, history, ethics, literature, art, economics, political the-

ory, and a high order of fundamental science. But mostly the chasm betrays a failure of the fire community to appreciate how the flames that it finds so compelling in the field—so *urgent* in its call to do—illuminate fascinating questions, and that such inquiries are ultimately vital to its mission, that the mind can experience a rush as stirring as anything wrought by a torching fir. Instead, a subject that goes to the heart of our identity as a species ends up as government reports, bowdlerized war stories, or a genre of juvenile sports literature.

So even as it admits its challenges are social and political (avoiding the thornier issues, which reside in the realms of philosophy, values, and matters of identity), the fire community continues to think with its hands, to search for technological fixes or to promote applied science that can translate quickly into practice. In recent years, for example, the fire guild has cranked out a metric ton of high-quality studies on policy without probing the core political ecology of fire. They insist on "science-based" solutions even though the crux of most disputes—the bottlenecks in moving plans into the field—lies in a politics charged by disputes over ethics, economics, and esthetics, with uncertainties over the proper place of humanity in nature, over nature's rights and humanity's responsibilities. Where and why should people intervene? With what means and to what ends should humanity apply and withhold fire? The fire guild, however, too often treats public opinion as though it were an overgrown woods, needing only a suitable prescription for silvi-social thinning in order for an agreement to emerge—a problem that can be solved by proper social science research. This mind-set only prolongs the agony.

Among the many tasks one might press upon America's fire community is the imperative to reconnect with intellectual culture, not only to incorporate more fields of scholarship but to engage the intelligentsia in fire issues. The fire guild might find the experience exciting, a jolt of mental adrenaline. The intelligentsia might discover that fire is not only fascinating but fun.

The fire community should know this. State-sponsored forestry, and the fire programs that it oversaw, got hammered over the past forty years not so much because their science or techniques were bad but because they had decoupled what they did from what the culture wanted. They could, in a basic sense, no longer speak to their sustaining society. A reengagement began with the debate over wilderness, whose fire subtext the Yellowstone conflagrations displayed spectacularly before the public; but the momentum really built only after Maclean published *Young Men and Fire* (that book, again). The national media witnessed the cataclysmic 1994 season through the prism of that extraordinary text: fire intrigued the literate public in ways it had not before. It is likely no coincidence that a year later a major consolidation of policy was published in the *Federal Register*.

The lesson was that the fire community needed more than pumps, policy briefings, training manuals, and applied science; it needed to be more than a trained guild. It needed to broker between free-burning fire and identity politics. It had to engage high culture by making the science fundamental and fascinating as science, not simply as an aide de camp for nifty gadgets. (It is hard to imagine a Crafoord or Nobel prize going to someone in fire research, although the subject deserves that kind of brilliance and should be able to inspire it.) But the fire community also, somehow, had to explain to its sustaining society why all this mattered, as it had to explain to itself why its most dazzling achievement had come from the William Rainey Harper Professor of Renaissance Literature at the University of Chicago. The fire community did not need another data set. It did not need another policy wonk. It needed novelists, artists, philosophers, pundits, critics. It needed a poet.

Consider, first, the question of suitable fire institutions. Any overhaul of American fire must examine the politics, not simply the policies, of fire. Yet the topic has been little studied, which seems positively weird when one considers that what to do about wildland fire is and has always been a political enterprise. Governments oversee the public wildlands, sponsor fire research, and determine bureaucracies and policies. The critical moments of reform occur when fire overlaps with political turmoil, when it joins other crises or comes to symbolize them. In simple terms, the fires must shock the system without killing it. Australia's bushfires have, as in 2003, provoked a political response. Indonesia's get lost in the chaos.

Wildland fire management, too, has its nation-building dimensions, the need to fashion institutions to understand and manage fire, particularly if old ones have collapsed. This would seem a natural subject for a profession joined at the hip to government, especially for the Big Four since all of them invented firefighting institutions as part and parcel of their drive to create a modern state. Yet the proliferation of new nations over the past decade highlights just how poorly understood fire politics is. What suite of fire institutions might suit Kazakhstan? What should Ukraine do about fire? Or for that matter, Russia? Does burning Brazil even have a wildland fire problem? Should wildland fire be an issue in Zimbabwe?

Foreign assistance in developing fire programs, however, typically means shipping equipment, training manuals, and videos, or sponsoring a research project or two, not advising what kind of new institutions might best match land and fire with society. The explosion of environmental NGOs and the politics of devolution argue that politics will matter more not less, and that its character will change. The imperial model will recede and its stepchildren, politics by presidential decree and court order, will likely if grudgingly yield ground to more openly democratic means of making decisions. Paradoxically, the problem of fire nation-building is exactly what the United States confronts internally as it seeks to recharter and redesign its national fire institutions. America has as much to learn as to export.

This suggests that any competent reformation must also examine the organs that exist for fire knowledge. Around the globe, government-sponsored fire science has receded over the past decade. South Africa and New Zealand have privatized their labs. Russia has downsized its facilities, including its formerly world-class fire lab at the Sukachev Institute. Canada has shrunken its commitment and redirected the vaunted facilities of the Canadian Forest Service into a mandate to "advise" Ottawa about matters regarding fire. Against this dismal trend Australia and America have mounted a resistance. Australia has granted its effervescent but diffuse fire-science community an institutional focus by establishing an Australasian Bushfire Cooperative Research Centre. The United States, beginning in 1998, sought to bolster its long-anorexic fire-research program with significant new funding, organized into a Joint Fire Science Program (JFSP) that would span all the federal agencies and collaborate with universities and the private sector. The funding involved was significant: $16 million by 2002. Fire research thus found that it had joined what critics were scorning as a "fire industry."

The JFSP illustrates the cultural-disconnect dilemma nicely. It has become a vehicle for funneling greater (much needed) funding into traditional themes. While it has expanded the domain of fire-research operatives beyond the old Forest Service hegemony, the money still comes from the federal government and goes to address questions about administering the public domain. This is only to be expected. (It doesn't take a cynic to ferret out that Congress's true purpose was to get those burning houses off TV screens.) The real problem is that the program assumes that given the right science, a solution will suggest itself, requiring only political will to make corrections happen on the ground. It shrinks scholarship to science. It assumes that the problem-solving powers of science can even solve problems beyond the scope of science.

What the JFSP has done it has done well enough. Most approved research designs have inherent limitations, some due to their origins in forestry. (They will fret over what diameter of tree to cut, for example, while ignoring the grazers and browsers that will compete with fire for the promised grass.) Most of the work is

applied science; many of the projects are experiments into slashing and burning—studies of fire's effects, not a full-gauge fire ecology. There is no drive for a truly biological theory of fire. The program's practical strengths are its probings and pokings about ways
to map and measure combustibles and their moisture content, and
about fire behavior models to link such fuels with flame. This is
the kind of detail that will make or break precision fire management. The country can be glad for every scrap.

The real lapse is that the program doesn't, perhaps can't,
address the fundamental questions because these are not
amenable to a science-based answer, even in the research space
grudgingly granted to the social sciences, which at least speak a
shared technocratic language. Instead these issues are about values; about how people see the world and themselves in it, about
who they think they are and how they should behave, about
how the acquire those conceptions, how they argue with others,
how they convey that sense; about literature, art, folklore, politics. The fact is, technology can enable but not advise, while science can advise but not decide. The disconnect is that we do not
have institutions to research the problem as it is but to do science, with the faith-based expectation that the accumulated
data will propel proper political decisions. All the evidence of
the culture wars over the national forests and fire policy suggest
otherwise.

The situation would seem to cry out for an applied humanities
of fire. While the humanities are not by nature a problem-solving
enterprise, they are problem-illuminators, and can enrich our
understanding about why the issues look as they do, what funda-
mentals are a stake, how and where scientific research might contribute (and where not). They help make it possible to parse diffuse discourses and rants based on abstract values into more
usable forms. At the simplest level philosophy, history, and literature can help translate the different conceptual languages of
competing parties into something more mutually intelligible.
Such an exercise will not resolve the disputes, but it would help

clarify the terms of disagreement and hence the political choices involved. (The multiple perceptions of "wilderness" is an obvious example.) If you want an interesting thought experiment, place a philosopher trained in ethics in charge of the JFSP, and see what kinds of research might be funded.

Consider the contemporary enthusiasm for "adaptive management" as a method for transferring scientific research into practice. This might seem, to the uninitiated, as simply an elaborate exercise in learning-by-doing. But one might also liken it to pragmatism, that school of formal philosophy which, a century ago, addressed the question of how to live in a pluralistic, contingent universe about what which we have incomplete knowledge. Instead of packing an experimental approach involving a give-and-take of information and action in technocratic language which either obscures the obvious or propounds the self-evident, why not also appeal to William James and John Dewey? The core strategic issues that adaptive management addresses American intellectuals have worked through before. It might help to learn how, to their minds, they resolved them. (It might also be useful to recall Dewey's observation that the really sticky questions of the day are never really solved in any technical sense. Society just moves on to new questions.)

What might history, in particular, contribute? To the more philistine practitioners, concerned solely with how a "history book" might help them do their prescribed burning, the only (if facetious) answer is, "Rip out the pages and use them for kindling." More thoughtful fire managers might apprehend that knowing how the present scene evolved will enrich their appreciation for what treatments might work or not, that the proposed practices must make sense to society, that they must work within the culture as well as on the landscape. Knowing how that culture has interacted with its land—and how it has perceived its own actions—is fundamental to such an understanding. Fire managers well educated in their culture will likely make better choices than those obsessed only with technical criteria. The fact is, history doesn't offer simple "lessons," readily coded into administrative guidelines. What it offers is thick-description context, but context is, finally, what fire is all about.

If the humanities don't propose an immediate payoff, neither does most basic science. No fire officer needs to master thermodynamics and Fourier equations to light a backfire, any more than a plumber needs to know the calculus behind Bernoulli's principle. One could even make a case against basic science. One could easily argue, for example, that a reason America's national fire-danger rating system works less well than competing systems is that it sought to found its equations on first principles and lab data instead of simple correlations between environmental conditions and fire behavior (as the Australian and Canadian systems do). Yet in intangible but real ways having that fundamental science in the background seems to matter. It nudges fire management out of the realm of craft and helps bond it to the larger culture.

And that social valence, however vague, is why fire management needs to engage a broader range of scholarship: history, literature, arts, philosophy, theology, folklore. Fire management is about choices, and more and more, it involves choices between competing environmental goods; between clean air and endangered species, or between different goals for fire's "restoration." A culturally illiterate fire manager will struggle. Fire protection in cities can remain a craft. Fire administration on the public lands cannot. Wildland fire management is not a stand-alone or outsourced service, but an integral element of land management. It touches on too many values and environmental choices. For its own practical survival, no less than its cultural coherence, the wildland fire community desperately needs to connect with scholarship beyond natural science and with questions beyond a three-year implementation horizon.

One suggestion made to the JFSP was to allocate 1 to 2 percent of its funds toward big questions and even some grounded in the humanities. Some samples: What is the interaction of industrial fire with other combustion sources? What is the global ecology of contemporary fire? How regular is the pyric transition? What is the history of fire science? Of fire technologies? What can we learn by comparing fire institutions among that club of countries with extensive burning but few public lands? Is a general model of anthropogenic burning possible? Since a century of efforts has failed to concoct a meaningful economic metric for fire, is an ecological metric possible? How might we expand fire ecology into a general theory of fire biology?

And if we truly wish to plunge into the humanities, one could begin examining choices according to philosophies of ethics or esthetics. Is there, for example, a better way to frame the debate about defensible space around communities than arguing, on the basis of radiant heat flux, whether that distance should be 100 feet or 200 feet or a mile? Or should that matter be sited within a discussion about the relative responsibilities of public and private ownership? Or about what kinds of landscaping might enhance biodiversity and natural beauty (and property values) while also establishing a fire-defensible space? Before such questions the sciences stand tongue-tied. The fact that the humanities have failed to seize upon such matters helps explain why, to the public mind, they so often seem irrelevant.

A model might be the setting aside of a similar proportion of publicly funded buildings for public art. (Or one could look to the Antarctic Artists and Writers Program underwritten by the National Science Foundation.) The proposal went nowhere, which should surprise no one. But unless someone begins the task of recentering fire and fire management within the larger culture, all its research will either become the political equivalent of money-laundering or a jobs program for scientists or just fritter away in a frenzy of intellectual hot-spotting.

Ultimately, the fire in the mind will be as significant as that on the ground.

Fire as Community

Who is the fire community? Not long ago, the quick answer was those who were employees of government-sponsored fire institutions. Yet even that defined group has waxed and waned over time. And as the institutions of fire management have shifted, it is time to consider a broader view.

In the early days, with their ranks thin, fire officers sought through cooperative ventures to expand the pool of available firefighters. Almost all those granted permits to the national forests were required to contribute labor and equipment in the event of a fire. Logging camps sent felling crews, railroads labor gangs, and ranchers their mounted hands. Citizens could be impressed into firefighting ranks by sheriffs under public-emergency statutes (not a few were flushed out of saloons). The various organs of government found ways to amplify their clout during big fires by pooling resources. And communities themselves, in time-honored pioneer fashion, turned out to fight fires that threatened them. Moreover, almost everyone living in rural landscapes control-burned—their yards, their pruned orchards, their fallow, their pastures. The fire community was a diffuse, ad hoc affair, mustered as needed.

As the federal government assumed more and more power, however, it took both torch and shovel away from local groups and transient users and replaced them with its own personnel. Fire was something that government institutions did (or did not do). The CCC choked off the flow of citizen exchange: the agencies had staff enough. In comparison, temporary laborers were unruly, unreliable, and inefficient, and as multiple-fatality fires came with almost metronomic clicks, unsafe. Like a vertically integrated company—a Ford or a GM—the government had its own facilities, its own workers, its own bulldozers and aircraft, its own internal research labs. Alternatives withered, save for rural volunteer fire departments where a federal presence was slight and the fires frequent. A few academics puzzled over fire in prairie restoration or game management, but outside private preserves or hunting plantations, their impact was negligible.

The military analogy, so often invoked (and misplaced), may actually here prove helpful. Today, fire management has a small corps of permanent-staff fire officers, a larger cadre of seasonally furloughed crew supervisors (firefighting's NCOs), and a horde of seasonal employees. Most seasonals work for a couple of summers. Beyond these regular forces the federal fire community relies on lightly trained reserves whose regular job in the agencies is not fire related. The states are different, dedicated to fire protection with an approach more akin to urban fire services. A national corps of hotshot crews (approximately seventy-eight) move where they are needed, mostly to large fires. The supervision of big fires relies on incident management teams, drafted from among the agencies. For major events, the community calls upon the national guard and the military. The latter is photogenic and suits a self-image of fire suppression as a moral equivalent to war, but the allusion is flawed and the exercise wasteful. Mostly the overall system exists to keep yearly costs down and the number of permanent government employees minimal. One can question whether staffing matches the tasks that fire management—as distinct from fire suppression—requires.

In fact, the whole matter of what constitutes the fire community deserves reconsideration. Like other enterprises, outsourcing has become normal, not only for catering and aircraft but even for staffing. Likewise, more groups are clamoring to participate in all aspects of fire management, and are being invited to join. Expense, a legacy of ill will, political fashions—all compromise the idea of a simple expansion of the Forest Service, or other federal land agencies, on the New Deal model. Will the federal agencies remain themselves the exclusive employer, with fire staff an inextricable part of land management? Or will a National Fire Corps evolve in emulation of the Corps of Engineers, an oversight body that contracts out for services? Or will NGOs like The Nature Conservancy, which already oversees for the feds its Fire

Learning Network, increasingly broker between the national government and the constituencies of the public lands, a kind of semichartered surrogate? Or will fire management return to something like what it was a century ago, a practice shared across a broad gamut of groups?

Consider some alternatives to the present arrangement of seasonal firefighters. Traditionally, fire staffing has been treated as though it were unskilled farm labor for planting and the harvest, not as a craft (much less a profession). But fire season extends beyond the summer recess, particularly where prescribed burning or site treatments are called for; fire crews need more training than they can normally receive in preseason fire schools; the reliance on called-up personnel with little direct experience in fire is asking for complications; and so on. Why not sign contracts for, say, three years? This would provide trained personnel without committing the government to lifetime employment. If the agencies do not move this way, the duties may be outsourced to private companies that can.

Consider, next, other sources of labor not yet tapped. The intermix landscape is a good place to start. The scene is curious: to protect citizens, whole communities are evacuated; to protect firefighters, the crews are also removed from risky settings or high-intensity fires. The result is to abandon those communities. Some locales may be indefensible by any objective standards; all such, however, become indefensible because there is no longer anyone on-site to defend them.

Who then could protect such landscapes? The residents, of course. Nothing demonstrates so utterly the government's fire monopoly than the practice of ordered mass evacuations. The reasoning behind the drill is self-evident: no fire officer would willingly place a community at risk to a fire under his direction. In the absence of serious preparations, a mass emptying of the community is the best of a desperate slate of choices. Once the practice becomes established, no incident management team would hazard the consequences of not following what has become standard practice. (One can imagine tort-claim lawyers drooling over a failure to do so.) But not all communities are indefensible; not all residents need to be hauled off to evacuation centers; not every evacuation under the rush of a firestorm is better than no evacuation.

Australia, for example, has devised another strategy, which grew out of studies of its most fatality-ridden conflagrations, beginning with Ash Wednesday in 1983. Most houses did not vanish into a maw of flame; they burned because of combustible roofs, because flames spread from the surface directly to the house, or because sparks blew into suitable niches. A surprising number of structures actually burned after the flaming front had passed. A sickening number of fatalities occurred during the panicked flight from the fast-approaching flames.[2]

What this recommended was the paradoxical logic of staying. Not for every house: only those with a reasonable degree of defensibility. Not for every resident: the infirm, the elderly, the very young, those without a crumb of training should all go. Those who stay, however, can survive the fire front and likely save their house. A related logic applied to those who choose to flee: they should do so early, or not at all, much as one should react to a hurricane. These practices are broadcast to the bush public, a kind of fire equivalent to emergency first-aid training. Residents know to flood their gutters, shut the blinds, stockpile water, and so on. They know the choice to stay or go is theirs. Apart from its volunteer bushfire brigades, which are the glory of Australian fire suppression, a complementary program has emerged in Victoria, the Community Fireguard Groups, to help during crises.[3]

There is no reason why, with modifications, a similar strategy could not apply to America's bush communities. The sticky part may be (as in so many areas) reforming liability law. The other knotty issue is that some communities most at risk are inhabited only seasonally, sometimes with a substantial fraction of retirees, not by the kind of permanent residents who normally sustain rural fire departments. (Increasingly, since fires have become rarer, most rural fire departments have evolved into an all-purpose crisis-response service, largely driven by medical emergencies and road accidents. Such crews require training well beyond firefighting; and few intermix hamlets have residents with the time or inclination to undergo such preparation and hence participate.) The communities must look elsewhere.

What may be needed is a kind of fire militia, a substantial body of the community drilled in basic fire protection, particularly for structures, that can be called out during major crises. A militia member might experience only one or two such call outs in his or her lifetime. That would be enough. Particularly with foam technologies and other options for shielding houses, a reasonably knowledgeable and disciplined corps of local residents could work with fire-dedicated crews to protect their community. Moreover, knowing that they might themselves have to defend a place would spark strong incentives to ensure it was as defensible as possible.

And then there is the *levée en masse* so characteristic of big fires and big-fire seasons. As crews pour in, more and more effort goes to servicing their burgeoning needs. Surely we could do more with fewer numbers if we leveraged those skilled crews with better technology. Besides, stripping people from other agency tasks only means those other tasks go undone. This is especially true where incident management teams are involved for extended tours. Perhaps, as some have suggested, we ought to treat big fires as extraordinary events—like other civilian disasters—and create a professional cadre to oversee them, perhaps within FEMA, which already rushes to the scene if housing or other private property is involved. Fire officers from the agencies might join the big-fire cadre for a several-year tour of duty as part of their professional development.

Splitting fire management from daily operations, and especially divorcing it from land planning, would be ruinous. But segregating big fires from the rest might help prevent the imbalances they provoke while key staff are siphoned off for indefinite periods to fight them. Removing big-fire campaigns from local control might also reduce the perverse incentives those fires provide to the public lands that experience them. At present, a big fire not only sends ripples through the national fire community, but can create a chain reaction of lost labor as it drafts in workers otherwise busy in the bureaucracy, even while showering the burned forest with emergency monies.

The flip side would be to enroll volunteers for assistance with prescribed fire or with the preparations that make them possible. The Healthy Forests Restoration Act provides for a Public Land Corps to assist with rehabilitation and fuel treatments. Administrative directives already stipulate that at least 50 percent of proposed thinning (primarily around existing settlements) should be done by contractors, not permanent government employees. It is only a question of time before outsourcing extends to the burning itself—already a small industry of prescribed-fire consultants is flourishing.

The process is likely to push a lot further. The detailed burning that sculpted presettlement landscapes came at the hands of seasonally mobile tribes. The equivalent today would be seasonal residents, or volunteer groups. They could burn as their predecessors did or as their suburban ancestors once did lawns and leaf piles. With suitable training there is no reason why local groups, or NGOs, could not participate under supervision. The consortia model that has served suppression can be extended to prescribed fire as well. Such an expansion of torch holders is helping to break the apparent monopoly over fire by the federal agencies. (Florida, for example, has passed legislation to encourage local landowners to burn, and burn better, by establishing criteria for liability and then shielding practitioners against nuisance suits.) Another sidebar is that such a move would expand the scope of the fire community at large. The prospect sounds radical only because we have lost our touch with flame and because we have come to treat prescribed fire as a government monopoly, as though it were nuclear power. It is not.

Some time ago critics noted a disparity between what the agencies as custodians of the public domain were supposed to do and what, in practice, they did with fire. There is a similar disconnect between mission and manpower. Whether wild or prescribed, fire is opportunistic, episodic, obedient to its own rhythms of wind and wet, and indifferent to labor laws and the customs of a white-collar workplace. Fire specialists must share those same traits.

Free-burning fire is not a bureaucratic category. It never will be.

CHAPTER FOUR

Flash Points

✖️ *Fire Scenarios for the Future*

LITTLE OF HUMAN LIFE escapes fire's touch. America's
future will continue to strike and receive sparks, some of
which will expire quietly, some of which will flare. The major
flashpoints, however, are likely to align with the three grand
narratives—the saga of fire, the drama of wholesale land-use
reforms including the public lands, and the chronicle of America's cultural engagement with fire. The intermix fire is the current obsession of America's national narrative, although
another problem fire may well replace it by the end of the
decade. How to restore and maintain ecosystem health on the
lands of the public domain—this is the question before the
imperial narrative, and it is likely to spark calls for more institutional reforms, perhaps affecting the fundamental character of
the lands themselves. And the matter of reconciling open flame
with closed combustion, that is, of global warming—which is at
heart a fire problem—is where the industrial fire narrative is
unfolding. Each has its own historical momentum. How they
braid together will decide the character of American fire in the
coming years.

The Fires This Time, and Next

For several decades Americans have been recolonizing their once rural lands. Satellite photos of settlement in Breckenridge, Colorado, look surprisingly like those from Rhondonia in southwestern Amazonia. The American newcomers, however, do not live off the land, only on it. They do not graze, prune, plow, slash, plant, or burn. They come from cities and carve small exurban enclaves out of abandoned farmland or platted ranchettes. In the eastern United States, the outcome is patches of subdivisions and woods, cloying perhaps but not intrinsically volatile. They are routinely blasted by wind and water, with vast damage (the ice storms of 2003, for example, acted like a kind of frozen fire). In the West, the resulting landscape quilt stitches houses to fire-prone public wildlands. Such places are primed to burn.

The urban and the wild—their compound is a kind of environmental nitroglycerine and when shaken by drought, wind, or spark, they explode. Fire is not alone: sprawl interbreeds with whatever indigenous hazards exist, but fire is the most visible. Over the past two decades the number of structures burned in the intermix (or wildland-urban interface, as officialdom prefers to call it) has escalated, the irrational exuberance of homeowners having helped the NASDAQ Nineties to create a bull market for burning. Even more, those enclaves have projected a vast fire protectorate of urban-centered values across the countryside (exurbanites particularly loath smoke, for example). Since 1990 the intermix issue has dominated the national discourse. When politicians and pundits speak of America's fire problem, this is usually what they mean, and it is why fire matters just now to the public at large.

This is a dumb problem to have because technical solutions exist. Banning wood-shingle roofs, attention to simple yard maintenance around structures, installing hydrants, the application of some basic codes for construction and zoning—such measures would eliminate the worst of the situation. In effect, one needs to treat such landscapes as periurban, not semiwild. Moreover, transitional eras are always the most dangerous: the land is neither one kind or the other, but held in perpetual, unstable suspension between the two, and this is unarguably the condition of the intermix zone, as such lands leap from a rural frying pan into an exurban fire.

For all the media fury expended and, occasionally, the extraordinary ferocity of these fires, it is possible to exaggerate the destructiveness the burns cause. Statistics are astonishingly poor (this is true for most fire-related issues). Rough figures only exist since 1998, and they show on average somewhat fewer than 900 houses and outbuildings burned each of the past five years (and that is distorted by the 2,381 structures burned in 2002). While significant, the number becomes vanishingly small when compared to the more than 300,000 residential fires across the country, a phenomenon that is declining nationally. Adding all the civilian fatalities associated with the intermix scene since 1980 amounts to less than one one-hundredth of the number of such fatalities in residential fires for a single year. While the intermix fire crosses the grain of the residential-fire trend, it will probably settle down over the coming five to ten years. Exurbanites' gamble with fire may be foolish but it is not irrational—certainly better odds than playing state lotteries.[1]

The shock value of course is different: intermix fires are like shark attacks, while garden-variety residential fires that take lives are like heart attacks. Still, even the largest fire outbreak is small compared with hurricanes, floods, and catastrophes located in densely inhabited areas. Windy and dry is less damaging than windy and wet. Of forty-six major weather disasters registered by the Bureau of the Census from 1980 to 2000, western wildfires accounted for three (or 6 percent). The Oakland firestorm of 1991 would add an expensive fourth; the October 2003 California outbreak will post a further fire contribution to the roster. Average loss due to each of these wildfires was about $1.3 billion, roughly equivalent to major tornado episodes. By contrast, some fourteen hurricanes slammed the United States, with an average loss of $4.8 billion each. (Hurricane Andrew in 1992 accounts for nearly 40 percent of the total losses.) The summed fire losses of the three seasons, including the seemingly staggering costs in 2000, equate with the 1993 ice storm that struck the Southeast. One explanation for the lesser damages is simply that the public domain is uninhabited and hence does not have the same values at risk. A hurricane in Nevada would not yield the damages of one in Texas or Florida. Moreover, with the government as insurer, a weaker metric to applies to the losses that do occur. But it is also true that firestorms, for all their telegenic grandeur, simply are not in the same league as water-powered storms.[2]

Yet neither is it likely that the intermix scene is simply an odd fad. Americans are creating a new kind of landscape, a postmodern pastoral, something neither urban nor wild nor rural. Like strip malls, these landscapes are destined to become permanent features that will not give way to "real" architecture. They are what they are and can be done well or poorly. Such communities need reasonable standards for fire codes, not simply the jeers and *schadenfreude* of the chattering classes, eager to gloat over the spectacle of tech-boom millionaires trying to protect log-plated trophy homes with garden sprinklers. And unless we want our intermix milieu to look like the parking lots of big box retailers mixed with woody trailer slums, we need to think about landscaping—settings that are fire-safe but biofriendly. We need an esthetic for ourselves in the scene. All of which argues that, once the transitional phase has passed, a new kind of fire will exist more or less permanently, and that the fire community should think about what kind of institutions and practices are suitable to cope with it.

To its credit the fire community early identified the intermix issue and is succeeding in taming it. This seems counterintuitive: the burning houses and evacuated towns crowd TV screens every summer. But the public has heard the message, new communities are incorporating fire safety into their design, and the crisis, stoked by the Long Drought, is cresting. The most stubborn problems involve those communities created early in the movement and under the worst circumstances; it is this backlog that is most vulnerable. (While California in the early 1990s legislated against shake-shingle roofs in new construction, the Cedar fire took those Scripps Ranch houses not yet retrofitted to the new code.) Probably the intermix fire wave will pass within the next five years, and it is plausible that within eight to ten years, the intermix fire scene will be sufficiently domesticated to no longer pose a startling challenge. It will take its place beside urban, wildland, and rural fire, overlapping with the others but with its own distinctive character.

All observers agree that the ultimate responsibility for solving the problem resides with local communities. Homeowners must create defensible houses; exurban hamlets and sprawling suburbias must enact and enforce appropriate standards for access, protection, and cleanup (even for absentee landowners); county boards must create fire districts; insurance companies ought to charge suitable rates based on hazard (where is competitive capitalism when we need it?). The scene may well demand new fire institutions, neither urban nor rural, welding both local and federal interests. It might argue for a national fire insurance, modeled on those for floods and crops, or for low-cost loans to help underwrite the expense of conversion. Increasingly, too, fire agencies are reluctant to risk firefighters by trying to defend places that they regard as indefensible. Much of the intermix they dismiss as hopeless.

But "defensible" is an elastic, even arbitrary designation. There is no absolute index for intermix fire as for other natural threats. There is no metric for design equivalent to one-hundred-year floods for bridges or magnitude 6 earthquakes for skyscrapers. We do not demand Midwestern houses withstand a direct hit from a tornado; we cannot insist that every outbuilding be able to withstand a millennial fire. Most houses, moreover, apparently burn from small ignition sources, which boil over because no one is there to snuff them out. The appropriate standard is that the structure be defensible, not that it be impregnable. That leaves a clear imperative for a firefighter on the scene, which is the logic behind a fire militia and the fire greenbelts that would help justify a stand against the flames.

If the intermix fire is climaxing, then what might replace it? Bet on the lands beyond and between, that vast unsettled public domain over the ridge from the pale of settlement and beneath the summits of legal wilderness and parks. Some reasonable agreement exists about what to do with fire at the poles of the urban and the wild; there is little regarding the ocean of land between those shores. Yet that is where the worst fires are flourishing, where the contest over thinning and burning is fiercest, and where the nation remains most irresolute. The Land Between will likely replace the intermix fire as fire's next new thing.

Because Americans cannot agree on what those lands should be, they cannot craft a consensual strategy for managing fire on them. One solution, of course, is to parcel those generic lands into particular purposes such as more nature reserves, recreational parks, or timber berths, which will decide the issue of what fire regimes are suitable. This will take time and may not, ultimately, ever happen. Meanwhile, wildfires will rip through vast landscapes more or less trashed ecologically. Regardless of their final disposition, these lands require some degree of active fire management, or at least of minimal protection, or they will ill serve whatever purpose the nation eventually elects for them.

It is possible to imagine a simple scenario by which "defensible space" around houses becomes "defensible habitats" located farther into the backcountry. Rather than protecting a house one protects a biota. Nearly two decades of fire-ecology propaganda has sensitized the public to regard fire as somehow natural while the intermix fire has taught it that active measures are necessary to make fire behave as we wish it to. Combining those two inclinations might yield a new problem fire, a successor to the intermix fire as the intermix was to the wilderness fire, that could inform a near future.

The sticky part is that there are many such landscapes—a score of "unhealthy" ecosystems. Each would require a separate treatment, which would unravel the sense of a shared problem for which a common strategy would be appropriate. The best known example, lower-montane forests (like ponderosa pine woodlands), should respond nicely to a mixture of thinning, burning, and controlled grazing. But those prescriptions might be meaningless (or damaging) elsewhere. They say nothing about higher-elevation forests or those that routinely burn with crown fires. They do not address issues of juniper encroachment on sagebrush and grasslands; they cannot cope with the invidious contagion of cheatgrass; they do not specify what fire regime is suitable for wetlands. Those fire-problematic biotas may not be, by themselves, sufficient to qualify as an informing issue; but they are vast in aggregate and they are certainly not going away.

The crux, however, is to link fire with ecology. Simply reducing fuel and thereby quelling wildfires is unlikely to serve as a sufficient justification for massive public-works projects, which is what a rehabilitation and burning program would demand. If cost is the issue, then the public may rightly decide to let wildfires free-burn when they erupt away from communities. If fire control is the problem, the public may determine that a beefed-up initial attack organization would be cheaper, and more effective. If fuel reduction is what the scene requires, then the public may opt for any number of means to chip, chew, or compress unruly combustibles. An argument for burning—for fire as a solution to a *fire* problem—must reside in fire's biochemical punch.

There must be a biotic imperative to the burning, and extensive preparations such as thinning or other ecological engineering are warranted in order to get the right mix of fires. In other words, fire is not so much a means to modulate fuel in order to further fire protection as fuel treatments are a way to modulate fire in order to advance ecological ends. The biota under consideration needs fire, as fire, not simply a better minced-up tray of landscape fuels. Otherwise the pressures for active fire management will expire once the flames move away from the intermix's frayed frontier or the rains return.

In a kind of political algebra, the strategy should proceed from the known to the unknown. This recommends the pale of the intermix as the point of departure. But where to move next? There is a biological argument for moving directly to the most degraded sites, whether they lie in the near orbit of communities or not, and this may happen. (A site or two would make a dandy exercise for Firestart I, for example.) There is also a case for plunging into even inviolable wilderness as places of inestimable value that, if left untouched, might immolate into oblivion. Such moves would stir—have stirred—powerful political reactions.

With tens of millions of acres in the Land Between, ripe for rehabilitation, there is scant urgency to move into wilderness. The call to rush into the wilderness reeks of symbolism, the identity politics of rival professions. Let the restorationists savor the irony if, years hence, the legally wild has lost much of its biodiversity or melted into a biotic lump, while the unremarkable Land Between blooms with ecological splendor. If the rehabilitation works, it will percolate in good time, out of its own logic, into the pristine.

Regardless, this is not a discourse that interests fire. Probably fire would welcome a long-overdue postironic culture, but only if it can be stated in the hieroglyphics of hydrocarbons, rock, and wind.

The Not-Quite Vestal Fire on the No-Longer Virgin Land

The great upheavals of land use continue. Among the Big Four both the recolonization of rural lands and the decolonization of public lands is accelerating, leaving, for the latter, only the rump of imperial institutions. The era of the public lands as a big-government commons overseen by state-sponsored forestry is dying on its feet. This is as true in the United States as it is in Australia, Canada, and the rest of a hollowed-out European imperium. The means and ends of fire management on those lands reflect these momentous trends. Whether by creep or rupture, from sheer accumulated internal strain or from sharp external stresses, the American way of fire has been significantly altered. Subjected to enough heat and pressure, even granite can melt and warp. The Forest Service that joined a national mobilization to fight the 2000 fires is not the organization that sought to suppress the Wenatchee and Southern California conflagrations of 1970.

Which is to say the institutions, not merely the policies, of fire protection have rapidly and probably irreversibly undergone a metamorphosis. The evidence lies all around. Privatization, partnerships, the devolution of political decision–making to more local jurisdictions, indigenous land claims, a near civil war over the destiny of the public domain—all are changing the attributes of how governments administer these lands and how they cope with fire. Such reforms have challenged not just the hegemony of the Forest Service but the command-and-control model of federal administration itself. They are not restricted to the quirks of fire management. In their aggregate they promise for public-land fire protection a reformation equivalent to welfare reform. (Interestingly, Social Security, the origin of an American welfare state, was announced the same year as the 10 AM policy out of a similar desire to establish a single national standard of protection. The December 1995 federal fire policy that finally repudiated the last vestiges of the 10 AM standard preceded by months the Welfare Reform Act.)

Consider: In 1970, its last hurrah as a fire hegemon, the Forest Service employed most of its crews, owned much of its equipment, supplied the bulk of its logistical needs, dominated fire research, and dispatched according to its own priorities, still under the 10 AM directive. Today, it relies on a national pool of equipment, crews, and aircraft; it exchanges personnel with other federal and state agencies, all trained according to national standards; it must compete for fire-science funding; it requests assistance through national dispatching procedures; and it is outsourcing many fire services to private contractors—food caterers, aircraft operators, equipment-rental companies, consultants. (Although cynics smell a sinister "fire industry," powered by emergency dollars, mostly this is no more than turning over to the private sector what the government had traditionally done at equivalent costs on its own. The scandal is the exorbitant cost of big-fire suppression.) Today, the Forest Service shares a generic policy of appropriate management response with all the other federal agencies. Aggressive suppression is but one option among many.

Behind these changes lie deeper reforms in the administration of public lands. Devolution is transferring the power to decide and act from the metropole to groups and institutions closer to the action, even if their values are fundamentally urban. Legislation to protect endangered species, native religious places, historical and cultural sites, and on and on—all restrict the ability of the federal agencies to act on their own. Instead, new partnerships, institutional collaborations, and communities are doing what the national government no longer has the money, staffing, or moral authority to do on its own. There is an easy irony in this. Community-based strategies are the norm for almost all sponsored conservation projects the world over—except in the American West, where any proposal to involve local communities is taken as a pretext for looting the land. This anomaly cannot stand. America is slowly joining this global strategy, however much variants such as the Healthy Forests Restoration Act may arouse the suspicion of environmental groups. It is merely the golden rule in reverse: we should do unto ourselves as we would do unto others.

We cannot revise how we govern public lands, however, without affecting how we manage fire. It is hard to imagine a reversal to what becomes a thirty-year trend in de facto decolonization—the deconstruction of fire's imperial legacy, the replacement of a monopolistic state-sponsored forestry with a more decentralized system. If anything, the push to more intensive management will quicken the tempo of reform. The outcome will influence all the authorities peculiar to fire's administration—who does scientific research, and to what ends; who supplies the crews, the helicopters, the air tankers, the tractors, the retardant and pumps; who conducts prescribed burns, furnishes weather forecasts, runs campaign-fire camps; who organizes the suppression of large fires; and who oversees and audits the entire fire enterprise. At issue is not merely what policy should direct our relationship with fire or who should decide that policy, but the very process of deciding and then of acting is on the line. The country is moving toward a mixed political economy for fire.

The reformation in fire is thus part and parcel of a broader reformation in administering the public lands. There is nothing intrinsically permanent about those lands, the agencies that govern them, or the reasons for which they exist. The decolonizing impulse is transforming them, bit by bit. For liberal critics, the good news is that the Forest Service no longer dominates the agenda. For conservative critics, the good news is that neither does the federal government. Wildland fire and its institutions will both reflect these changes and force them. The future of wildland fire will depend on the future of the public lands—they are free-burning fire's prime habitat. Equally, the future of those lands will depend in good measure on how they cope with such fires.

Begin with a consideration of existing fire institutions. From the beginning two countervailing trends have existed. One was centrifugal, as each agency pursued its own agenda with its own means. The federal bureaus have different missions—that is why they exist as separate bodies. Doing things differently is how they are supposed to act. The other trend, though, was centripetal, a drawing together of diverse interests to face a common challenge.

That challenge had been wildfire, which compelled the bureaus to seek out cooperation because fires ignored political boundaries and no agency had the resources to fight the big fire on its own. Until the 1960s the two opposing forces could be held together. Wildfire was a common threat, which required a common response, which the Forest Service controlled.

By the early 1970s the Forest Service was fast losing its grip. The agency's collapse as a dominant presence liberated fire management from dogma and uniformity, but it also tore apart the old mechanisms for interagency coordination. Fortunately, for each new centrifugal pull, there was a centripetal tug. Interagency institutions emerged to hold the restless pieces together, from the Boise (later, National) Interagency Fire Center to the National Wildfire Coordinating Group to the Wildland Fire Leadership Council established to oversee the National Fire Plan. Throughout, however, there was a further trend that began to diminish the firepower of the federal government overall. The most obvious development has been that even fire suppression looks more and more like other government activities, which is to say, less and less like a Big Government program—outsourced, partially privatized, devolved, searching out new alliances for cooperative cost sharing, unable to impose its will on a multicultural stew of incommensurable values.

The push for less government and the pull of a common policy may combine. As *fire* institutions, the federal agencies have less and less to distinguish among themselves, and one can legitimately ask why they should not consolidate altogether. An economic logic exists to merge the federal fire establishment completely into a National Fire Service, a kind of Coast Guard for the interior. Models for such a consolidation exist—the Alaska Fire Service, for one. (It helps if one agency dominates land ownership.) So, too, there are off-the-shelf models for a stand-alone fire program available from the Canadian provinces. The attractions are again fiscal: such programs have the virtues of specialization, which makes them cost-efficient, effective at their target mission, and modern. There is little to separate such a goverment agency from private contractors. (Before the 2003 fire bust shocked it, British Columbia was on the verge of simply privatizing its fire service altogether.) The United States already has common standards for training and job certification, collective facilities for dispatching, and a shared policy. Why not create a single agency to absorb this unruly swarm, apply the discipline of a common mission, and achieve the real efficiencies of specialization?

The reason why not is that it would shatter one of the genuine accomplishments of America's fire revolution, the fierce bonding of fire to land management. While that achievement is far from complete, it exists as an axiom in the American fire community—an American contribution to global fire management far more significant than smokejumpers or air tankers. The tasks of routine fire management need to be integrated with everything else done on the land, relying on people who know intimately the local settings and working hand in glove with planning. If all one needed was to dump water on flames, one could certainly contract out for firefighting, as one could garbage collection, road paving, or campground reservations. Intensive fire management, however, comes from on-the-ground knowledge and that expertise must interbreed with every other activity. That is why Canada can boast of better initial attack forces, while America has a surer grasp of fire management. Moreover, fire crews rightly have dual allegiances, one to fire and the other to their host agency. A single federal agency for fire would shred those institutional ties as much as it would knowledge of the land under protection. Probably a national fire service would not work better than a national police force for all the public domain. Probably, though, there is a credible case for splitting off the administration of big fires as an emergency that should not be allowed to paralyze a forest or park, or federal lands far removed from the flames.

The thrust, in brief, should be for a better intertwining of fire with agency missions rather than teasing fire jobs out of the mix. There are other ways to contain costs. And for integrating the various missions of fire management beyond the problem of big fires, additional venues would be more appropriate. One could, for example, establish formal fire districts akin to those devised for water and soil conservation. This would allow the agencies and interested parties outside to pool knowledge and to bond fire practices more firmly within an ecologically informed plan.

What the federal agencies require more than reorganization and fiscal efficiency is accountability. The fire establishment cries out for a system of deliberate review.

Until the last decade, the fire community—whatever its internal squabbles and petty rivalries—policed itself. If a fire ran up an inordinate bill, a board of review might examine why. If firefighters died, another board would convene and pass judgment. If their varied policies did not mesh with their common missions, the agencies would thrash out their differences in-house. They were long accustomed to pooling crews, engines, and shovels, and later, other venues of cooperation, from certification to terminology. However savage their infighting, they circled their engines when a crisis struck the guild.

To a degree rare outside professional organizations, the fire community has evolved without having to answer to an outside body of regulators, auditors, and overseers, other than Congress itself and an occasional wrongful-death suit. There is no equivalent to the National Transportation Safety Board, for example, to investigate fatal incidents; there should be. There is no routine auditing of accounts, particularly the slippery emergency funds; there ought to be. There is no equivalent to medical boards or the investigative arm of a state bar to review and censure professional misconduct or to ban unsuitable members from further practice; this should happen.

The issue goes beyond fatalities. It involves the conduct of all fire practices. While environmental groups often raise concerns—and from within its ranks a Forest Service Employees for Environmental Ethics organization has arisen—there remains no formal source of impartial investigation. Because wildland fire protection has always been a duty of government, very few persons knowledgeable about fire are not directly or indirectly in the service of the agencies under review. This benign conspiracy applies not only to outright employees but to fire researchers and academics, dependent on the agencies for grants and contracts. Even with celebrity fires like those at Yellowstone in 1988, the fire community (or the involved agency itself) has been allowed to investigate its own conduct, and the suitability of its policies and practices, or to oversee the appointment of reviewers and to control the publication of their report.

This state of affairs changed only with the tremendous notoriety of the 1994 season. The fatalities at the South Canyon fire prompted OSHA to rouse itself for a report on workplace safety (other investigations have followed, in a desultory way). As the prospects loomed for a massive investment in restoration forestry, Congress requested a GAO inquiry. Yet the chief source of criticism about its fire practices remains the fire community itself. However well intentioned, the deference to the fire guild to superintend itself—particularly to scrutinize disasters—creates a conflict of interest. For its own benefit, the fire community needs to urge the creation of independent oversight boards. This is not simply a matter of credibility, but of fresh outlooks.

The reach beyond itself has begun, with the oft maligned Forest Service in the vanguard. Increasingly, the powerful story is not the constant reshufflings among the federal deck, but the introduction of new players to the table. Here, decolonization is becoming something more than evolution by default.

Arguably, the momentum for fire management no longer resides with the large bureaus at all, but with private landowners, NGOs, and the like, which stand outside the blood feuds. The comfortable polarization that has dominated discourse for the past few decades and mustered every interested party to one polarity or the other is an anachronism. (So fixated are some critics on hindering misuse that they prevent legitimate use as well. Fearful, for example, that good forest thinning and burning might lead to bad, they would rather ban the practice altogether.) Increasingly, fire management is the work of consortia, of projects conceived, staffed, and funded by public, private, and non-governmental organizations. In this game no one holds a stronger hand than The Nature Conservancy (TNC).

TNC's reach is astonishing. It cultivated fire expertise, originally, because many of its holdings were prairie or fire-adapted savanna and required burning. What astounds, first, is not the volume of burning, however, but its variety—from Kansas prairie to Carolina sandhills to Albany scrubland; and what astonishes, secondly, is the density of the institutional support behind it. TNC trains its own crews, devises its own fire plans, negotiates with neighbors about its fires (and their smoke), contracts for what science it requires—the whole constellation of fire practices. In effect, it has created an NGO that does what, over the past century, only government institutions had increasingly claimed for themselves alone. Perhaps not surprisingly, TNC's fire offices are sited on the grounds of the Tall Timbers Research Station, that vital critic of state-sponsored fire programs.

Now the *coup de main*: TNC is expanding those tasks in ways that complement and supplement, and in some instances may make possible, duties that had traditionally resided solely within governmental bureaus. TNC is becoming a general institutional medium for brokering among various public and private landowners; it is evolving into the grand facilitator—the task the old Forest Service used to perform. TNC is doing what the legacy of the environmental culture wars makes difficult for the public-land agencies to do. It is filling the institutional vacuum, not only in America but globally.

Almost all collaborative fire programs now have TNC as a partner. One can sample virtually anywhere in the United States. TNC contributed a member to the Joint Fire Science Program stakeholders advisory council (who quickly became chair). As a landowner, it bridges with neighbors. A model arrangement emerged with the Malpais Borderlands Group in southeastern Arizona, which joined private ranchers, TNC's Gray Ranch, the Coronado National Forest, state trust lands, BLM-administered lands, and the Natural Resource Conservation Service, and had, with Forest Service funding, a five-year Borderlands Ecosystem Management Research Project that involved several regional universities and the U.S. Geological Survey Desert Lab; in 2003 the Malpais Group collectively conducted a 43,000-acre prescribed burn. In 2003 all the federal land agencies and TNC signed an agreement for a two-year collaborative project for Restoring Fire-Adapted Ecosystems. The emphasis was on areas of mixed land ownership, all of them with corrupted fire regimes, with about half of the fifty sites from the Intermountain West. Among the tasks was a North American Fire Learning Network designed "to help isolated community-based groups overcome a variety of scientific, social, and logistical barriers"; enhanced fire education; and a Fire Training Network that increased fire-management training, with TNC doubling the availability of its own courses, similar to standard national offerings with "an ecological bent."[3]

Remarkably, TNC has expanded these ambitions into a Fire Initiative with global sweep. Some sites TNC owns, or manages in collaboration. Mostly, TNC facilitates—for example, by establishing Global Fire Partnerships with the International Union for the Conservation of Nature and the World Wildlife Fund, and by crafting multilateral agreements. In particular TNC has created, as a kind of demonstration program, a Latin American and Caribbean Fire Network, again catalyzing local programs in practical fire ecology (the Forest Service assisted). The torch is passing.

More and more, arguments over Forest Service administration especially have a ritualistic quality. Sometimes the stakes are real, ofttimes symbolic. The forty-year conflict begun over wilderness and then expanded into logging on public lands has created polarized, cold-war-like blocs—the scene belongs more with the Department of State than with those of Agriculture and the Interior. Yet for all the sound and the fury, the action is happening elsewhere. Certainly in the realm of restoration ecology the public lands claim only a fraction of the labor being invested. To its credit the Forest Service is doing what it has always done best: it is allying with potential collaborators, widening the arena of fire knowledge and craft, even if it has to reach beyond the federal government to do so.

The more profound issue, however, concerns not fire-specific institutions but their deeper political setting. The decolonizing shock wave is propagating through the parent bureaucracies; it may well force a reordering of the public lands themselves.

A radical revolution is unlikely. For all its dysfunctions the present regime suits both national parties. Each exploits the public domain for the benefit of its core constituencies. The interior West generally votes Republican, so Republican administrations are keen to develop the public lands to support the livelihood of those communities, promoting forest industry, ranching, tourism. Community-based conservation could thus become the environmental equivalent of compassionate conservatism. Democratic administrations look to the coasts, and to large metropolitan areas, whose economic vitality is far removed from the public lands. They are keen on preservationist programs, pushed by the old imperial methods—capturing the executive-branch elite, issuing presidential proclamations, mandating court rulings; far removed from the messy compromises of legislative politics, they dismiss the sparsely settled West as the environmental equivalent of the segregated South. Democrats tend to create parks. Republicans try to pay for their operation. Besides, imply the Democrats, the cost of the preserves appears minor and in any event will be manifest in the form of lost income by local communities—hardscrabble hamlets, rural whites, or politically incorrect Mormons.

What is difficult for many Americans residing outside the West to appreciate is the extent to which the public domain distorts the region's political geography. Arizona, for example, is by area the fifth largest state, but less than 17 percent of its lands are private; and much of that is scattered in an unusable checkerboard of ownership, all of which grants the state an aggregate nonpublic area roughly equal to New Hampshire and Vermont combined. The residents of Show Low, evacuated before the threat of the Rodeo-Chediski fire, were later chastised for not making their community more fire defensible. But the borders of the town were national forest; any citizen of Louisiana or New Hampshire had as much say over those lands as anyone in Show Low and was unlikely to wish federal monies spent on such remote scenes. Western states are powerless in ways that eastern states are not.

Easterners may stew about the amount of federal monies lavished on the West, but any federal funding on the public domain is almost certainly far less than the region would earn (or pluck from the public till) if the lands were private, or in truth less than it would gain if it had a large resident population of voters. What, for example, would be the political standing of Iowa if 70 percent of its landscape were allocated into a National Farm System? Any decision about what to plant would become a national issue—residents of Show Low would help determine if a farmer outside Cedar Rapids planted soy or corn, or whether genetically modified crops could be sown without an environmental impact statement. Farmers would have to bid on rights to plow and harvest, as ranchers and loggers do in the Southwest. Environmental groups might welcome the chance to cordon off large chunks of the public domain in order to restore the pristine prairie. National Environmental Policy Act guidelines could further complicate, if not compromise, what residents could do. Towns would see their tax revenue shrivel or become subject to the political fashions of Congress. In fact, the farm system is heavily subsidized—far more than any public lands in the West. The difference lies in the politics of those subsidies and the relative power of the residents to decide about land use.

Many westerners have not forgotten how the Carter administration declared the West a "national sacrifice area," suitable for strip mining coal for energy and siting the MX missile facility. That decision could be made because the federal government owned the lands and there were few voters on-site to object. The Clinton administration created the Grand Staircase/Escalante National Monument by presidential order, announcing the scheme on the photogenic rim of the Grand Canyon. The Utah residents affected were dismissed; these were, after all, the same people who had been downwind, and ignored, during the nuclear blasts from the Nevada Test Site. They were too few and too different to reckon with. It is interesting to imagine what aftershocks might have shaken the White House had President Clinton instead declared the Adirondacks a national monument, particularly with his wife planning to run for a New York senate seat.

Both parties, counting votes, know that they can land more political punches by spending on prescription drugs than on prescribed burns, and on farm subsidies than on thinning contracts. Neither owns up to the expense of intensive, ecological management. Neither has a fire platform, or recognizes a fire *qua* fire constituency. The Republicans paid the exorbitant costs of the Yellowstone fires. The Democrats had, in Bruce Babbitt, a secretary of the interior who did more than any other to promote fire reforms, yet was granted little power to move his larger ecological agenda. The Clinton administration conceived the National Fire Plan. The Bush administration morphed it into the Healthy Forests Restoration Act. Had the big fires of the Long Drought broken out during odd-numbered years rather than even-numbered years with national elections, little political movement of any sort may have been the outcome.

All in all, a cynic might conclude that proposing what to do on the public domain is like spending other peoples' money. The political parties may matter less, however, than the evolving mechanics of the political process, galvanized by the emergence of fast-breeding interest groups and NGOs. This is changing how the issues are debated and what kind of actions the government—

a government controlled by either party—might take. Ultimately, the new dynamics may alter the structure of the public lands altogether. Only a few fringe groups would wish the dissolution of public domain lands or the stripping of their assets. Most citizens know that, once eliminated, those national commons would never be restored. They appreciate the ultimate political precariousness of these lands. There is ample room, however, for reforming what gets done and who decides. At some point the country will have to own up to the costs of its estate. These lands cannot be indefinitely plundered, nor can they be left abandoned. Yet the means by which they are administered may well change their ends as well.

How far might the process go? Since the early 1960s, notably with the Wilderness Act, the federal land agencies have had their missions restated and their legislative charters (or organic acts) reissued. Probably the majority of citizens would like still more recreational sites and more nature protection (and at less cost). At some point, the cumulative strains might argue for a wholesale reorganization of the public lands, a constitutional convention as it were, for the national estate. At this point, even the most ardent critic might hesitate about unleashing the passions of the citizenry in an open-ended forum. Most likely the public would prefer an incremental give-and-take of reforms, a continued transfusion of new purposes and personnel.

Still, the specter of the Forest Service—an agency in limbo, as even its own professionals admit—should give pause. Although foresters no longer run the agency as they once did, and the forest industry is no longer its primary clientele, the culture wars have so crippled the institution that a case can be made for a kind of bureaucratic euthanasia. One could imagine, on the occasion of its centennial, simply retiring it. With honors—it deserves that from the country. It did what the nation demanded and in general has served the country according to Congress's wishes. It did what it was paid to do, and more. Better a gold watch and a handshake than another few decades of chronic debilitation. While that outcome is unlikely, the agency may retain little beyond its name.

What is needed, however, may be less a redesignation of agencies, or their reorganization, than a review of the political process. More is involved than the replacement of forestry by ecology as the intellectual administrator behind public lands management. The implicit assumption is that forestry was, in fact, "wrong," while ecology is "right." Yet, a century ago, forestry correctly claimed that it spoke with the authority of Progressive science. Today's ecology has no more fundamental claim, and it would be a bitter pill if we merely replaced state-sponsored forestry with state-sponsored ecology. The flaws lie with the public domain's inherited imperial design. And that—the political process governing the public lands—is the wheel that is turning.

No longer can one single entity control the agenda concerning the public domain. No one group can define itself as the fire community; and fire-affected communities need not be solely those that live adjacent to the public lands and their free-burning flames. They may be interest groups, volunteers, seasonal residents, recreational birders, scientists. The problem is not that the Forest Service, or some successor federal agency, may rule this community, but that none do—that a working consensus becomes impossible. While appeals to NGOs like The Nature Conservancy may or may not prove a partial solution, they are certainly a symptom of profound distress.

Wildlands and wildland fire—what affects one affects the other. Whatever institutions emerge or survive to administer the public lands, whatever their titles and legislated charges, they will remain fire institutions, whether by choice or by force of fact. In the future, administrators of the public lands may or may not separately manage for soil, old-growth Douglas–fir, Mexican grey wolves, watersheds, spotted owls, rangelands, riparian habitats, outdoor recreation, airsheds, or archeological sites; they may or may not administer legal wilderness, national recreation sites, or wildlife refuges. But inevitably they will have to tend fire. They would be wise to see that obligation as an opportunity, for fire is a synthesis of all the rest.

Only a mass privatization of the public domain might alter this reality, and then fire management would become a duty of private institutions, either to protect against wildfire or to promote ecological integrity. The former would be more likely. It is hard to imagine a Bitterroot Range owned by Bill Gates that would tolerate much fire, or a Blue Mountains under the management of Rupert Murdoch that would waste much money on prescribed burning for ecological intangibles. Fire's "naturalness" has little to do with it.

The bald fact is worth repeating: much of the West remains fire-prone not only because of El Niño's flutterings, but because its lands are public. The way in which they are public will shape what kinds of fire will happen. And the kinds of fires may, unexpectedly, shape the ways in which those lands remain public.

The Big Burn

The burning of fossil biomass set in motion a cascade of environmental changes, the variety and magnitude of which we barely appreciate. By means both overt and covert, these changes have redrawn the cartography and refigured the calculus of combustion. Virtually no aspect of contemporary fire management—from its mechanized forces for suppression to its mindless removal of open flame—remains unaffected by earthly fire's new prime mover. This is why suppression will remain the norm, and why controlled burning will struggle, save in special reserves. But the aspect that is beginning to grip the imagination of the populace is the prospect of climate change, specifically global warming.

Global warming is, at base, a question of combustion. It involves not only the direct release of greenhouse gases from fossil biomass but the indirect consequences of wholesale logging and land clearing and other measures that, through the technology of internal combustion, have liberated carbon from its lithic and organic bonds and set it loose on the planet. A pittance returns to the soil as black carbon. More gets recaptured by plants, where it may be burned over and over again. (Probably the woody crust over the West's public lands is as much a by-product of carbon dioxide fertilization and carbon storage as of attempts to exclude fire.) Most of the liberated carbon goes into the ocean and, with special malevolence, into the atmosphere. Here the combustion effluent of all sources merges into one colossal gassy cocktail.

On the Earth's surface, combustion is fissioning into two geographic domains—those in which people burn living biomass and those in which they burn fossil biomass. Each is apparently exclusive and incommensurate with the other. In the atmosphere, however, the two combustion realms recombine. Here they compete not over fuel but over airshed. From the perspective of greenhouse warming, a molecule of carbon dioxide from a charcoal brazier is identical to one from a slashed-and-burned rain forest, a field of burned fallow, a wildfire in Yosemite National Park, or from a sulfur-coal power plant. The pressures are thus keen to reduce the overload caused by burning fossil biomass by reducing the burning of living biomass. Better to leave it stockpiled as woods and peat. Europe, especially, views with horror any open fire, which it regards as dangerous, wasteful, and slovenly, the mark of Cain of a careless society and inadequate institutions.

One problem with this conception is that, as of 1990, 60 percent or more of the planet's combustion comes from fossil fuels. Living biomass constitutes a shrinking source of contamination. Most of its burning gets recaptured by plants, a long-fallow recycling rather than a net transfer. A deeper problem is that organic fuels are not carbon bullion, to be stacked like bricks or hoarded like gold. They exist within living systems, subject to evolutionary selection and ecological stresses. In particular, many ecosystems require some regular rhythm of fire in order to remain rudely healthy. To enlarge the dominion of industrial fire by shutting down anthropogenic (and natural) fire will ripple through such biotas in generally unhelpful ways.

The economic and political costs, in the short term, may favor clamping down on open burning. The United States could conceivably try to shrink free-burning fire in Alaska (a million acres a year burn, on average) as an expedient to offset industrial combustion in the Lower 48. The experiment would fail, eventually, but its cost might be acceptable for a couple of decades until other measures come into effect. Still, the ecological expense, and in the long term, economics, favors renegotiating a space for flame.

Industrial combustion's Big Burn is unprecedented. No one knows its dynamics or how it will reshape the planet. Many countries, including such megastates as India and China, are just beginning their pyric transition. Already anthropogenic fire practices are being evaluated for their impact on the planetary carbon budget. Unless, soon, alternative power sources emerge, the Big Burn and its emissions will saturate the ecological sponges for combustion and smother the intricate history of fire on Earth under its enormous pall.

Several trends are apparent. The pyric transition argues for more fire in the short term, less—perhaps—in the long. As more countries industrialize, burning will metastasize, the combustion equivalent of a blowup fire. Vastly more fossil fuels will burn, while traditional biomass will continue to flame for a half century or more. The developed world meanwhile will likely continue along another trajectory, burning more but with less combustion output. The decarbonization of fuel is reducing carbon-based emissions, a happy convergence of efficiency and economics. The Bush administration's push for a hydrogen-powered car may do more than its Healthy Forests Restoration Act to counter the consequences of America's combustion imbalances because it could begin removing some of the deep pressures. The near future, though, is alarming.

The other tack is political. From its origins with reserved lands, wildland fire has been a political creature. It has always been politicized, but over the past decade, the politics has become more overt nationally, and it has gone global. It seems clear that unilateral fire programs will be increasingly untenable. By its threat to human habitations and livelihood, wildfire has joined other natural disasters of humanitarian interest; by its effluent, fire has become planetary in its effects; and through international commitments to biodiversity and nature reserves of various kinds, fire management must justify its practices to a world community. The competing values that swirl around every fire program in the American West will become a global vortex.

It is not simple to explain why smoke should be banned from California restaurants but made obligatory across the Sierra Nevada; yet American fire programs will have a much harder sell around the planet. Proposals to uproot and burn trees over tens of millions of acres of public land in the American West must answer why this regional ecological good is superior to the global good of reducing greenhouse gases in the atmospheric commons shared by all. Why is it beneficial to burn a million acres of old-growth forest in Yellowstone, but not in Amazonia, or Borneo? Why is it deemed obligatory to reinstate fire in the Cascade Range, but to denounce it in Botswana or the Sahel? While there are good answers possible, they must be based on ecological values—a green equivalent of universal human rights—not on national self-interest. It will not be long before conventions, treaties, and international regulatory institutions appear to oversee the Earth's combustion commons.

The Kyoto Accord that fell apart during the Clinton administration before being dismissed outright by the Bush administration is only the most visible point of discord. In reality, America is already engaged with other nations. We have treaties with Canada, Mexico, and Russia for mutual assistance in fire suppression; we have active season-long exchanges of personnel with a handful of countries, and we imported fire specialists from Australia and New Zealand during the 2000 and 2002 fire seasons. We have sent advisors to Brazil, Ghana, the Galapagos, and a score of other countries; we have mutual research projects with Brazil, Russia, Canada, and Australia, and, under auspices of the UN's Food and Agriculture Organization, an exchange of regular fire-study tours with the latter. We dispatch fire assistance through the Agency for International Development. The UN has added wildfire to its agenda for its International Strategy for Disaster Reduction. The most comprehensive fire-science programs are international, for example fusing nations that share the boreal forest or crown fires. And so on. As in other matters, the world looks to the United States for leadership in fire technology, science, and practice. The globalization of fire began long ago.

What is new is the shift away from fire only as emergency—as assisted suppression in another guise—and into fire as a topic of global environmentalism. As in the United States, fire may become hostage to other agendas, and fire policy will enter a briar patch of international politics; American fire habits and mores could easily become another club for anti-Americanism. A suite of fire-management treaties will be inevitable, however. One can only hope we apply to those accords the experience of our flawed fumblings with fire politics nationally so that those conventions can speak in a language that fire understands. The most plausible outcome is that collective humanity will pressure the United States to squelch open burning except where we can establish fire's indisputable and unique ecological significance. Americans will be forced to choose between cars and drip torches. The more we want to burn, or allow to burn, the less we can drive. That is not a formula for wholesale fire by prescription.

If our wanton combustion does force a permanent shift of climate, we could be witnessing a massive realignment of fire regimes, imposed by an indifferent fire planet on an improvident fire creature. A wave of extraordinary burning, lasting for decades, will leave in its ash landscapes far removed from what existed before. Until the Earth passes through its collective pyric transition, probably another fifty years or so, anthropogenic fire may split into two extremes: the ceremonial flame of a guttering candle and the malicious blaze of an arsonist's torch. The only free-burning fire allowed may, paradoxically, be wildfire.

So we would end where we began. There are lands with too much fire and lands with too little. There are places with scrambled fire regimes. There is a planet slow-cooking in its combustion effluent. There is a creature with a species monopoly over fire to whom almost all aspects of the contemporary scene converge, like the focal point of a parabolic antenna. The Earth's fire scene is largely the outcome of what this creature has done, and not done, and the species operates not according to strict evolutionary selection but in the realm of culture, which is to say, of choice and confusion. We are truly the weak link in the great chain of combustion, and the missing link in modern theories of earthly fire. Whether the Earth ends as hearth or holocaust will depend on us.

Imagining Fire

ᴋ.

SINCE THE ONSET of the twenty-first century, three images of fire have haunted the American imagination. One is an evening photo taken on the Burgdorf fire, part of the 2000 fire season in the Northern Rockies, that shows a hillside lit by snag fires like a battery of votary candles while elk, gleaming, stand in the East Fork of the Bitterroot River. It is a transcendental tableau: the fires, like the elk, stand on display as a gorgeous and benevolent part of nature's ensemble. The second image is the twin towers of the World Trade Center in Manhattan, ablaze with violent reds and the sinister black smoke of burning oil. Here is fire as a force of unremitting destruction, of human malevolence amid a wholly human-made landscape. The third image is the evolving cyclorama of western conflagrations, like dispatches from the fronts of a war on nature. It is a kind of Exodus in reverse, with pillars of smoke by day and flame by night driving an almost-chosen people away from their not-quite-promised land.

All are images peculiar to an urban imagination. More vitally, none show people in their most elemental ecological role, as unique fire creatures, as beings who use fire to make their world habitable. People are absent, they are villains, or they are victims. But none of these images show them as residing within a world their fires have usefully made. Their fires are vengeful, malignant, and destructive; or nature's fires proceed without their presence. The boast of Prometheus, that by giving fire to humanity he founded "all the arts of men," is gone, along with the agent who would so use fire.

How Should We Think about Fire?

We can begin by thinking in more deeply *biological* ways. The traditional prism of fire protection is to envision fire within a hierarchy of physical frames. Life matters because it spawns fuels and complicates predictions of what will happen after the flames have passed, but grand physical parameters really control fire, and they must be countered by physical forces of similar type and greater power. Fire management means manipulating fuel, wind, aridity, and heat flux. Yet it is possible to turn this conventional conception inside-out. One can, instead, define fire as primarily a phenomenon of the biosphere, subject to biological controls both tiny and huge, with the well-known physical constraints internal and secondary to that scaffolding.

The justification goes like this. Fire is a creation of the living world. Life supplies its oxygen, life furnishes its fuel, and through ourselves, life kindles most ignitions. Wind, lightning, drought, upper-level highs, El Niño episodes, ridges and ravines—in the absence of life, such physical parameters constrain nothing but themselves. They exercise influence only through the medium of a biosphere that makes combustion possible and that profoundly shapes its properties. Fire propagates through living matter, not air or rock. All this is not a plea for a Gaian fire. It simply states a reality lost in the fury of quenching flames, forecasting winds, and chopping fuel.

At every scale a suite of biological controls shapes how combustion's core chemistry behaves. From the level of molecules and mitochondria to individual particles to landscape patches to the planet itself as an abode for fire—genetic, ecological, and evolutionary processes sculpt what kind of fire exists, when, and where. Pick almost any aspect of earthly fire, and its biological character is fundamental, for without life, fire would not exist. Moreover, a biological theory of fire would reserve pride of place to ourselves as uniquely fire creatures, as the one species to claim a monopoly over fire's direct manipulation. Fire ecology, as presently conceived, encompasses only a fraction of what a general theory of fire biology would embrace. Such a redefinition of fire as a subject would allow for a redefinition of fire as a problem.

What would such a biologically based theory mean for practice? For actual firefighting, it might mean little. Coping with the intermix fire will still depend on simple, mechanical treatments like raking needles and shearing off ladder fuels. Firefights will still resort to water, pulaskis, and retardants in an effort to break the chain of combustion chemistry. But the context of protection could shift from simple mechanical tools to more ecological engineering, from confronting flame to controlling the fuels—which is to say, the biota—that shape flame. What is likely is that the search will integrate fire management with everything else that happens on the land.

It is improbable that the search for biological controls would plunge into the molecular level—hard to conceive of genetically modified fuels, for example—but in principle it is possible. A biological theory could, however, redefine prescribed fire away from simple hazard reduction, as though it were merely a flaming woodchipper. The purpose of burning is to ensure that fire does the ecological work demanded of it; the purpose of fuels management is to get that fire. (If all one wants is fuel reduction, there are plenty of techniques available other than burning.) A biological theory could recharter fire as a biotechnology, one in which "control" depends on context. A biological theory would promote big fires because, in places, they are necessary, but it would also boost small fires because they may be useful in sites that cannot tolerate much flame or smoke—a kind of fire gardening as an alternative to mindless mowing and the application of chemical herbicides and pesticides. A biological theory of fire would suggest such sites as opportunities; a mechanical conception lashed to the needs of the public lands would necessarily overlook such fire niches or view them only as points of vulnerability for fire escapes.

More profoundly, a biological theory would allow a place for ourselves as an ecological presence—in fact, as the biosphere's designated fire agent. Landscapes forged in anthropogenic fire would be the norm, and sites from which humans have chosen to absent themselves would become, properly, ecological outliers. The arguments for such a recentering (or refocusing, *focus* being the Latin word for hearth) are two, one theoretical, the other practical.

The theoretical case is that we hold a species monopoly over fire's manipulation, that we very nearly close the circle of life for fire's cycle. Other creatures knock over trees, dig holes in the ground, eat plants, hunt: we do fire. This is who we are as ecological agents. We may choose to remove ourselves from the scene in select wilderness areas, but this is our choice, not a natural state. Removing ourselves from theory, however, is nonsense. No one would argue that we ought to delete lightning from fire-ecology models because it complicates ignition rhythms, yet humans start many more fires than lightning. No one would suggest that we erase grazers and browsers from models of fire-frequented ecosystems since they muddy the fuel scene, yet people affect fuels far more than any other organism. No comprehensive theory can ignore how we conceive of the world and our place in it, any more than a grand unified theory of physics can ignore gravity, however inconvenient to quantum calculations. A biological theory of fire demands a place for ourselves.

The practical issue is that fire ecology includes the flow of ideas and information as much as carbon and that institutions structure landscapes as fully as mountains and seasons. Because humans are such powerful fire agents—starting and stopping ignitions, forever fiddling with fuels—the means by which they decide what to do powerfully influence how fire appears on the land. People choose fire practices on the basis of what they know (or perceive, or believe), and they act on those choices through institutions. The programmatic crashes that followed the 1988 Yellowstone fires illustrates nicely how a fire's effects can be broadcast through journals, reports, and institutions as well as through air, water, and soil. By such means landscapes far removed from the Northern Rockies felt the impact of Yellowstone's burns. This is as real as fire ecology gets.

The point should be obvious: ideas, data, misinformation, perceptions, and beliefs all mold how people behave, directly with fire or indirectly with the landscape that fire must act in. Increasingly information is the power behind fire applications. For decades, fire management has resembled a commodity economy. More and more, however, it has recreated itself as a kind of service economy for which information has become a medium of exchange. Although the likely prospect is that fire management must become more not less intensive in the future, this need not simply mean more axes and pumps. It should mean denser data and contextual knowledge that can guide more specific decisions about particular places. Intensity of management will depend on intensity of information.

A biological theory would, finally, compel us to address industrial fire. This species of combustion exists only because humans tend it, and it interacts with other varieties through the medium of human societies. Not least, industrial fire, which seems so abstracted from the living world, challenges the assumption that physical parameters are paramount. Burning, both of living and fossil biomass, is progressing to the point that it is perturbing the global climate. At its core, global warming is a problem of combustion, and of people. Even climate can no longer be considered an absolute, a physical condition beyond the influence of anthropogenic fire practices.

Why Should We Think about Fire?

After all, America is rife with pathologies. The good causes to which one can devote time and money are bottomless. Why should fire, which seems so remote from the daily lives of Americans, almost all of whom live in pyrophobic cities and suburbs, command special attention, which can only come by not attending to some other cause?

One reason is that fire poses an immediate crisis. Hundreds of homes are burning annually, thousands of citizens are forced into evacuations, many thousands more are inconvenienced or, if smoke pools into catchments, suffer ill health. But a response to the immediate crisis can be done with modest effort and little thought. It means controlling careless or malicious fire setting by people—closing public lands during periods of extreme danger can do that. It means striking quickly those ignitions that lightning, arcing power lines, accident, or shrewd arsonists kindle—a beefed-up initial attack force can handle that, at least in the short term. It means cleaning up around houses and hamlets, abating the worst hazards. It means waiting out the cruel Long Drought and hoping that it is not the harbinger of a permanent climatic dislocation. A few years, a couple billion dollars, and the urgency may pass.

A deeper reason is that fire management is fundamental to our obligations as environmental stewards and is an obligation of civil society to its members and the future. The public has a duty of care for its estate, as a collective enterprise of the commonwealth. If we cannot muster the money and resolve to calm and cure fire, then we should turn those lands over to some institution that can, instead of hanging on to them in vague expectation, like speculators holding to a vacant weedy lot. The public domain is an expression of American nationalism; those lands deserve our attention as much as our courts and highways. For those federal agencies with lands in the West, fire management is their core mission—not something that must be done before the real work can begin, but the essence of that job and the measure of their success. This is a complicated purpose that demands in mind and field a relentless tending. It requires lighting fires as well as fighting them, letting them roam and shutting them off, cultivating, if coarsely, the combustibles that sustain them. It demands mixed institutions, muddled choices, endless negotiation. It will continue in perpetuity. That is what a relationship means.

The more profound reason for attention is that we, as a species, do fire. It is our hominid heritage, the signature of our ecological agency, even if in recent times we have gone from being keepers of the flame to custodians of the combustion chamber. The complication of course is that, while we come hardwired to handle fire, we do not come programmed with the software to run it. That depends on beliefs, politics, knowledge, values, ignorance—the whole maddening moral universe that we must inhabit. We cannot know exactly what to do. We stumble. We make mistakes. But this does not change the charge. We should manage fire and do whatever is necessary to make fire work as best we see it, because that is how the biosphere very nearly completes the cycle of burning. Nature gave that task to us: we should not be ready to hand it back. Our firepower is not discretionary: it is who we are. And while we might choose to renounce that right, the evolutionary birthright and its obligations remain. Our burning can cause problems; so can our not burning. The fact is, if we cannot get fire right, we might as well resign from the great chain of being.

Yes, that's what I'd try to do, if I ran the zoo.

Fire's American Century

➤ *By the Numbers*

The Pyric Transition: Technology and Geography

Figure 1 shows the replacement of biomass fuel by fossil fuels, which is the essence of industrialization's pyric transition. Normally we consider this transformation within the context of technological change, but it extends to landscapes as well, as various mechanical devices and artificial fertilizers, pesticides, and so on, replace open burning. Figures 2a and 2b show the global outcome of the transition up to 1990, a fissioning of the planet into two great combustion realms, one that burns living biomass and the other, fossil fuel. Note that the indices of carbon emissions differ for the two, with fossil-fuel combustion far the larger. Sources: (Fig. 1) Smil 1994; (Fig. 2) Lim and Renberg 1997, redrawn.

An Imperial Narrative: Creating a Habitat for Wildland Fire

The creation of the American public domain was part of a global movement by which, in places subject to European colonization, lands were reserved for the common good. Almost everywhere state-sponsored forestry spearheaded the endeavor. Their greatest administrative chal-

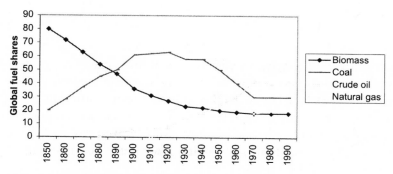

Figure 1 Earth's pyric transition (1850–1990)

a. Living-biomass combustion

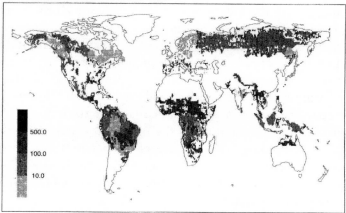

b. Fossil-fuel combustion

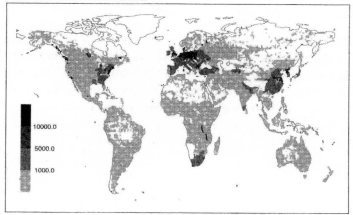

Figure 2 The two geographies of combustion

lenge was fire, which helps account for the prominence of fire protection within forestry and for the peculiar way in which free-burning fire
on such lands was understood. By the mid-twentieth century the reservation process had ended, and since then has reversed, not so much in
actual land transfers as in their administration. Figure 3 tracks the
process for the United States and figure 4 for India. Sources: (Fig. 3)
Dana 1956; (Fig. 4) Ribbentrop 1900.

The U.S. Forest Service, however, controlled only a portion of the
national estate and had to cope with only a fraction of the total fires on
the land. Its solution was to broker cooperative programs with the
states, beginning with the Weeks Act of 1911. By 1965 all the states
had joined. Figure 5 measures the relative contributions, as indexed by
expenditures, for federal, state, and private fire programs. The states
dominate the overall system and handle proportionately the largest
number of fires. Cooperative fire protection continues, to good effect.
In 1985, for example, the Forest Service and the National Fire Protection Association launched a Wildland-Urban Interface Initiative,
which sought a collective solution to the problem of fires along the
urban fringe. Interestingly, the process of cooperation has more
recently reversed, with outside institutions and NGOs like The
Nature Conservancy assisting the administration of public lands.
Source: Bureau of the Census 1975.

The Changing Geography of American Fire

Figure 6 maps the distribution of forest fires kindled by lightning,
which traces the "natural" geography of fire. A map of thunderstorms
(or lightning flashes) would concentrate in the Midwest and Southeast,
with Florida a virtual lightning rod. What matters is not the number of
lightning bolts but the patterns of wet storms and dry strikes. By this
measure the Southwest is the natural epicenter of American fire.
Source: Schroeder and Buck 1970.

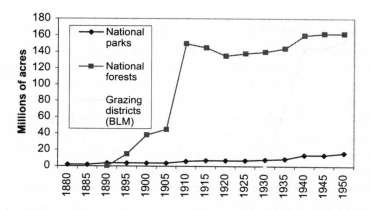

Figure 3 Creating America's public domain (1880–1950)

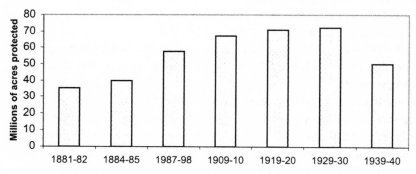

Figure 4 India's forest reserves (1881–1940)

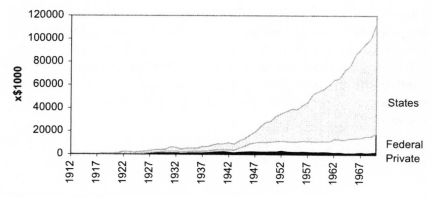

Figure 5 U.S. fire protection expenditures (1912–1970)

By 1880, as recorded by Charles S. Sargent for the census, human fire practices had fashioned a very different geography of burning (figure 7). Note the heavy association (indicated by darker shading) with logging, land clearing, and agriculture except where the conversion is more or less complete in a naturally fire-intolerant area (e.g., the Ohio Valley). Also, the map does not include predominantly prairie sites, since they do not fit the definition of "forest" fire, nor does it include many areas with very sparse settlement, since Sargent relied on correspondents. Yet the Great Plains held, year after year, the greatest proportion of North American fire until farms and ranches throttled flame from the scene. South Florida, too, is conspicuous by its apparent fire void, the outcome of sparse settlement until the 1920s. (Early in the twentieth century the state forester of Florida announced that by his estimation 105 percent of the state had burned over the past year, the result of herders burning in the spring and then reburning many of the same sites in the fall.)

By the early 1990s most fire remained in the Southeast, especially prescribed fire, as indicated by figure 8. The West (defined as everything west of the Mississippi River) is a distant second, mostly because of wildfire on the public lands. The Northeast and Lake States barely register, in striking contrast to Sargent's map. The Great Plains have only vestigial flames. When the survey was made, it was believed that another half million hectares had burned in the Southeast that were not officially reported. Source: Ward et al. 1993.

Convergence to Conflagration: The Intermix Fire Scene

The problem of fire and the urban fringe—the mixing of something like wildlands with something like cities—dominates contemporary concerns about fire. In one variant, wildlands come to cities, as former rural landscapes overgrow with both houses and vegetation. In another, the city in the form of exurban enclaves comes to the wild, etching borders to public lands. Call it, collectively, the intermix fire scene.

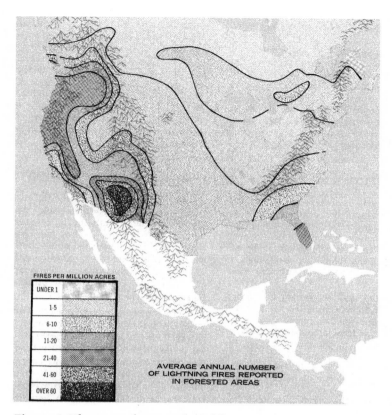

FIRES PER MILLION ACRES

| UNDER 1 |
| 1-5 |
| 6-10 |
| 11-20 |
| 21-40 |
| 41-60 |
| OVER 60 |

AVERAGE ANNUAL NUMBER
OF LIGHTNING FIRES REPORTED
IN FORESTED AREAS

Figure 6 The natural geography of fire

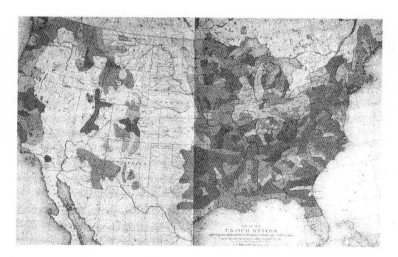

Figure 7 Geography of fire in 1880 America

Figure 9 tracks two trends for Oakland, California. The top curve traces the shrinking of open space. Originally Oakland was a hilly countryside of grasses, with wooded copses in wetter niches. Development began in earnest after the 1906 earthquake and fire, which shattered San Francisco. The second curve plots the growth of tree cover. The two rapidly converged, leaving less open land and crowding the city with combustibles in the form of woods and wooden houses. The two curves cross around 1988. Three years later, Oakland exploded in one of the worst urban fire catastrophes of the twentieth century. Yet there is a sense in which the disaster was less a traditional urban fire than an intermix one, the first of a new era. Certainly, the loss of open space and the crowding with combustibles is a miniature for the American West. Source: Nowak 1993.

Letting It Burn: Yellowstone 1988

First, the ecology of the fires. Large, intense burns are of course not alien to Yellowstone. Its dominant forest, lodgepole pine, has adapted to crown fires and will in fact become unstable in their absence. The 1988 fires that commanded so much media attention were a composite, not a solitary flaming front, and they burned in a typically spotty way, stripping some sites to bare soil while leaving others green. Apologists thus argued that the fires were "natural."

But statistics on the burned area over several hundred years and on the percentage of old-growth forest in the park suggest that the past century of fire protection had been effective in distorting the historical trends. Figure 10 shows the historic burned area for the park. One reckoning of the 1988 fires is that they burned off a century's backlog, fueled by an unusual surplus of old-growth lodgepole. Undoubtedly the park had achieved its protection not by outright suppression of high-intensity fires but by eliminating the fire-littering by people, some of whose loitering fires would have blown up. The pre-1886 data comes from calculating the age of stands that regenerated after large burns, and that by sampling. Source: Romme and Despain 1989.

Figure 8 Geography of prescribed fire (1989)

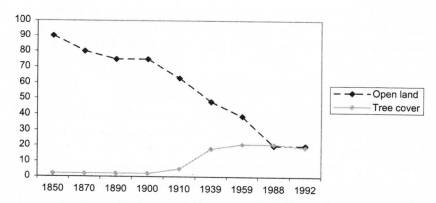

Figure 9 Convergence to conflagration (Oakland, 1850–1992)

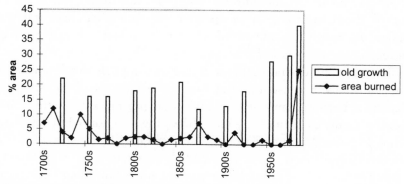

Figure 10 Fire and fuel at Yellowstone (1700–1990)

Second, the administrative anthropology of the fires. Figure 11 plots the number of fires started in the Greater Yellowstone Area, that is, in the park and on its surrounding public lands. After tolerating a few early prescribed natural fires (PNFs), every park and forest outside Yellowstone declared the season so extreme that each new start would be considered outside prescription and declared a wildfire. Every Yellowstone fire was accepted as a PNF, however, until the secretary of the interior intervened in mid-July. Of the twenty-eight fires Yellowstone had designated as PNFs, sixteen became official wildfires. Of course not every fire attacked was controlled. But the regional differences in burned area reflect administrative biases as much as ecological ones. Source: Wakimoto 1990.

Equally revealing is figure 12, which documents the growth of natural fire programs for both the National Park Service and the Forest Service. The Yellowstone events caused the momentum of such programs to crash. Some places recovered relatively quickly, most did not. Within ten years the concept of wildland fire use replaced the PNF.

Suppression, and Its Discontents

Figure 13 shows the power of suppression as measured by a rapid decline in burned area. For federal lands, this happened by the early 1930s, and even as cooperators (such as state forestry bureaus) added to the lands under protection, the overall area burned quickly reached an equilibrium. The vast bulk of burning occurred on unprotected lands. The thrust of the next twenty years was to transfer such lands into protection, so that even as the total number of acres subject to suppression shot up, the number of acres burned from wildfire plummeted. From an ecological perspective, this plunging curve traces a deficit in burning, some of which certain biotas require. Source: Bureau of the Census 1975.

This task the federal agencies did not accomplish alone, nor did it happen solely because running fires were suppressed. Mostly the expunged burning happened because rural fire practices were transformed. Consider figure 14, which shows the area burned in southern Ohio. Organized fire protection in southern Ohio (inspired by the 1924 Clarke-McNary Act, which granted federal aid to state cooperators), caused an immediate drop in burned area. Source: Sutherland, Hutchinson, and Yaussy 2003.

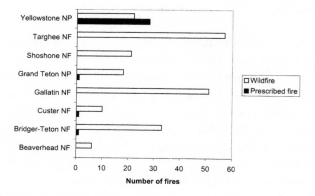

Figure 11 Greater Yellowstone Area Fires (1988)

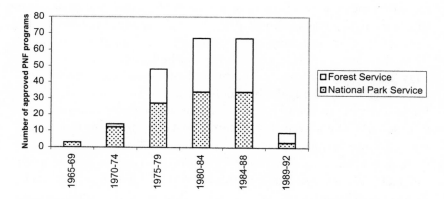

Figure 12 Yellowstone's off-site fire ecology

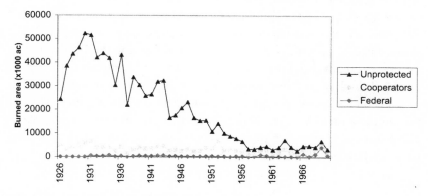

Figure 13 America's fields of fire (1926–1970)

Similarly, agricultural practices either abandoned burning or were discouraged from continuing it. Figure 15 tracks the area burned in California under permit from 1945 to 1975. Interest in burning revived after World War II, but then entered a terminal decline. Again, it was not active suppression that removed fire but the abolition of traditional burning practices. Source: Biswell 1989.

By 1970 the costs of fire exclusion had become undeniable. One measure was ecological, of which the overcrowded, scarce-regenerating sequoia groves were a poster child. But economic costs were also out of control, although these numbers can be almost as opaque as ecological measures. Figure 16 plots the costs, calibrated in 1995 dollars, since the era of policy reform. The abolition of the emergency *pre*suppression funds led to a jump in budgeted funds, which occurred when the 10 AM policy was scrapped. (The jump was intended to bring under control the ever-escalating rise in emergency *pre*suppression funds.) Thus the curves of emergency funds and budgeted funds crossed in 1977. But as drought returned in the mid-1980s, now acting on exceptional fuel loads, the regular budget began a slow rise while emergency funds reach unprecedented heights. Large seasons now run over a billion dollars. The system has become unstable, prone to binges and busts. Source: Schuster 1999.

And, not least, as illustrated by figure 17, there was that other melancholy cost associated with suppression: firefighter fatalities. The sad saga begins with the cataclysm of 1910, when the Big Blowup claimed seventy-eight lives. There were others who perished, some of them fighting fires, but the records concern themselves with those who were hired officially. This begins the trend by which responsibility for fire control has moved from civilians to government-sponsored fire crews. The worst era of crew-fatality fires coincides with the war years, beginning with the CCC and extending for thirty years. The other significant trend is the rising proportion of fatalities collateral to actual firefighting. These mostly reflect accidents involving mechanized vehicles, especially aircraft. Even so, two to three times as many people die annually in the United States from lightning strikes. Probably one is at greater risk on a golf course during a thunderstorm than on a fire line. Source: Ensely 1995.

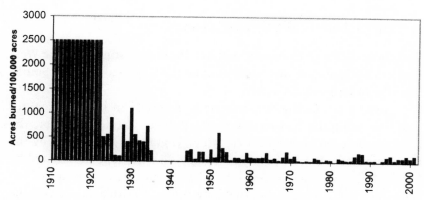

Figure 14 Rural fire protection (southern Ohio, 1910–2001)

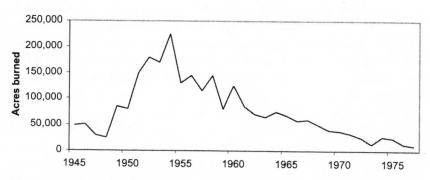

Figure 15 California burning by permit (1945–1977)

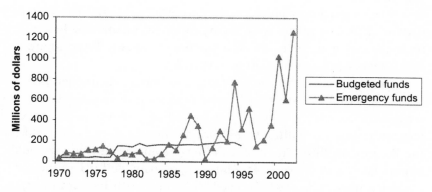

Figure 16 U.S. Forest Service fire funding (1970–1995)

A Tale of Two Forests, 1940–1995

Was the eruption of extensive, extreme burning that plagued the West inevitable? Consider two examples of public land, one from the Southeast, the other from the West.

Figure 18 tracks the fire history, as recorded in burned area, for Carolina Sandhills National Wildlife Refuge. Created in 1941, the refuge suffered serious wildfires, which it gradually beat back by the usual methods. But its peculiar ecology—a landscape dominated by longleaf pine and wiregrass—argued for controlled burning, which the refuge staff attempted in the early 1960s. A critical factor was the presence of the red-cockaded woodpecker, which was dependent on the longleaf and which eventually became listed as an endangered species. The program had problems, including an ice storm that trashed a large chunk of its woods, but after adopting aerial ignition in the late 1980s, it now burns approximately one-third of the refuge annually. The few wildfires that occur blend almost inconspicuously into the mix of patchy burns. In effect, prescribed fires replaced wildfires, and the woodpecker got the habitat it required. Source: Ingram and Robinson 1998.

A similar profile of burning characterizes the eleven western states (figure 19). The war years saw a small spike in wildfire because of reduced staffing and an exceptional season in 1941, but then the composite chronicle reaches equilibrium until 1970. From then on the background burning rises, and by the mid-1980s the land begins to binge burn, with two million acres common in serious fire years. Historically, upward spikes appeared during droughts; now downward spikes of reduced burning occurred during wet periods. The pattern had inverted. The causes were many, although the increase in woody fuels, readied by drought, seems fundamental. Source: Intermountain Fire Sciences Lab, courtesy Robert Mutch.

Viewed in profile, the two fire chronicles mirror each other. Probably the last time the West could have plunged into an aggressive prescribed-fire program was around 1970. In fact, this was when policy was reforming. The failure to get that burning on the ground yielded the field to wildfire. The refuge did have some advantages: it could manipulate its vegetation, and did so rigorously; and it had the red-cockaded woodpecker, whose needs coincided with its burning regimens. The refuge was not burning simply for fuel reduction but for

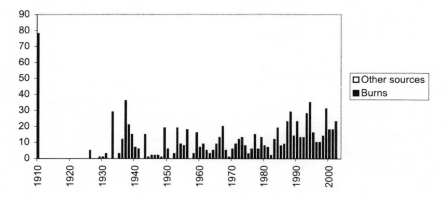

Figure 17 Firefighter fatalities (1910–2003)

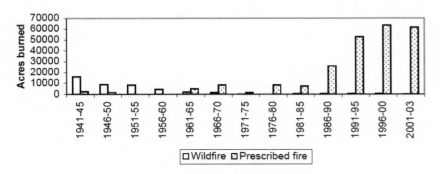

Figure 18 Fire in Carolina Sandhills NWR (1941–2003)

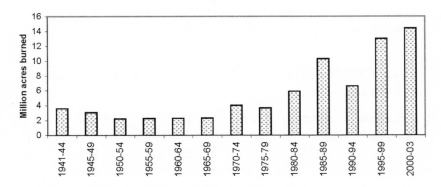

Figure 19 Western states wildfires (1941–2003)

habitat. The western forests tried to reintroduce flame unaided, and in the name of fuels reduction, while environmental legislation often worked against fire's reintroduction.

Southwest Synecdoche

Fewer fires, larger burned area, more intense fires—the Southwest bears grim testimony to this nightmarish scenario. Figure 20 shows the number of sites documenting fires as recorded by fire-scarred ponderosa pines in the region, which measures how widespread burning is. The variance is wide, tracking the rhythms of El Niño, but the pattern holds until the late nineteenth century, when the overall count of places burning drops precipitously. One primary reason is the arrival of American settlement, bringing with it livestock that cropped off the grassy cover, relocating the indigenes to reservations, instigating the pyric transition, and generally restricting fires to reserved lands of the public domain. Here, around 1905–1910, active fire suppression commences. Source: Swetnam and Baison 1996.

For a while—for a few decades—it was possible to keep a lid on any revival of burning. But around 1970 that illusion vanishes (see figure 21). Big fire seasons returned, powered by drought, an accumulation of accessible combustibles, and a suppression organization that had built out to its limits. Decade by decade, the number of big fires has increased. With the monstrous Rodeo-Chediski fire of 2002, Arizona recorded its largest fire. (Probably fires larger in area had swept the state previously, but they had burned in grasses, not dense forests.) The fire regime was changing, and doing so in ways that the indigenous pine forests could ill cope with. Source: compiled figures courtesy of Tom Swetnam, Laboratory of Tree-Ring Research.

Aggressive Measures: The Case for and against Roads and Logging

The example of thinning as a remedial treatment in ponderosa pine suggested, to some, that the country should put that program on steroids and push it generally into the backcountry. Roads into roadless areas could open those lands to more rapid fire control, and logging would remove "fuel" and pay for other projects, as well as support local communities. Critics objected that these were cynical devices to

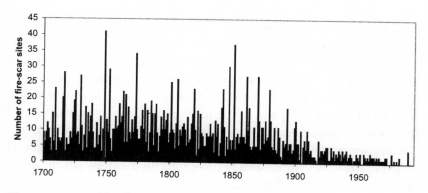

Figure 20 Breadth of fire in the Southwest (1700–1993)

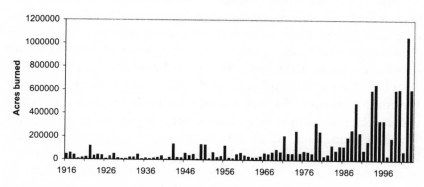

Figure 21 Intensity of fire in the Southwest (1916–2003)

ruin wilderness and reintroduce logging, when the national mood, over several decades, had favored nature reserves.

Figure 22 plots the distribution of fires from roads and settlements, as recorded in 1990s Russia. The closer a route of transit, the more fires. The exception is the immediate environs of a town, a scene for which fires are understandably rarer. The more people, the more starts, until the density of settlement is such that fuels disappear or consist only of a landscape built to fire codes. While roads would improve ground access to fires, they are essentially mopping up the fires that the roads themselves encourage. This is also the record of railways. Roads, moreover, promote fire-flashy weeds along their rights-of-way, thus further worsening the fire hazard. If initial attack needs improvement, then aerial means are probably the preferable alternative. Source: Korovin 1996.

Almost any map that segregates anthropogenic from lightning-caused fires reveals the same geography: people-caused fires follow people. Although dated, the two Alaska maps of figure 23 illustrate the dynamics nicely. Where, unlike Alaska, people are allowed to sprawl over the landscape, they gradually replace the natural fire mosaic with their own lines of fire and fields of fire. For roads to be effective as a fire-control measure, fire suppression must be able to patrol them and contain the fires along their corridors, but also must be able to rapidly attack lightning fires, which are not associated with the roading network. To put in sufficient roads for suppression would saturate the countryside. The cost alone of maintaining such a system would be exorbitant. Source: Gabriel and Tande 1983.

What about logging? Until the twentieth century, most large fires in the United States fed on the refuse of logging and land clearing. Improved fire protection and access have reduced the scale of those conflagrations, but slash remains a prime detonator, and landscapes recovering from clear-cutting are ideal for the low brush and reproduction that propel reburns. "Large fuels" like trunks are not the same as "large quantities of available fuel." The big-diameter boles, particularly if green, are more fire sink than source. What matters is the small stuff that logging leaves behind.

Yet logging as a part of intensive silviculture—a part of wholesale landscape gardening—can quell fires. A good example is Sweden, a place not naturally prone to fires, a well-behaved society, a country largely remade into a tree farm and intensively cultivated for cellulose. Figure 24 shows the record of burned area as organized fire protection

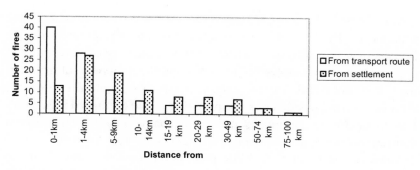

Figure 22 Roads and Russian fires

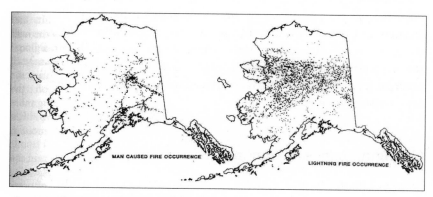

Figure 23 Alaska's two geographies of fire

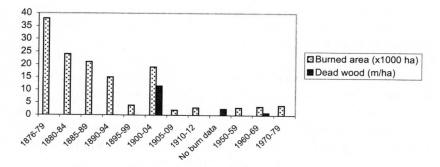

Figure 24 Fuel and flame in Sweden (1876–1976)

spread—a typical curve for the typical narrative of first-contact fire suppression. By the mid-1980s Sweden ceased to tabulate statistics on fire, dismissing it as though it were of only archeological interest. The protection methods employed went beyond the mustering of firefighting crews and engines; it involved extensive roads and the intensive removal of dead wood. Thus the plunging curve of burned area parallels the declining presence of dead wood, as recorded on two forests. Sources: Stocks 1991; Lundberg 1915; Östlund 1993.

Sweden's problem is that the process has expunged much of the country's biodiversity. Over the past decade, Swedish ecologists have begun experimenting with the reintroduction of fire—on a small scale, but symbolically revolutionary. It is worth recalling that Sweden's vast pineries sprouted on the ash of fires. Left to rude nature, these occurred once a century or so. But most grew on plots that had been slashed and burned for agriculture (in Swedish, *svedjebruk*). During the 1930s some Swedish foresters adapted this practice to logging by leaving a few seed trees, then firing the residue. Between the time this practice ceased and concerns surfaced over reinstating some fire, roughly sixty years passed.

Changing Lands, Changing Institutions

Reserved lands are undergoing a shift in purpose and hence in administration, which translates into different fire regimes, fires practices, and fire policies. Figure 25 documents the international movement of public lands into nature reserves and recreational parks. Just as the creation of public forests was a global enterprise, so now is the gazetting of lands under ecological protection, a good chunk of it from lands previously allocated to state-sponsored forestry. Source: World Conservation Monitoring Centre 1990.

The sharpest illustration within the United States, as recorded in figure 26, was the creation of a National Wilderness Preservation System, beginning in 1964. The big leap in lands came with a resolution to the Alaska lands question. Note, however, that the Forest Service dominates the number of individual units. It is easy to see why wilderness fire dominated the thinking of fire scientists and administrators from 1970 to 1990. Source: Landres and Meyer 2000.

The mosaic of fire institutions is also changing. Consider The

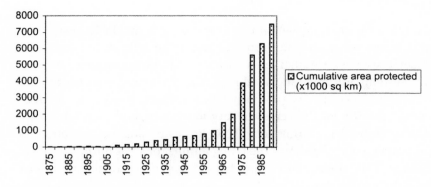

Figure 25 Global nature reserves (1875–1990)

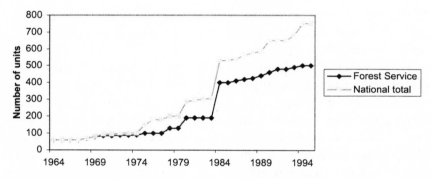

Figure 26 National Wilderness Preservation System

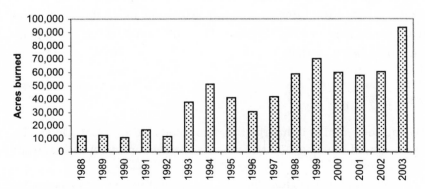

Figure 27 The Nature Conservancy as fire agency (1988–2003)

Nature Conservancy, which not only manages fire on its own lands, but is serving as a medium for public-private cooperation across the federal agencies through such means as the Restoring Fire-Adapted Ecosystems Initiative in the United States One component, the Fire Learning Network, is promoting "community-based fire management" in forty locales across twenty-four states, and even bridges the Canadian border. During 2003 TNC has even launched a global Fire Initiative. Figure 27 shows the rising number of acres burned by TNC. Source: TNC fire statistics from Paula Seamon, personal communication, 26 August 2003.

Restored Fire: Active and Passive Measures

The two primary means for reintroducing fire are to allow more room for fire to roam, even while nominally under control, and to set them under prescribed conditions.

Figure 28 shows the former. The numbers for wildfire fire use will probably rise and fall with the boom and bust of fire seasons. Figure 29 shows the latter strategy, one of deliberate burning. The agencies' commitment clearly shows, although it is uncertain how far they can push burning and how much burning will occur in the West or in places whose fire regimes are most desperately upset. Source: National Interagency Fire Center 2004b.

Interestingly, most of the burning is done by the states (the influence of the Southeast, again). Among the federal agencies, the Forest Service dominates the statistics. Most of the restored burning by the Department of the Interior occurs in Alaska or in a handful of parks (e.g., Everglades and Big Cypress). National statistics on these practices only begin in 1998.

The Big Burn

Within the realm of industrial fire, two trends are apparent. One is the expansion of burning, and the other is the decoupling of carbon from combustion.

Figure 30 plots the global growth in carbon flux (where Pg is a petagram, which equals 10^{15} grams). As more of the world industrializes,

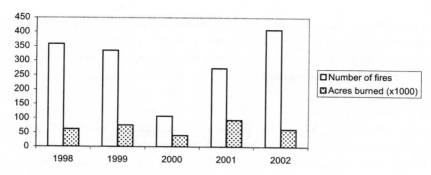

Figure 28 Wildland fire use (1998–2002)

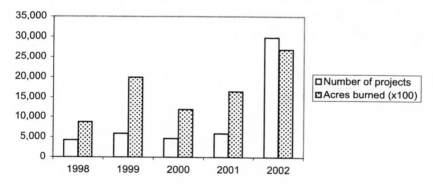

Figure 29 Prescribed fire by federal agencies (1998–2002)

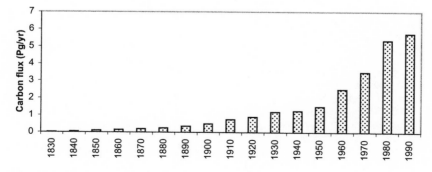

Figure 30 Global carbon flux (1830–1990)

especially in Asia, the curve will continue sharply upward as greater quantities of fossil hydrocarbons are burned. Yet there is a countervailing trend in fuel technology by which successive fuels are reducing the proportion of carbon to hydrogen. Coal has less than wood, oil less than coal, methane less than oil. A methane economy would reduce the burden of greenhouse gases unleashed by combustion, at least on a per capita basis. (Since 1860 the decarbonizing trend has been 1.3 percent per year, but the greater growth in combustion leaves a net difference of 1.7 percent per year, which is what is being loosed onto the Earth.) If a pure hydrogen economy evolves, not only would greenhouse-gas emissions disappear, so possibly would combustion, save for that needed to generate hydrogen from fossil biomass. The overall effects, might well reduce pressures on open fire (allowing for necessary biological burning), but overall shrink further the presence of fire on the planet. Source: Smil 1994.

NOTES

Prologue

1. National Interagency Fire Center, "Wildland Fire Accidents by Year," http://www.nifc.gov/reports/index.html (May 2004). Up to 1994, see Pam Ensely, *Historical Wildland Fire-Fighter Fatalities, 1910–1993* (Boise, ID: National Wildfire Coordinating Group, Safety and Health Working Team, 1995).
2. Data from Global Fire Monitoring Center, posted on its Web site, http://www.fire.uni-freiburg.de/current/globalfire.htm. The site is also the most comprehensive chronicle of each year's evolving season.
3. Data from Global Fire Monitoring Center, "Extract of Summary of Global Wildland Fire Data: Status of End of the Year 2002," http://www.fire.uni-freiburg.de/media/WaldbrandeinEuropaimSommer2003.pdf. A richer background source is available in Johann Goldammer and Robert W. Mutch, *Global Forest Fire Assessment: 1990–2000*, UN Food and Agriculture Organization, 2001.
4. Anspach, Allen J., et al. *Sawtooth Mountain Prescribed Fire Burnover Fatality. Factual Report.* Bureau of Indian Affairs, Fort Apache Agency, Arizona. (May 14, 2003).

Chapter 1

1. Personal communication from Gordon Schmidt and Al Hyde, Brookings Institution.
2. Rhys Jones, "Fire-Stick Farming," *Australian Natural History* 16 (1969): 224–228.

3. Meinrat O. Andreae, "Biomass Burning: Its History, Use, and Distribution and Its Impact on Environmental Quality and Global Climate," in *Global Biomass Burning: Atmospheric, Climatic, and Biospheric Implication*, ed. Joel S. Levine (Cambridge, MA: MIT Press, 1991), 3–21.

4. Vernon Louis Parrington quote from his *Main Currents in American Thought*, vol. 3 (New York: Harcourt, Brace, 1958), 23.

5. On Brandis: Gifford Pinchot, *Breaking New Ground* (1947; repr., Seattle: University of Washington Press, 1972), 9; on Algeria: Theodore S. Woolsey, Jr., and William B. Greeley, *Studies in French Forestry* (New York: John Wiley and Sons, 1920), vi.

6. Henry Clepper, *Crusade for Conservation: The Centennial History of the American Forestry Association* (Washington, DC: American Forestry Association, 1975), 3.

7. Berthold Ribbentrop, *Forestry in British India* (1900; repr., New Delhi: Indus Publishing Co., 1989), especially pages 125–133.

8. Rudyard Kipling, *The Jungle Books* (New York: Oxford University Press, 1992), 343.

9. Fernow: Andrew Denny Rodgers III, *Bernhard Eduard Fernow: A Story of North American Forestry* (New York: Hafner, 1968), 167; Pinchot: Gifford Pinchot, "Study of Forest Fires and Wood Protection in Southern New Jersey," in *Annual Report of Geological Survey of New Jersey* (Trenton, 1898), appendix p. 11; Graves: see, for example, Henry S. Graves, *Protection of Forests from Fire*, Forest Service Bulletin 82 (Washington, DC: Government Printing Office, 1910).

10. Inman Eldredge, "Fire Problem of the Florida National Forest," Society of American Foresters, *Proceedings* 6 (1910): 166–170.

11. The best review of the light-burning controversy, complete with copious quotes, is still Stephen J. Pyne, *Fire in America* (1982; repr., Seattle: University of Washington Press, 1995), 100–122.

12. Theodore Roosevelt, "The Strenuous Life," in *The Works of Theodore Roosevelt*, vol. 13 (New York: Charles Scribner's Sons, 1923–26), 20–21; William James, "The Moral Equivalent of War," in *The Writings of William James*, ed. John McDermott (New York: Modern Library, 1967), 669–670.

13. A synopsis of the debate leading to the 10 AM policy is available in Pyne, *Fire in America*, 281–284.

14. A. S. Leopold, S. A. Cain, C. M. Cottan, I. N. Gabrielson, and T. L. Kimball, "Wildlife Management in the National Parks," (March 4, 1963), reproduced in *Compilation of the Administrative Policies for the National Parks and National Monuments of Scientific Significance*, rev. ed. (Washington, DC: Government Printing Office, 1970) and available online at http://www.cr.nps.gov/history/online_books/leopold/leopold2.htm.

Chapter 2

1. Etymology explained in letter from Len Dems to author, October 26, 2003.
2. Coert duBois, *Systematic Fire Protection in the California Forests* (Washington, DC: Government Printing Office, 1914), 3. This and other pieces published by duBois constitute forestry's answer to Emerson's "American Scholar" address.
3. See, again, National Interagency Fire Center, "Wildland Fire Accidents by Year," http://www.nifc.gov/reports/index.html (May 2004). Up to 1994, see Pam Ensely, *Historical Wildland Fire-Fighter Fatalities, 1910–1993* (Boise, ID: National Wildfire Coordinating Group, Safety and Health Working Team, 1995).
4. George L. Hoxie, "How Fire Helps Forestry," *Sunset*, August 1910, 145–149.
5. This is an argument I myself have made, twice, in two editions of *Introduction to Wildland Fire* (1984, 1996). Consider it another case of logic and fire colliding.
6. An excellent summary of this program is available in Peter Friederici, ed., *Ecological Restoration of Southwestern Ponderosa Pine Forests* (Washington, DC: Island Press, 2003).
7. A succinct summary of the "home ignition zone" can be found in Jack Cohen, "Thoughts on the Wildland-Urban Interface Fire Problem," memo to Chief Forester, June 2003, available at http://www.wildfirelessons.net/Library/I_zone/Cohen_WUI_Thoughts_062003.pdf.
8. The seminal study remains Andrew A. G. Wilson, *Assessing the Bushfire Hazard of Houses: A Quantitative Approach*, Technical Paper No. 6. (Melbourne: National Center for Rural Fire Research, Chisholm Institute of Technology, 1984). A good example of contemporary research in the United States, all the more impressive for being preliminary, is Jack D. Cohen, "An Examination of the Summerhaven, Arizona Home Destruction Related to the Local Wildland Fire Behavior during the June 2003 Aspen Fire." Unpublished report, Intermountain Fire Sciences Lab, August 1, 2003.

Chapter 3

1. In May 2004, while this manuscript was in production, the Forest Service announced that it was grounding all its old contract air tankers for safety reasons. Proposals floated to covert C-130 Hercules for delivering retardants, or even Boeing 747s.
2. The modern classic of assessing fire risk is still Andrew A. G. Wilson, *Assessing the Bushfire Hazard of Houses: A Quantitative Approach*, Technical Paper No. 6 (Melbourne: National Centre for Rural Fire Research, Chisholm Institute of Technology, 1984).
3. See, for example, Victoria's Country Fire Authority program, online at http://www.cfa.vic.gov/au/residents/programs/index.htm (May 2004).

Chapter 4

1. For statistics, see Michael J. Karter, Jr., *Fire Losses in the United States during 2002* (Quincy, MA: National Fire Protection Association, 2003); and Jack Cohen, personal communication regarding fire losses, mostly from NFPA data, July 2003.
2. Comparative statistics from U.S. Bureau of the Census, *Statistical Abstract of the U.S.* (Washington, DC: Government Printing Office, 2001).
3. The best description is at The Nature Conservancy's Web site, http://www.tncfire.org.

FURTHER READING

The literature on fire is vast, although almost all of it consists of scientific works, government-sponsored studies, and the proceedings of technical conferences. More recently, a raft of general-audience books has seen print, inspired first by the Yellowstone outbreak, then by Norman Maclean's meditation, and finally by a steady cycle of media attention on the worsening western fire scene over the past decade. The highly select roster that follows attempts to list the major documents, some of the general-audience literature, and those publications cited in the notes or figures.

The other striking development of recent years is the transfer of information onto the Internet. One could Google for years without exhausting the potential URLs, but the interlinking character of the official sites means that only a handful are vital as portals. In particular, I have not attempted to list the thicket of sustaining reports, or the evolving iterations of the National Fire Plan. These are easily captured through the relevant websites. For the purposes of this book, we can reduce this register of URLs to two. The first is the Global Fire Monitoring Center at http://www.fire.uni-freiburg.de. From here one can leap to virtually any fire-related site on the planet, access much of the visual and numerical databases, and find an astonishing array of country reports that help contextualize the American scene. The second Web site is the National Interagency Fire Center at http://www.nifc.gov. From daily fire situation reports to the National Fire Plan to photo galleries to published surveys to the separate Web pages of each of the agencies—this portal can access them all.

Andreae, Meinrat O. "Biomass Burning: Its History, Use, and Distribution and Its Impact on Environmental Quality and Global Climate." In *Global Biomass Burning: Atmospheric, Climatic, and Biospheric Implication*, ed. Joel S. Levine, 3–21. Cambridge, MA: MIT Press, 1991.

Anspach, Allen J., et al. *Sawtooth Mountain Prescribed Fire Burnover Fatality Factual Report* (Bureau of Indian Affairs, Fort Apache Agency, Arizona, May 14, 2003).

Arno, Stephen F., and Steven Allison-Bunnell. *Flames in Our Forest: Disaster or Renewal?* Washington, DC: Island Press, 2002.

Biswell, Harold. *Prescribed Burning in California's Wildlands Vegetation Management.* Berkeley: University of California Press, 1989.

Carle, David. *Burning Questions: America's Fight with Nature's Fire.* New York: Praeger Publishers, 2002.

Clepper, Henry. *Crusade for Conservation: The Centennial History of the American Forestry Association.* Washington, DC: American Forestry Association, 1975.

Cohen, Jack D. "An Examination of Summerhaven, Arizona Home Destruction Related to the Local Wildland Fire Behavior during the June 2003 Aspen Fire." Unpublished report, Intermountain Fire Sciences Lab, August 1, 2003.

Cohen, Jack. "Thoughts on the Wildland-Urban Interface Fire Problem." Memo to Chief Forester, June 2003, available at http://www.wildfirelessons.net/Library/I_zone/_Cohen_WUI_Thoughts_062003.pdf.

Dana, Samuel T. *Forest and Range Policy: Its Development in the United States.* New York: McGraw-Hill, 1956.

duBois, Coert. *Systematic Fire Protection in the California Forests.* Washington, DC: Government Printing Office, 1914.

Eldredge, Inman. "Fire Problem of the Florida National Forest." Society of American Foresters. *Proceedings* 6 (1910): 166–170.

Ensely, Pam. *Historical Wildland Fire-Fighter Fatalities, 1910–1993* (Boise, ID: National Wildfire Coordinating Group, Safety and Health Team, 1995).

Friederici, Peter, ed. *Ecological Restoration of Southwestern Ponderosa Pine Forests.* Washington, DC: Island Press, 2003.

Gabriel, H. W., and F. Tande. *A Regional Approach to Fire History in Alaska.* BLM-Alaska Technical Report 9. Anchorage: Bureau of Land Management, 1983.

Goldammer, Johann, and Robert W. Mutch. *Global Forest Fire Assessment: 1990–2000.* UN Food and Agriculture Organization, 2001. http://www.fao.org/

forestry/include/frames/english.asp?section=http://www.fao.org:80/forestry/
fo/fra/docs/Wp55_eng.pdf.

Graves, Henry S. *Protection of Forests from Fire.* Forest Service Bulletin 82. Washington, DC: Government Printing Office, 1910.

Hoxie, George L. "How Fire Helps Forestry." *Sunset,* August 1910, 145–149.

Ingram, Richard P., and David H. Robinson, "Evolution of a Burning Program on Carolina Sandhills National Wildlife Refuge." In *Fire in Ecosystem Management: Shifting the Paradigm from Suppression to Prescription,* Tall Timbers Fire Ecology Conference Proceedings, No. 20, eds. Teresa L. Pruden and Leonard A. Brennan, 161–166. Tallahassee, FL: Tall Timbers Research Station, 1998.

James, William. "The Moral Equivalent of War." In *The Writings of William James,* ed. John McDermott, 669–670. New York: Modern Library, 1967.

Jones, Rhys. "Fire-Stick Farming." *Australian Natural History* 16 (1969): 224–228.

Kailidis, D. "Forest Fires in Greece." *In Seminar on Forest Fire Prevention, Land Use and People,* ed. joint FAO/ECE/ILO Committee on Forest Management, Technology and Training, 27–40. Athens, Greece: Ministry of Agriculture, 1992.

Karter, Michael J., Jr. *Fire Loss in the United States during 2002.* Quincy, MA: National Fire Protection Association, 2003.

Kipling, Rudyard. *The Jungle Books.* New York: Oxford University Press, 1992.

Korovin, G. N. "Analysis of the Distribution of Forest Fires in Russia" in *Fire in Ecosystems of Boreal Eurasia,* eds. J. G. Goldammer and V. V. Furyaev, 112–128. Dordrecht, Netherlands: Klumer Academic Publishers, 1996.

Landres, P., and S. Meyer. *National Wilderness Preservation System Database: Key Attributes and Trends, 1964 through 1999.* General Technical Report RMRS-GTR-18-Revised Edition. U.S. Forest Service, 2000.

Laverty, Lyle, and Tim Hartzell. *Managing the Impact of Wildfires on Communities and the Environment: A Report to the President in Response to the Wildfires of 2000, September 8, 2000.* (U.S. Department of the Interior and U.S. Forest Service, May 2001).

Leopold, A. S., S. A. Cain, C. M. Cottam, I. N. Gabrielson, and T. L. Kimball, "Wildlife Management in the National Parks," March 4, 1963. In *Compilation of the Administrative Policies for the National Parks and National Monuments of Scientific Significance.* Rev. ed. Washington, DC: Government Printing Office, 1970. http://www.cr.nps.gov/history/online_books/leopold/leopold2.htm.

Lim, B., and I. Renberg. "Lake Sediment Records of Sissil Fuel-Derived Carbonaceous Aerosols from Combustion." In *Sediment Records of Biomass*

Burning and Global Change, eds. James S. Clark, Hélène Cachier, Johann G. Goldammer, and Brian Stocks, 443–459. Berlin: Springer-Verlag, 1997.

Lundberg, Gustaf. "Om skogseld, dess förbyggande och bekämpande." In *Skogsvårdföreningens tidskrift*, 114–156. 1915.

Maclean, Norman. *Young Men and Fire*. Chicago: University of Chicago Press, 1992.

Nakicenovic, Nebojsa. "Decarbonization as a Long-Term Energy Strategy." In *Environment, Energy, and Economy: Strategies for Sustainability*, ed. Toichi Kaya and Keiichi Tokobori, part 4, p. 13. New York: United Nations University, 1997.

National Interagency Fire Center, a. "Wildland Fire Accidents by Year." http://www.nifc.gov/reports/index.html (accessed July 2003).

National Interagency Fire Center, b. "2003 Statistics and Summary." http://www.nifc.gov/news/2003_statssumm/intro_summary.pdf (accessed May 2004).

The Nature Conservancy. *The Nature Conservancy's Fire Initiative*. Tallahassee, FL: The Nature Conservancy, 2003. Available at http://nature.org/initiatives/fire.

Nowak, D. J. "Historical Vegetation Change in Oakland and its Implications for Urban Forest Management." *Journal of Arboriculture* 19, no. 5 (1993): 313–319.

Östlund, Lars. *Exploitation and Structural Changes in the North Swedish Boreal Forest, 1800–1992*. Dissertations in Forest Vegetation Ecology, 4. Umeå, Sweden: University of Umeå, 1993.

Parrington, Vernon Louis. *Main Currents in American Thought*. Vol. 3. New York: Harcourt, Brace, 1958.

Pierce, E., and W. Stahl. *Cooperative Forest Fire Control: A History of Its Origin and Development under the Weeks and Clarke-McNary Acts*. Washington, DC: U.S. Forest Service, 1964.

Pinchot, Gifford. *Breaking New Ground*. 1947. Repr., Seattle: University of Washington Press, 1972.

———. "Study of Forest Fires and Wood Protection in Southern New Jersey." In *Annual Report of Geological Survey of New Jersey*. Trenton, 1898.

Pyne, Stephen J. *Fire: A Brief History*. Seattle: University of Washington Press, 2001.

———. *Fire in America*. 1982. Repr., Seattle: University of Washington Press, 1995.

———. *World Fire*. Seattle: University of Washington Press, 1997.

Pyne, Stephen J., Patricia L. Andrews, and Richard Laven. *Introduction to Wildland Fire*. 2nd ed. New York: Wiley and Sons, Inc., 1996.

Ribbentrop, Berthold. *Forestry in British India.* 1900. Repr., New Delhi: Indus Publishing Co., 1989.

Rodgers, Andrew Denny, III. *Bernhard Eduard Fernow: A Story of North American Forestry.* New York: Hafner, 1968.

Romme, William, and Don G. Despain. "Historical Perspective on the Yellowstone Fires of 1998." *BioScience* 39, no. 10 (November 1989): 695–699.

Roosevelt, Theodore. "The Strenuous Life." In *The Works of Theodore Roosevelt.* Vol. 13. New York: Charles Scribner's Sons, 1923–26.

Schroeder, M. J., and C. C. Buck. *Fire Weather.* Agriculture Handbook 360. Washington, DC: Government Printing Office, 1970.

Schuster, Ervin G. "Analysis of Forest Service Wildland Fire Management Expenditures: An Update." In *Proceedings of the Symposium on Fire Economics, Planning, and Policy: Bottom Lines,* General Technical Report PSW-GTR-173, technical coordinators Armando Gonzales-Caban and Philip N. Omi, 37–49. U.S. Forest Service, 1999.

Simard, Albert J., fire coordinator. *Workshop Report: A National Workshop on Wildland Fire Activity in Canada.* Canadian Forest Service, 1996.

Smil, Vaclav. *Energy in World History.* Boulder: Westview Press, 1994.

Stocks, Brian J. "The Extent and Impact of Forest Fires in Northern Circumpolar Countries." In *Global Biomass Burning: Atmospheric, Climatic, and Biospheric Implications,* ed. Joel S. Levine, 197–202. Cambridge, MA: MIT Press, 1991.

Sutherland, Elaine Kennedy, Toddy Hutchinson, and Daniel Yaussy. "Introduction, Study Area Description, and Experimental Design." In *Characteristics of Mixed-Oak Forest Ecosystems in Southern Ohio Prior to the Reintroduction of Fire,* General Technical Report NE-299, eds. Elaine Kennedy Sutherland and Todd F. Hutchinson, 1–16. U.S. Forest Service, 2003.

Swetnam, Thomas W., and Christopher H. Baisan. "Historical Fire Regime Patterns in the Southwestern United States Since AD 1700." In *Proceedings of the Second La Mesa Fire Symposium,* ed. Craig Allen, 11–32. General Technical Report RM-GTR-286, U. S. Forest Service, 1996.

Swetnam, Thomas W., and Julio L. Betancourt. "Mesoscale Ecological Responses to Climatic Variability in the American Southwest." Impacts of Climate Change and Land Use in the Southwestern United States. http:// geochange.er.usgs.gov/ sw/impacts/biology/fires_SOI/ (accessed May 2004).

Tall Timbers Research Station. *Proceedings, Fire Ecology Conferences.* 22 vols. Tallahassee: Tall Timbers Research Station, 1962–2001.

U.S. Bureau of the Census. *Historical Statistics of the United States: Colonial Times to 1970.* Washington, DC: Government Printing Office, 1975.

U.S. Bureau of the Census. *Statistical Abstract of the U.S.* Washington, DC: Government Printing Office, 2001.

U.S. Department of Agriculture. *Climate and Man.* Yearbook of Agriculture. Washington, DC: Government Printing Office, 1941.

U.S. Forest Service. *Protecting People and Sustaining Resources in Fire-Adapted Ecosystems—A Cohesive Strategy.* U.S. Forest Service, 2000. Available at http://www.fs.fed.us/publications/2000/cohesive_strategy10132000.pdf (accessed May 2004).

U.S. General Accounting Office. *Western National Forests: A Cohesive Strategy is Needed to Address Catastrophic Wildland Fire Threats.* GAO/RCED-99-65. Washington, DC: U.S. General Accounting Office, April 1999.

Wakimoto, R. H. "The Yellowstone Fire of 1988: Natural Processes and National Policy." *Northwest Science* 64 (1990): 239–242.

Ward, D. E. et al. "An Inventory of Particulate Matter and Air Toxic Emissions from Prescribed Fires in the USA for 1989." In *Proceedings of the Air and Waste Management Association 1993 Annual Meeting and Exhibition,* 93-MP-6.04, Denver, CO. 1993.

Williams, Michael. *Americans and Their Forests: An Historical Geography* (Cambridge: Cambridge University Press, 1992).

Wilson, Andrew A. G. *Assessing the Bushfire Hazard of Houses: A Quantitative Approach.* Technical Paper No. 6. Melbourne: National Centre for Rural Fire Research, Chisholm Institute of Technology, 1984.

Woolsey, Theodore S., Jr., and William B. Greeley. *Studies in French Forestry.* New York: John Wiley and Sons, 1920.

World Conservation Monitoring Centre. *United Nations List of National Parks and Protected Areas.* Gland, Switzerland: International Union for the Conservation of Nature, 1990.

Index

Note: page numbers in *italics* refer to illustrations

STEPHEN PYNE is a professor in the Human Dimensions Faculty, School of Life Sciences, Arizona State University, and the author of sixteen books, including *Year of the Fires: The Story of the Great Fires of 1910*; *The Ice: A Journey to Antarctica*; *How the Canyon Became Grand*; and a six-volume suite of global fire histories, *Cycle of Fire*. He spent fifteen seasons with the North Rim Longshots, a fire crew at Grand Canyon National Park, and several seasons writing plans for other national parks. He is the owner of a cabin on a tidily landscaped lot adjacent to the Apache National Forest.